GRADES 2–3

Beyond the BUBBLE

GRADES 2–3

Beyond the BUBBLE

How to Use Multiple-Choice Tests to Improve Math Instruction

Maryann **Wickett** and Eunice **Hendrix-Martin**

Stenhouse
PUBLISHERS
www.stenhouse.com

Stenhouse Publishers
www.stenhouse.com

Library of Congress Cataloging-in-Publication Data
Wickett, Maryann.
Beyond the bubble : how to use multiple-choice tests to improve math instruction, grades 2-3 / Maryann Wickett and Eunice Hendrix-Martin.
p. cm.
ISBN 978-1-57110-817-3 (alk. paper) -- ISBN 978-1-57110-911-8 (e-book)
1. Mathematics--Study and teaching (Primary) 2. Multiple-choice examinations.
I. Hendrix-Martin, Eunice 1957- II. Title.
QA135.6.W53 2011
372.7--dc22

2010038929

Cover design, interior design, and typesetting by designboy Creative Group

Manufactured in the United States of America

PRINTED ON 30% PCW
RECYCLED PAPER

17 16 15 14 13 12 11 9 8 7 6 5 4 3 2 1

We wish to thank our families for their support
during all the endless weekends it took to create this book.

Contents

Introduction 1

Number 3
Problem One 4
Problem Two 11
Problem Three 18
Problem Four 25
Problem Five 31
Problem Six 38

Measurement 45
Problem One 46
Problem Two 54
Problem Three 61
Problem Four 68
Problem Five 75
Problem Six 83

Algebra 93
Problem One 94
Problem Two 101
Problem Three 108
Problem Four 115
Problem Five 123
Problem Six 131

Geometry 139
Problem One 140
Problem Two 148
Problem Three 156
Problem Four 165
Problem Five 173
Problem Six 192

Probability 193

Problem One 194

Problem Two 203

Problem Three 211

Problem Four 219

Problem Five 228

Problem Six 236

Appendix A: Generic Conversation Starters 243

Appendix B: Reproducible Problems 245

General Resources 277

Acknowledgments

We wish to thank all of the second- and third-grade students of Carrillo Elementary School in Carlsbad, California, for sharing their learning and thinking with us. Without you, this book would not have been possible. Thank you for helping us to learn and grow as teachers.

Introduction

Multiple-choice testing is an educational reality for students and teachers. Rather than continue to complain about how these tests can adversely affect teaching and learning, we thought it better to turn the testing situation on its head—that is, to take full advantage of all that multiple-choice testing can offer. The purpose of *Beyond the Bubble* is to do just that: show teachers how to get more from multiple-choice tests. By asking students just a few carefully chosen questions, teachers can gain valuable insight into students' mathematical thinking.

Many schools and districts rely on multiple-choice testing to assess students' math progress. The assumption is that if a student marks a correct answer—if he or she fills in the *right* bubble—that student is proficient in the corresponding skill or objective. However, a correct answer can often mask fragile knowledge or misconceptions, or it may have been just a lucky guess. (There are many examples of this throughout the book.) The inverse is also true. If a student marks an incorrect answer—if he or she fills in the *wrong* bubble—that student is considered to be in need of remediation. But the student may have just misread the problem or made a mistake when selecting an answer. Both "correct" and "incorrect" answers reveal little about what a student truly does or doesn't understand. Consequently, instructional decisions based on this testing information may be misguided. Again, taking just a few moments to probe students' thinking can provide valuable insight leading to more effective instruction for all students.

Using typical multiple-choice questions often found on second- and third-grade assessments and in test-prep materials, we asked hundreds of students to explain their answer choices in writing and verbally. We found that both correct and incorrect multiple-choice responses often painted an inaccurate or incomplete picture of students' mathematical understanding. For example, we assumed students who answered questions correctly would consistently show strong understanding and demonstrate logical thinking, but they just as often showed partial understanding, confusion, or no understanding at all. We were surprised to find the same was also true for students who marked incorrect responses. But using these test questions and probing with a few additional questions allowed us to get "beyond the bubble"—suddenly we were using the questions to our (and our students') advantage, uncovering understanding and misconceptions, which, in turn, allowed us to make more effective instructional decisions as we considered what our students needed next.

Beyond the Bubble is divided into five strands: number, measurement, algebra, geometry, and probability. There are six problems per strand. Each problem begins with a brief overview of the test question's objective, followed by the sample test question, typical student strategies used to solve the problem, conversation starters, actual student work, student-teacher conversations along with teachers' insights, and suggestions for instructional strategies that should help advance individual students' learning. Reassessment questions are also provided.

Each strand is followed by a brief list of additional resources to support your instruction. At the end of the book there is a more general list of teaching resources as well as a general list of questions for you to use to start conversations with your students. We've found that posting these questions on the back wall of your classroom provides a quick and easy way to use them with students when having conversations throughout the school day.

Some Dos and Don'ts

- Do take the time to ask questions and listen carefully to students' responses. They will provide you with valuable opportunities to understand and appreciate their strengths and weaknesses.
- Don't rely on a single multiple-choice response alone. It may mask true understanding or misunderstanding, making purposeful instruction difficult.
- Do discuss what you find out with colleagues. Talk about surprises, victories, and methods to engage students and help them move forward with understanding.
- Don't be afraid to follow a child's lead. You may not understand his or her thinking initially, but by listening carefully with an open mind, you may discover brilliance in ways you've never before considered.
- Do reflect on our examples and see if you can find similar outcomes in your class. The more connections you make to your children, the more comfortable you will be in engaging students in meaningful mathematical conversations, ultimately improving your instruction and children's learning.
- Do keep asking good questions that uncover students' learning and understanding, providing you with valuable insights. Children deserve our attention and our best instructional decisions.

As educators, the more information we can gather, the better instructional decisions we can make for our students. We wrote *Beyond the Bubble* for all educators who want better, more focused mathematics instruction for their students. This includes teachers, administrators, and preservice teachers. The results of our work with students provide the basis for excellent inservice discussions or professional learning community (PLC) planning and conversations. When instructional decision makers, both teachers and administrators, examine students' written and verbal explanations, differentiation becomes quicker, easier, and more targeted. It is our hope that *Beyond the Bubble* will be used as a tool for insightful, engaging mathematics instruction for you and your students.

Number

PROBLEM ONE

Overview

This problem asks students to identify and apply a pattern to find a missing number. The ability to recognize and apply patterns supports students' number sense and is an underlying idea of algebraic thinking. An important challenge of this problem is that students must continue the pattern from two-digit numbers to three-digit numbers.

Sample Problem

If you are counting by tens to make this pattern, what is the next number in the pattern?
71, 81, 91, ________

A. 110
B. 111
C. 101
D. 121

Show how you know.

Possible Student Solution Strategies

- Students continue the pattern by adding ten to ninety-one.
- Students continue the pattern by counting on by tens.
- Students use a number line to show the pattern of counting on or adding ten.
- Students continue the pattern by counting by ones from 91 to 101.
- Students use the pattern of adding one ten to the tens place and leaving the ones place as is.
- Students are unable to see a pattern and guess.
- Students misapply their knowledge of counting by tens, believing that when counting by tens, all numbers in the sequence end in zero.

Conversation Starters

- Why did you choose the answer you did?
- Select one of the answers you didn't choose. What was wrong with it?
- Select one of the answers you didn't choose and explain how someone might get that answer.
- What patterns did you notice?
- What always happens to the ones place when ten is added to any number?
- What always happens to the tens place when ten is added to any number?
- Tell me about your thinking.

Student Work Sample: Tyron

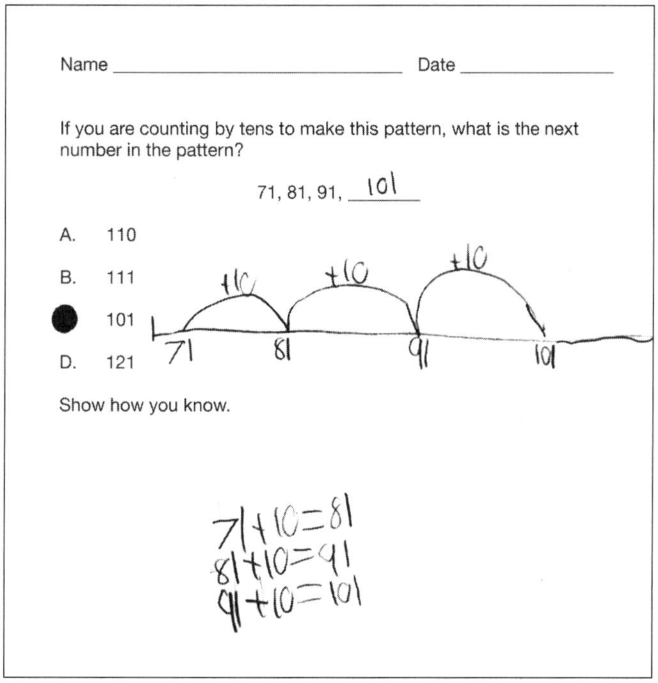

Name ______________________ Date ____________

If you are counting by tens to make this pattern, what is the next number in the pattern?

71, 81, 91, 101

A. 110

B. 111

C. 101

D. 121

Show how you know.

A Conversation with Tyron	Teacher Insights
T: The work on your paper looks as if you found a pattern to these numbers. What pattern did you notice? **Tyron:** The numbers were going up by ten. **T:** Tell me more about your thinking. **Tyron:** If I count on my fingers from 71 to 81, that's ten fingers. The same thing if I count from 81 to 91. I showed that on my number line. I knew I had to add 10 to 91, and I got 101.	**T:** *Tyron's written work and his verbal explanation about his thinking indicated strong understanding. He was able to see a pattern that helped him find the answer. He was also able to represent his thinking clearly on his paper by using a number line and indicating the additions using appropriate equations.*
T: What do you notice about the ones place when ten is added to these numbers? **Tyron:** Ah . . . I'm not sure. Maybe there is always a one in the ones place? **T:** That seems to be true for these numbers. Do you think if the first number had been seventy-two, there would always be a two in the ones place when ten was added? **Tyron:** I am not really too sure. [Tyron pauses and appears to be counting on ten from seventy-two, using his fingers to keep track.] Maybe, but I really don't know.	**T:** *Tyron demonstrated very tentative understanding about the pattern that occurs in the ones place when ten is added to any number. He seemed to be thinking about the notion that adding ten to any number will not change the digit in the ones place, but he was not at all certain about this.*

Informed Instructional Suggestions

Tyron's work indicates he can find a pattern and use it in a counting sequence involving addition to find a correct answer. But Tyron is not clear about patterns that occur in the ones place when ten is added to any number. We plan to provide him with additional similar problems and focus a line of questioning to help Tyron make this connection. Once Tyron understands this idea, he can investigate what happens to the tens place when ten is added to any number.

Student Work Sample: Bonita

Name ______________________ Date ____________

If you are counting by tens to make this pattern, what is the next number in the pattern?

71, 81, 91, ______

A. 110

B. 111 71, 81 91,

(C.) 101 so it's like 7 8 9 then 10

D. 121

Show how you know.

A Conversation with Bonita	Teacher Insights
T: It looks like you might have seen a pattern. What pattern are you noticing? **Bonita:** I noticed a pattern in the tens place. It went seven tens, eight tens, nine tens. I knew the next number had to have ten tens. **T:** Did you notice anything else? **Bonita:** The ones place always had a one in it, so the next number had to have a one in the ones place. So ten tens and one one is 101.	**T:** *Bonita's written explanation does not indicate clear understanding of place value. She indicates a pattern in the tens place, but her written explanation doesn't indicate understanding that the 7, 8, 9, and 10 are tens rather than ones. In other words, she is writing about the pattern in the tens place as if it were in the ones place. However, Bonita's verbal explanation makes it clear that she recognizes the value of the digits in the tens place, which indicates solid understanding.*

Informed Instructional Suggestions

Conversation is critical for understanding Bonita's thinking. Her written explanations are typically weak or unclear, as was this one, but she was able to communicate strong understanding in her verbal explanation. We need to continue to provide Bonita frequent opportunities to present written explanations and guide her in making her thinking clear on paper. It may be helpful for Bonita to partner with other students who are more proficient at writing explanations so that she can see this process modeled while participating in it. We will also provide modeling of written explanations to illustrate the qualities of good math writing.

Student Work Sample: Ming

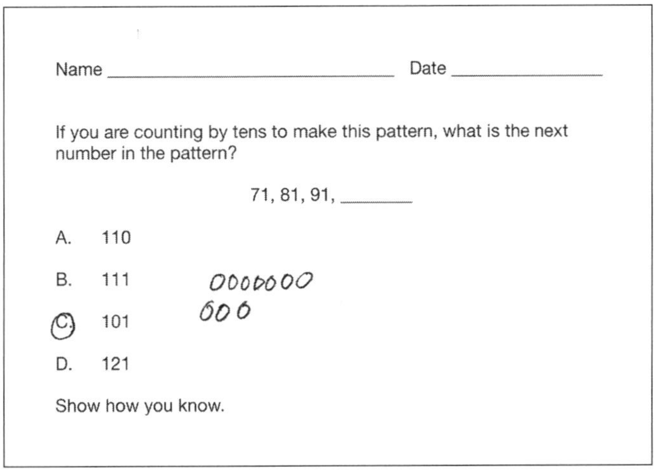

Name ______________________ Date ____________

If you are counting by tens to make this pattern, what is the next number in the pattern?

71, 81, 91, ______

A. 110

B. 111 0000000

(C) 101 000

D. 121

Show how you know.

A Conversation with Ming	Teacher Insights
T: Tell me about your thinking, Ming. **Ming:** Well, I don't know. Answer C seemed right. I tried to show it, but I got stuck. **T:** Do you still think answer C is correct? **Ming:** [Shrugging] Maybe; I'm not really sure. It might be 111. I don't know.	**T:** *Ming marked the correct answer, but her written and verbal explanations revealed no understanding. Essentially, her correct answer was a lucky guess. Ming did not understand the problem.*

Informed Instructional Suggestions

Ming marked the correct answer but was unable to show any understanding. Without reading or hearing explanations from Ming, we would have assumed that she understood the concepts involved in this problem, and her needs would have gone unmet. Ming needs many opportunities to create patterns and recognize that mathematics is the study of patterns. To achieve this goal, we can offer activities that require her to use a hundreds chart, count by tens from various one- and two-digit numbers, recognize the pattern in both the tens and the ones place when ten is added to any number, and move back and forth on a number line.

Student Work Sample: Lacie

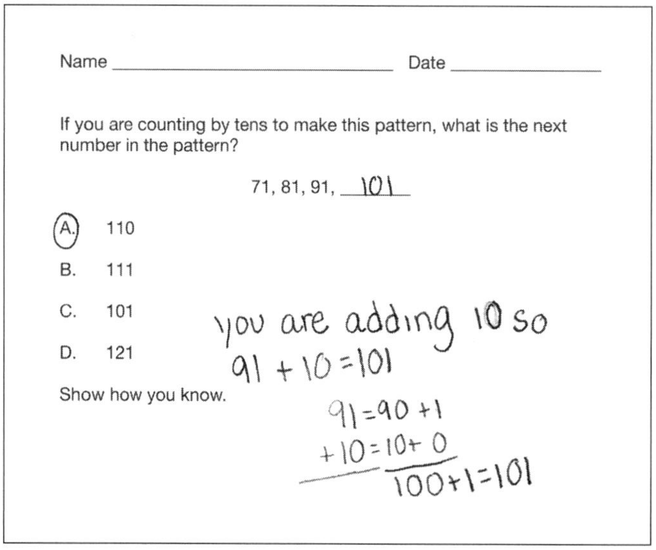
Name ______________________ Date ______________

If you are counting by tens to make this pattern, what is the next number in the pattern?

71, 81, 91, 101

(A.) 110

B. 111

C. 101

D. 121

Show how you know.

you are adding 10 so
91 + 10 = 101

91 = 90 + 1
+10 = 10 + 0
100 + 1 = 101

A Conversation with Lacie	Teacher Insights
T: I noticed that the answer you chose is different than the answer you got in your figuring. Why do you think this is so? **Lacie:** [Pauses a moment] Oh no, I got mixed up! It should be choice C!	**T:** *Lacie is typically a capable student who has indicated in the past strong understanding of pattern and place value. An incorrectly marked answer was a surprise.*
T: Why not choice A like you marked on your paper? **Lacie:** [Pointing to her written explanation] Because 90 plus 10 is 100, and 1 more is 101. Choice A says 110, and it should be 101.	**T:** *Lacie's explanation indicated understanding more typical of her.*

Informed Instructional Suggestions

Had Lacie not provided a written explanation of her thinking followed by our conversation, we would have assumed she did not understand the problem. In fact, she understood the problem and found her own error. The information in Lacie's written work and verbal explanation suggests that Lacie needs reinforcement opportunities involving reading and writing numbers accurately in the hundreds to strengthen her understanding and ensure accuracy when applying her understanding. It would also be helpful to have Lacie explore patterns that occur in the ones and tens places when ten is added to any number.

Student Work Sample: Sarita

Name ______________________ Date ____________

If you are counting by tens to make this pattern, what is the next number in the pattern?

71, 81, 91, ______

(A) 110

B. 111

C. 101

D. 121

I think it is 110 because it was counting by tens.

Show how you know.

A Conversation with Sarita	Teacher Insights
T: Why did you choose choice A, 110? **Sarita:** Well, from 71 to 81 is 10, and 81 to 91 is 10. That's counting by tens. So when I count by tens, the number always ends in zero, and 110 is the only one that ends in zero.	**T:** *Sarita's explanation revealed important clues about her misunderstanding. She believes when counting by tens, the numbers always end in zero!*

Informed Instructional Strategies

Sarita needs experience with counting by tens from numbers that do not have a zero in the ones place. In addition, she needs guidance to recognize the pattern that occurs in the ones and tens places when ten is added to two-digit numbers and, later, to larger numbers.

Reassessment

1. Use a similar problem at the same level of difficulty.

   If you are counting by tens to make this pattern, what is the next number in the pattern?
   67, 77, 87, 97, ________

   A. 117
   B. 107
   C. 170
   D. 98

   Show how you know.

2. Use a problem that is similar but slightly more challenging. (Note: The use of larger numbers makes the following problem more difficult for this age group—many students this age can handle two-digit numbers, but not three digits. Sometimes, additional information is more confusing.)

   If you are counting by tens to make this pattern, what is the missing number in the pattern?
   117, 127, 137, __________, 157

   A. 147
   B. 247
   C. 140
   D. 167

   Show how you know.

3. Have students create their own number pattern and complete it. Ask students to explain what it is that makes their number pattern a pattern. Then ask students to exchange and complete each other's patterns.

PROBLEM TWO

Overview

Students must first find the sum of two numbers and then select the response that is closest to the sum. Students with well-developed number sense and experiences with 0–99 or 1–100 charts have little difficulty determining which ten is closest to the sum of the problem. Students who have learned rounding as a procedure may have more difficulty. These students may forget the rules of the procedure, use the incorrect digit to round, or fail to recognize which tens the sum falls between.

Sample Problem

Which of the following is closest to 15 + 18?

A. 40
B. 30
C. 20
D. 50

Show how you know.

Possible Student Solution Strategies

- Students use an addition strategy to find the correct sum and then select the best choice by using comparison or a number line.
- Students find the correct sum but make a guess to select their answer.
- Students find the correct sum and have partial understanding of the process of rounding.
- Students find the correct sum but round up to the incorrect ten.
- Students find the correct sum, but their explanation indicates little understanding of place value.
- Students first round each addend to the nearest ten and then add the rounded numbers to find the sum.
- Students find an incorrect sum and consequently round to an incorrect ten.

Conversation Starters

- How did you find the sum?
- Why is it important in this problem to know about when and how to use rounding?
- How did you think about the problem?
- How can you prove your answer choice is reasonable?
- What have we learned before that helped you solve this problem?
- Why is five ones important in choosing your answer for this problem?

Student Work Sample: Neal

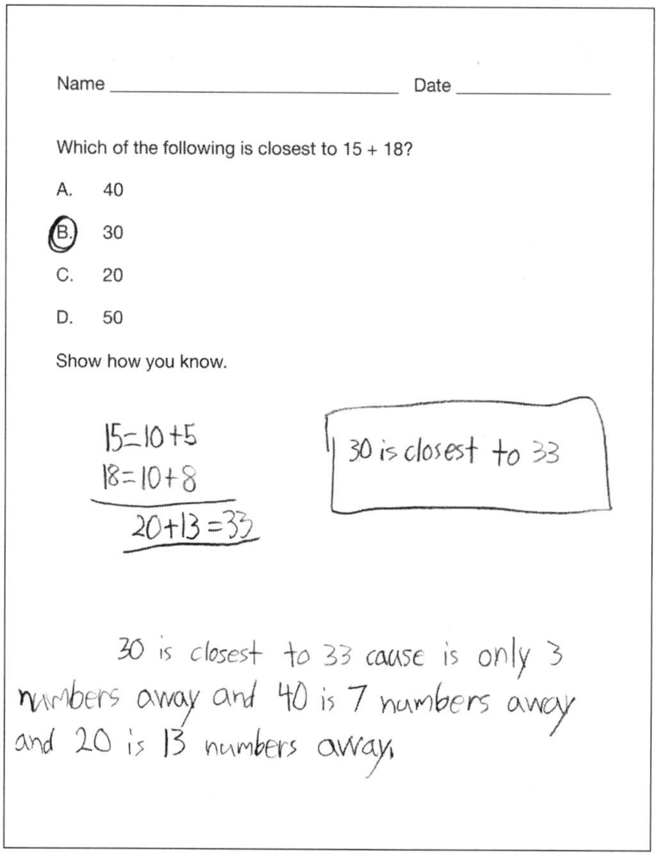
Name ______________ Date ______________

Which of the following is closest to 15 + 18?

A. 40

(B.) 30

C. 20

D. 50

Show how you know.

15=10+5
18=10+8
20+13=33

30 is closest to 33

30 is closest to 33 cause is only 3 numbers away and 40 is 7 numbers away and 20 is 13 numbers away.

A Conversation with Neal	Teacher Insights
T: Tell me about how you thought about this problem. **Neal:** First I added and got 33. But 33 wasn't a choice and so I knew I had to find the one that was closest. Thirty-three is only 3 away from 30 and 7 away from 40, so I knew the answer had to be 30.	**T:** *Neal has an efficient and accurate strategy for addition. He used comparison to determine that thirty-three is closest to thirty. He was able to explain his thinking clearly and confidently in both his written and his verbal explanations.*

Informed Instructional Suggestions

Neal has strong understanding of addition, place value, and rounding using ones and tens. He is ready to take on similar tasks involving hundreds.

Student Work Sample: David

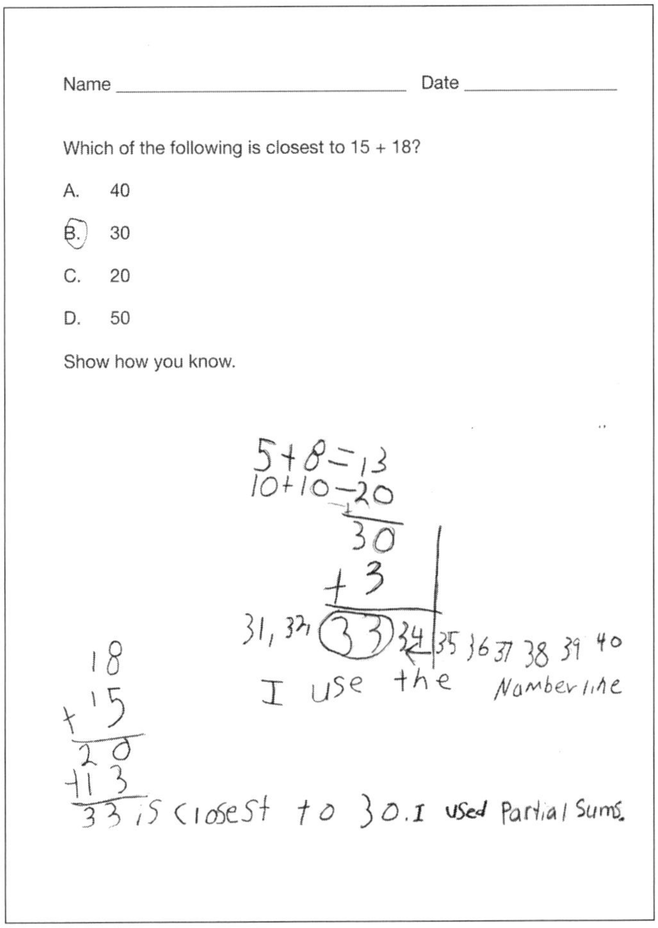
Name ______________________ Date ____________

Which of the following is closest to 15 + 18?

A. 40

(B.) 30

C. 20

D. 50

Show how you know.

5+8=13
10+10=20
30
+3
31, 32, (33) 34 35 36 37 38 39 40
I use the Numberline

18
+15
20
+13
33 is closest to 30. I used Partial Sums.

A Conversation with David	Teacher Insights
T: How can you prove your choice is reasonable? **David:** I used two strategies to find the sum. Then to find out which choice is best, I used a number line to show that thirty-three is closer to thirty than to forty. See?	**T:** *David had clear understanding of the problem and was able to solve it easily.*

Informed Instructional Suggestions

Like Neal, David showed strong understanding, although he used different strategies than Neal. He is also ready to move on to working with hundreds.

Student Work Sample: Greta

Name ____________________ Date ______________

Which of the following is closest to 15 + 18?

A. 40

(B.) 30

C. 20

D. 50

Show how you know.

1
15
18
+ ——
33

I Know that 30 is the Closest too 33 because they are both in the 30's. I'm not good Rounding So this all had to do is add and think Wich was the best.

A Conversation with Greta	Teacher Insights
T: On your paper, you said you weren't good at rounding. What makes you believe that your answer is best? **Greta:** I noticed that fifty is too big. It's far away from thirty-three. **T:** What do you think rounding is about? **Greta:** I know that the number has to go to a ten, but I don't know why. **T:** You chose thirty on your paper. Why didn't you choose twenty or forty? **Greta:** Because thirty-three is in the thirties and so is thirty.	**T:** *Greta found the sum of fifteen and eighteen correctly but has little understanding of rounding. She made an accurate guess and knew fifty was too far away from thirty-three. She indicated another potential misunderstanding when she stated that she chose thirty because thirty-three is in the thirties. Her thinking would have led her to an incorrect guess if the sum had been thirty-five to thirty-nine.*

Informed Instructional Strategies

Greta can accurately add, so we need to focus our work with her on rounding. Working with a number line or hundreds chart would provide concrete ways for her to see which ten a given number is closer to.

Student Work Sample: Norm

Name ______________________ Date ____________

Which of the following is closest to 15 + 18?

A. 40
B. 30 (circled)
C. 20
D. 50

Show how you know.

15
+18
33

33 is the closest to is because is ha3 and not 5 if you have 5 you would do 40 but it it 3 and that is low that is why.

A Conversation with Norm	Teacher Insights
T: I see that you have mentioned the number five in your explanation. What have you learned before that makes you think that five has something to do with this problem? **Norm:** I know that three is less than five, so I have to go down. **T:** The sum you found is thirty-three. Which three do you mean? **Norm:** Um . . . this one. [Norm points to the 3 in the ones place.] **T:** What does the other three represent? **Norm:** Three tens.	**T:** *While Norm's written explanation lacked clarity, his verbal answers indicated an understanding of place value.*
T: So what does five have to do with the answer you chose? **Norm:** If the ones place has a 1, 2, 3, or 4, you have to go down. If it has a 5, 6, 7, 8, or 9, you have to go up. **T:** Go up or down to what? **Norm:** The next ten.	**T:** *Norm indicates in his verbal explanation that he knows how to round accurately based on the digit in the ones place.*

Informed Instructional Suggestions

Norm can add accurately and was able to verbally justify his answer choice. Providing him with additional similar problems will help him further clarify his understanding, thus giving him the opportunity to write clearer explanations. Modeling of clear written explanations by his teacher and classmates would also be helpful to Norm.

Student Work Sample: Ellen

Name ______________________ Date ______________

Which of the following is closest to 15 + 18?

A. 40

(B) 30

C. 20

D. 50

$$\begin{array}{r} 15 \\ +\,18 \\ \hline 33 \end{array}$$

Show how you know.

because if 5+8 = 13 you Know that 1+1=2 so put the 1 the on the 2 and the 2 tis now a 3 and it is 33 and it is closest to 30!

A Conversation with Ellen	Teacher Insights
T: You say one plus one is two, but I don't see a 2 anywhere in your computation. Please explain what you mean. **Ellen:** Oh! There's a 1 in 15 and a 1 in 18. So one plus one is two.	**T:** *While Ellen found the correct sum, she indicates no understanding of place value. She needs to recognize that the 1 in 15 represents a ten, not one. The same is true for the 1 in 18. Additional work to support number sense and place-value understanding is necessary before moving forward.*

Informed Instructional Suggestions

Ellen needs to construct one- and two-digit numbers using base ten blocks to help her visually and kinesthetically build understanding of our base ten number system. It will be important to help Ellen make the connection between the concrete representation of the base ten blocks and the abstract written numbers and what each place represents. Another tool we could use to help develop Ellen's understanding is the hundreds chart.

Reassessment

1. Use a similar problem at the same level of difficulty.

   Which of the following is closest to 32 + 36?

   A. 60
   B. 50
   C. 80
   D. 70

   Show how you know.

2. Choose a problem that is similar but slightly more challenging.

   Which of the following is closest to 131 + 42?

   A. 170
   B. 550
   C. 180
   D. 70

   Show how you know.

PROBLEM THREE

Overview

This problem asks students to consider the most reasonable sum for two large numbers. The numbers do not have the same number of digits, adding a twist to the problem. Students with good number sense can mark the correct answer without doing any computation at all because three of the answers are unreasonable.

Sample Problem

Last weekend a gas station sold 2,487 gallons of gas on Saturday and 935 gallons of gas on Sunday. What was the total number of gallons of gas sold over the weekend?

A. 2,312
B. 1,552
C. 11,837
D. 3,422

Show how you know.

Possible Student Solution Strategies

- Students recognize that this problem requires addition to solve it and then correctly add the two quantities of gas to find the total gallons sold, 3,422.
- Students use their number sense and estimation skills to realize that 935 is close to 1,000, and 1,000 plus 2,487 is closest to the answer of 3,422.
- Students may not recognize that addition is needed and may subtract to find the difference, 1,552.
- Students may align the two addends incorrectly without regard to place value, then add to get the sum of 11,827.
- Students may fail to regroup and fail to recognize that their answer is smaller than the larger addend to get the answer of 2,312.

Conversation Starters

- In your own words, what do you think this problem is asking you to do?
- How can you use estimation to find the correct answer?
- Why doesn't the first answer choice make sense?
- What is another way to solve this problem to verify your answer?

Student Work Sample: Tam

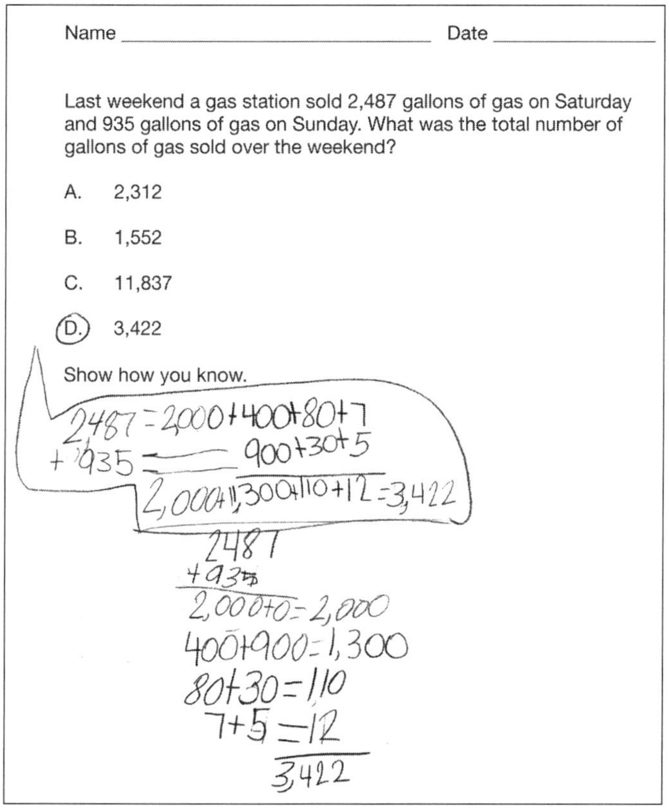
Name ______________________ Date ____________

Last weekend a gas station sold 2,487 gallons of gas on Saturday and 935 gallons of gas on Sunday. What was the total number of gallons of gas sold over the weekend?

A. 2,312

B. 1,552

C. 11,837

(D.) 3,422

Show how you know.

2487 = 2000+400+80+7
+ 935 = 900+30+5
2,000+1,300+110+12 = 3,422

2487
+935
2,000+0 = 2,000
400+900 = 1,300
80+30 = 110
7+5 = 12
3,422

A Conversation with Tam	Teacher Insights
T: I see you have solved the problem using addition and circled choice D. What is a second way you could solve the problem to verify that your answer is correct? **Tam:** When I did the problem, I decomposed the numbers and then figured out how many ones, tens, hundreds, and thousands. Then I added all those up to get 3,422. Instead of starting with the ones, I could start with the thousands and go the other way.	**T:** *Tam has a strong understanding of an addition procedure and was able to apply it effectively and efficiently to solve this problem. I asked Tam to use a second method to solve the problem again to push her thinking, to keep her thinking flexible, and to establish the value of checking results by using a second method. She was able to use a second method to solve the problem and arrived at the same answer.*

Informed Instructional Strategies

Tam clearly understood how to solve this problem. As a new challenge she would benefit from doing missing-addend problems with numbers of the same magnitude. Then Tam needs to have new opportunities to explore addition of larger numbers to further strengthen her understanding and confidence. When possible, the context of the problems should link directly to Tam's interest. Also, Tam should have experiences with adding more than two multidigit numbers.

Student Work Sample: Ned

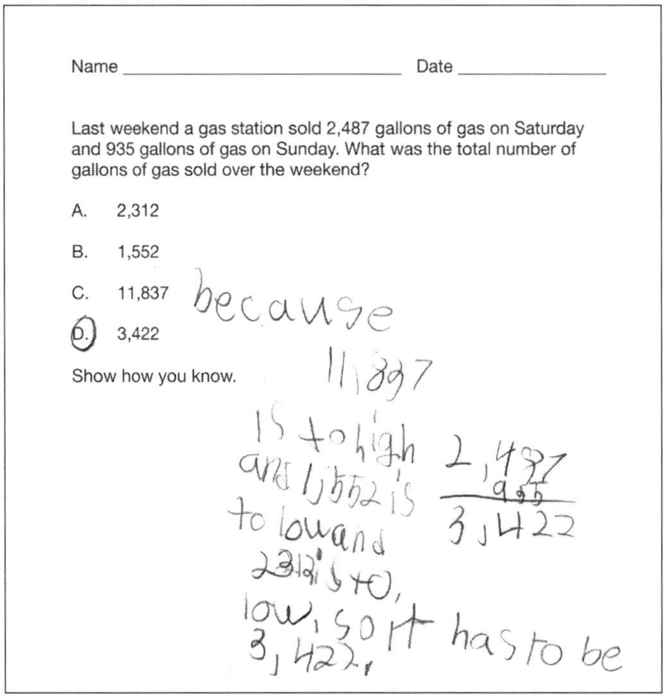
Name ______________________________ Date _______________

Last weekend a gas station sold 2,487 gallons of gas on Saturday and 935 gallons of gas on Sunday. What was the total number of gallons of gas sold over the weekend?

A. 2,312

B. 1,552

C. 11,837

(D.) 3,422

Show how you know.

because 11,837 is to high and 1,552 is to low and 2312 is to low, so it has to be 3,422.

2,487
935
3,422

A Conversation with Ned	Teacher Insights
T: It looks to me like you used estimation to find your answer. Would you please explain your thinking further? **Ned:** Two thousand four hundred eighty-seven is close to 2,000 and 935 is close to 1,000. Two thousand plus 1,000 is 3,000. So I know the answer has to be somewhere around 3,000. Eleven thousand eight hundred thirty-seven is way too high, and 1,552 and 2,312 are too low, so the only choice is 3,422. I didn't actually have to add the real numbers. **T:** It helped me a lot to better understand your thinking when you explained about the 2,000 and the 1,000 and how you were able to use that information to know which choices were too high or too low.	**T:** *Ned's written explanation did not clearly reveal how he knew that some answer choices were too high while others were too low. His verbal explanation clarified what he knew. Although he wrote the addition problem complete with a correct answer, he did not show clearly how he got the answer. He could have written the problem after solving it using his number sense as he explained. Ned's habit of mind to estimate and save himself the work of computing is a good disposition. Not only is it efficient, but he can use his estimate to see whether his sum is reasonable if he does the actual computation.*

Informed Instructional Suggestions

While Ned was able to easily use his number sense to solve this problem, we plan to give him similar problems with answer choices that encourage him to actually compute the sum correctly to verify that he can compute efficiently and accurately. For example, if all the choices for this problem were in the 3,000s, he probably would have had to compute the sum to choose the correct answer.

Student Work Sample: Konner

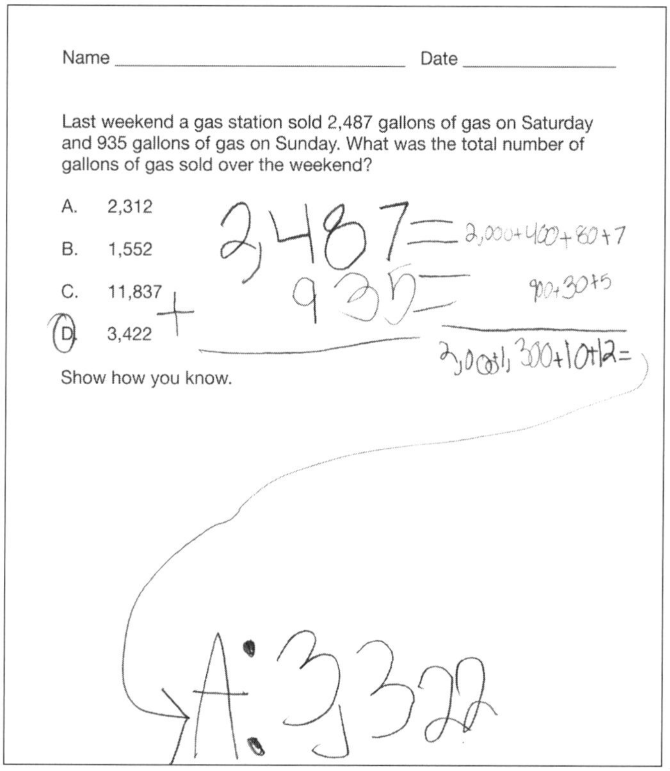

Name ________________________ Date ____________

Last weekend a gas station sold 2,487 gallons of gas on Saturday and 935 gallons of gas on Sunday. What was the total number of gallons of gas sold over the weekend?

A. 2,312

B. 1,552

C. 11,837

D. 3,422

Show how you know.

A Conversation with Konner	Teacher Insights
T: I notice that your written answer is 3,322, but you circled choice D, which is 3,422. Why does that make sense to you? **Konner:** Well, choice D is the closest choice to what I got, so I figured that was probably the right one. **T:** Does it concern you that your answer and the answer you chose aren't the same? **Konner:** Maybe, a little bit. **T:** What can you do about the fact they aren't the same? **Konner:** Check my work? Oh, I see a mistake. I added 80 and 30 and said it was 10. That's ridiculous! It's really 110. I'm missing 100 and my answer is 100 off.	**T:** *Konner's number sense helped him find the correct answer, but he didn't accurately figure it out. If the goal of the question were to learn if Konner could add accurately, his choice could have been misleading. If he hadn't shown his thinking, I wouldn't have known about his error. In order to find out if Konner can add accurately, I need to offer more problems involving addition.*

Informed Instructional Suggestions

Konner needs to continue to practice adding and checking his work to ensure its accuracy. He should learn that when his answer does not match any choices, he should double-check his work.

Student Work Sample: Bella

Name ______________________ Date ______________

Last weekend a gas station sold 2,487 gallons of gas on Saturday and 935 gallons of gas on Sunday. What was the total number of gallons of gas sold over the weekend?

A. 2,312

B. 1,552

C. 11,837

(D.) 3,422

Show how you know.

2,487
+ 935

7+5=12
80+30=110
400+900 = 130

3,422

A Conversation with Bella	Teacher Insights
T: I see that when you added 7 plus 5, you got 12. I agree with this. I also see that when you added 80 and 30, you got 110. I agree with this also. But when you added 400 plus 900, you got 130. I disagree. Why do you think I disagree? **Bella:** Um, I don't know. Because I know my basic facts, I added the 4 and the 9 and got 13 and then because they are both really hundreds, I stuck on a zero because 400 plus 900 is 130.	**T:** *Bella marked the correct answer; however, Bella has struggled with addition of numbers greater than two digits. Her verbal response showed a lack of understanding of place value. Her work was confused and incomplete. Without Bella's written and verbal explanations, I would have assumed that Bella could accurately add a three-digit number to a four-digit number. With that belief, I would have failed to meet Bella's needs.*

Informed Instructional Suggestions

Bella's previous work has shown she can consistently and accurately add two two-digit numbers. She needs to build on this knowledge and understanding as she moves forward with adding three-digit numbers. She knows how to accurately decompose numbers to find a sum, so we should help her extend this understanding to addition with three-digit numbers. It is also important that Bella spend more time learning the underpinnings of place value because she indicated confusion about this in her verbal explanation.

Student Work Sample: Cara

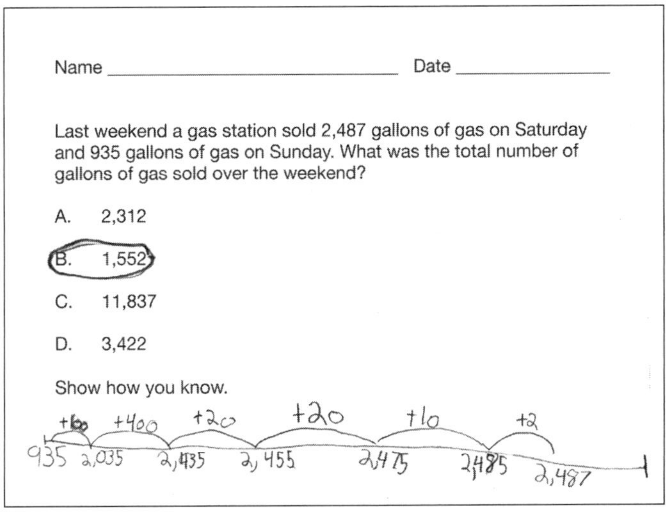
Name ______________________ Date ____________

Last weekend a gas station sold 2,487 gallons of gas on Saturday and 935 gallons of gas on Sunday. What was the total number of gallons of gas sold over the weekend?

A. 2,312

B. 1,552

C. 11,837

D. 3,422

Show how you know.

A Conversation with Cara	Teacher Insights
T: What is this problem asking you to do? **Cara:** Ah, find out how many gallons of gas were sold. **T:** What information does the problem give you? **Cara:** Two thousand four hundred eighty-seven gallons were sold on Saturday and 935 were sold on Sunday. **T:** Read the question aloud please. **Cara:** "What was the total number of gallons of gas sold over the weekend?" Oh no, I think I did it wrong. I figured out how many more were sold on Saturday than on Sunday. I found out the answer to a different question! **T:** What would you do differently? **Cara:** I started at 935 and used the number line to find out how many jumps to take to get to 2,487. But I should put 935 together with 2,487, which means the answer has to be about 1,000 larger than 2,487, which is somewhere around 3,487. It has to be choice D, which is close to 3,487.	**T:** *Cara attempted to find the difference between the two numbers involved in the problem but was unsuccessful. As well as finding an incorrect difference, she did not understand that this particular problem required addition rather than subtraction. Cara needs more experience with determining when addition is needed to solve a problem and when subtraction is appropriate.*

Informed Instructional Suggestions

We need to provide Cara with many tasks involving addition and subtraction situations and guide her in comparing them to further understand what makes a problem an addition problem or a subtraction problem. To further develop her understanding, we'll ask Cara to write her own addition and subtraction word problems.

Reassessment

1. Use a similar problem at the same level of difficulty.

   Oak Hill Elementary School bought 2,424 pencils in August and in January it bought 852 pencils. What was the total number of pencils bought?

   A. 2,276
   B. 10,944
   C. 3,276
   D. 3,476

   Show how you know.

2. Choose a problem that is similar but slightly more challenging.

   In May, Juarez Elementary School bought 6,745 cartons of chocolate milk and 2,336 cartons of regular milk. How many cartons of milk were bought in May?

   A. 9,071
   B. 8,071
   C. 8,081
   D. 9,081

   Show how you know.

3. Ask students to solve a problem without multiple-choice answers.

   The Tigers soccer team sold 3,497 soft drinks during October. In November they sold 2,805. How many more soft drinks did they sell in October than in November? Solve the problem in two different ways.

PROBLEM FOUR

Overview

For this problem, students must be able to select an appropriate operation: multiplication or repeated addition. Prior to computing, students with good number sense and understanding of operations can eliminate two of the answer choices (44 and 2,448), as they make no sense in this situation.

Sample Problem

Stacy bought 8 flats of eggs. Each flat held 36 eggs. What was the total number of eggs she bought?

A. 44
B. 2,448
C. 288
D. 248

Show how you know.

Possible Student Solution Strategies

- Students use one of the following strategies to correctly solve the problem: repeated addition, skip-counting, drawing a picture, alternative strategies based on decomposing thirty-six, or the standard multiplication algorithm.
- Students add eight to thirty-six to get forty-four.
- Students make a regrouping error when applying the standard multiplication algorithm to get 2,448 or 248.
- Students regroup four tens with the three tens in thirty-six and add to get seven tens and then multiply to get an incorrect answer of 568, a common error, although this result is not one of the answer choices.

Conversation Starters

- What is this problem asking you to do?
- What strategies can you use to solve it?
- Why does your solution make sense?
- Why does one of the answers you didn't choose not make sense?
- What's a second way you could show your thinking?
- Does your solution match the answer you chose?
- Which answer choice makes no sense at all?

Student Work Sample: Boyd

Name ______________________ Date ____________

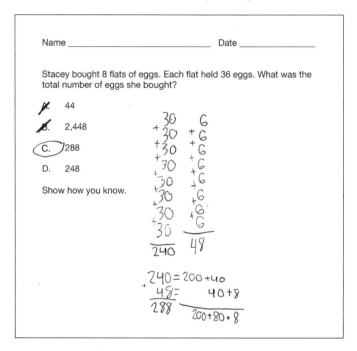

Stacey bought 8 flats of eggs. Each flat held 36 eggs. What was the total number of eggs she bought?

~~A.~~ 44

~~B.~~ 2,448

(C.) 288

D. 248

Show how you know.

30 + 30 + 30 + 30 + 30 + 30 + 30 + 30 = 240

6 + 6 + 6 + 6 + 6 + 6 + 6 + 6 = 48

240 = 200 + 40

\+ 48 = 40 + 8

288 = 200 + 80 + 8

A Conversation with Boyd	Teacher Insights
T: I noticed that you crossed off choices A and B. Why don't they make sense? **Boyd:** Well, it's because 44, choice A, is way too small. Two flats of eggs would be 72 because 36 plus 36 equals 72. And choice B can't be right because it is way too big. I know 8 times 3 equals 24, so 8 times 30 is 240. Two thousand four hundred forty-eight is way bigger than that. **T:** Why does your answer make sense? **Boyd:** I looked at choices C and D and saw that they are both very close. So then I used repeated addition and decomposing to find which one was correct.	**T:** *Boyd loves to do computation and has strong number sense. His paper showed evidence of his strengths and his verbal comments added further proof of his knowledge.*

Informed Instructional Strategies

Boyd used his number sense as well as his computational skills to solve this problem accurately. He was able to find unreasonable answers and eliminate them quickly. He had a strategy to help him solve the multiplication accurately, although it is not particularly efficient. Next steps could include exploring more-efficient strategies that would strengthen his understanding. Also, it would benefit Boyd to write and solve his own word problems involving multiplication.

Student Work Sample: JD

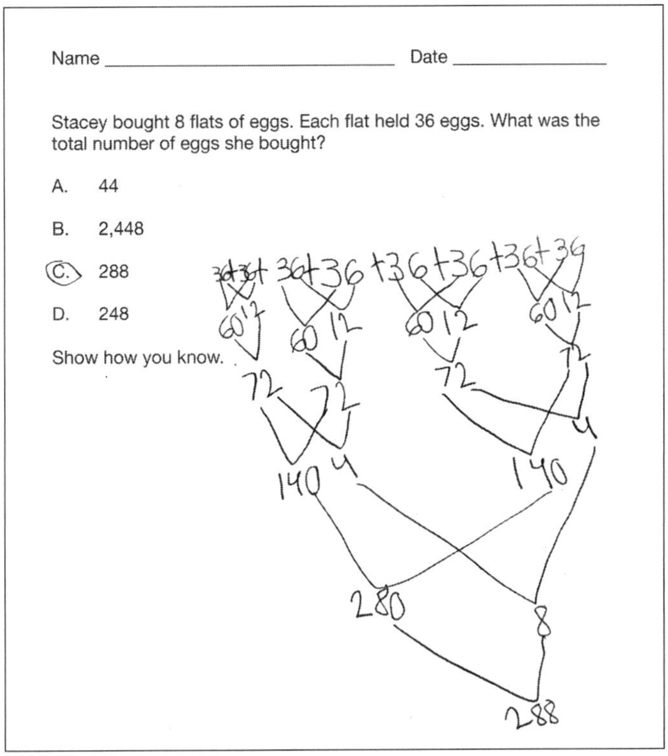
Name ______________________ Date ____________

Stacey bought 8 flats of eggs. Each flat held 36 eggs. What was the total number of eggs she bought?

A. 44

B. 2,448

C. 288

D. 248

Show how you know.

A Conversation with JD	Teacher Insights
T: Tell me about the strategy you used to solve this problem. **JD:** I used repeated addition because I know that I need to add 36 eight times. But that was a lot of times. So I drew branches to connect two numbers. Then I added the tens and then the ones. Thirty plus 30 equals 60 and 6 plus 6 equals 12. Then I added 60 plus 12 to get 72. I had to do that four times. Then I added 72 plus 72. Seventy plus 70 is 140 and 2 plus 2 is 4. I did that two times. Then I added 140 plus 140, which is 280. Then I added 4 plus 4, which is 8. Two hundred eighty plus 8 is 288. That's how I got my answer. And it was a choice!	**T:** *JD understands that repeated addition is a strategy that can be used to solve whole number multiplication problems. Although his strategy is not particularly efficient, he was able to get the correct answer and demonstrate his understanding and thinking.*

Informed Instructional Strategies

JD needs more experience with multiplication and the opportunity to explore more efficient strategies that would strengthen his understanding. Also, it would benefit JD to write and solve his own word problems involving multiplication.

Student Work Sample: Carman

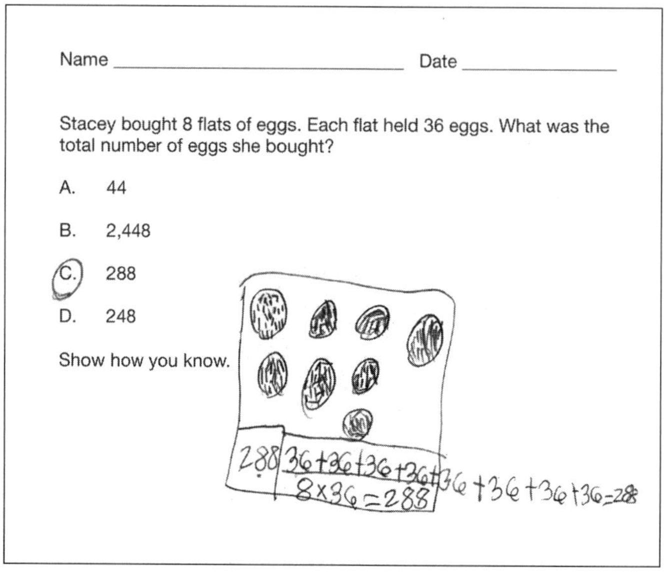
Name ______________________ Date ____________

Stacey bought 8 flats of eggs. Each flat held 36 eggs. What was the total number of eggs she bought?

A. 44

B. 2,448

C. 288

D. 248

Show how you know.

288 36+36+36+36+36+36+36+36=288

8×36=288

A Conversation with Carman	Teacher Insights
T: I see you used two solutions to find the answer to this problem. Why do your solutions make sense to you? **Carman:** I drew eight circles and put thirty-six dots in each circle. **T:** Did you count each dot in the circles? **Carman:** No. That was too hard. So I wrote *36 + 36 + 36 + 36 + 36 + 36 + 36 + 36 = 288.* **T:** How do you know that it equals 288, because I don't see evidence of how you figured it out? I also see you wrote *8 × 36 = 288* but also included no evidence of how you know. You show that this problem asks you to add 36 eight times, but I don't see how you got the answer of 288. **Carman:** I looked at Brian's paper. He got 288.	**T:** Carman appeared to understand the problem, according to her paper. She also appeared to have strategies to solve the problem. She was able to verbalize and verify the strategies indicated in her written work. But she failed to show how she got her answer. When pressed to explain, she was honest and stated she copied her neighbor, Brian. Had this conversation not taken place, I would have assumed that Carman was competent and solved this problem accurately and independently, and I would not have taken the appropriate next instructional steps.

Informed Instructional Suggestions

The first step is to follow up with Carman and find out if she indeed can add thirty-six eight times. Her ability to do this will indicate further steps. If she cannot accurately add thirty-six eight times, she needs more work with addition of two-digit numbers. If she can accurately add thirty-six eight times, she needs to learn how to show evidence of her ability and then work on more efficient strategies, such as multiplication.

Student Work Sample: Suzie

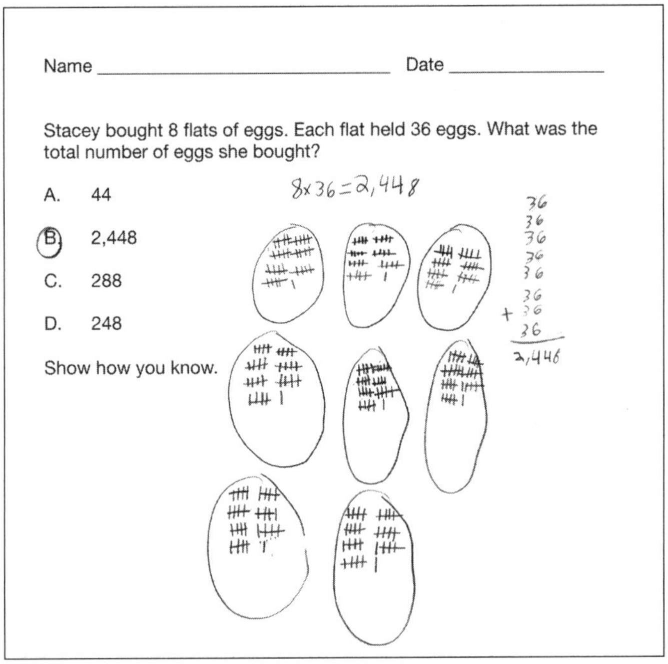

Name ______________________ Date ______________

Stacey bought 8 flats of eggs. Each flat held 36 eggs. What was the total number of eggs she bought?

A. 44

(B.) 2,448

C. 288

D. 248

Show how you know.

A Conversation with Suzie	Teacher Insights
T: Wow, Suzie, I see a lot of tally marks on your paper. What does each one stand for? **Suzie:** Each one stands for an egg. **T:** Why did you put them in circles? **Suzie:** Because that's the group of eggs in each flat. **T:** You chose choice B. Why does that answer make sense to you? **Suzie:** I don't really know. Actually, I just got tired from all the tally marks and picked it. All of the tally marks seemed like a lot, and that's a big answer. **T:** Does it look like there are really 2,448 tally marks on your paper? **Suzie:** Well, maybe not. [Suzie starts to quietly count the tally marks by ten.] **T:** What are you doing now? **Suzie:** Counting by tens because, actually, that's easy. I'm on 110, so I know 44 is wrong. I have more to go, but I don't think I have thousands more to go. I bet 2,448 is too many. Maybe it's 288 or 248.	**T:** *In her picture of tally marks, Suzie demonstrated an understanding of what the problem was asking her. Her symbolic representations also indicated awareness that multiplication was involved. Although her written explanation implied weak number sense, during our conversation she did recognize that 2,448 was much too large, indicating greater understanding than shown on her paper.*

Informed Instructional Suggestions

Suzie needs additional experiences with multiplying small two-digit numbers by one-digit numbers to help her strengthen her number sense while continuing to develop her multiplicative reasoning.

Reassessment

1. Use a similar problem at the same level of difficulty.

   Mr. Stanley bought 9 boxes of crayons for his craft class. Each box had 24 crayons. What was the total number of crayons that Mr. Stanley bought?

   A. 186
   B. 216
   C. 35
   D. 1,836

   Show how you know.

2. Choose a problem that is similar but slightly more challenging.

   Gladys bought 7 reams of paper. Each ream had 500 sheets. What is the total number of sheets of paper that Gladys bought?

   A. 350
   B. 35,000
   C. 3,500
   D. 3,050

   Show how you know.

3. Ask students to solve a problem with no multiple-choice responses.

   Susie bought 4 bags of valentine erasers. Each bag had 144 erasers. How many erasers did she buy? Show how you know using words, pictures, and numbers.

PROBLEM FIVE

Overview

This problem requires students to find a combination of two numbers that equal one hundred, an important landmark number. Students may apply their skills of computation, number sense, and estimation to correctly solve this problem.

Sample Problem

Which of the following is another way to write 100?

A. 45 + 65 =
B. 63 + 38 =
C. 72 + 28 =
D. 84 + 26 =

Show how you know.

Possible Student Solution Strategies

- Students use an addition strategy such as partial sums, decomposing, a number line, estimating skills, or the standard algorithm to find the correct answer.
- Students use a mental math strategy such as their knowledge of combinations that make one hundred or an efficient mental decomposing strategy.
- Students fail to regroup the ones into tens when appropriate.
- Students make a computational error.

Conversation Starters

- Select an answer you didn't choose and explain why it is wrong.
- What is another way you can show that your answer choice is correct?

Student Work Sample: Jackson

Name ______________________ Date ____________

Which of the following is another way to write 100?

A. 45 + 65 =

B. 63 + 38 =

(C.) 72 + 28 =

D. 84 + 26 =

Show how you know.

First, I added A. and got 110 so I crossed that out, because A. is 10 more than 100. Secondly, I added B. and got 101 so I crossed that out because B. is 1 more than 100. Thirdly, I did C. and got 100! But still, I need to add D. just in case, and I got the same answer as A. 110! So, I circled C..

A Conversation with Jackson	Teacher Insights
T: Wow, you did a lot of figuring. Tell me about your thinking. How did you know which choices were wrong? **Jackson:** Well, first I looked at all of the problems to try to figure out where to start. I knew the right answer had to equal 100. So I looked at the tens place of each of the numbers in choice A. I noticed that 60 and 40 were 100 and I still hadn't added the ones, so I knew that problem would be greater than 100. Then I did the same thing for choice B. Sixty plus 30 is only 90, but 3 plus 8 is 11, so I knew that sum would have a 1 in the ones place, and 100 doesn't have a 1 in the ones place, so I didn't choose it. Then I thought about choice C. It did equal 100! Yeah! I did choice D, too, just in case! It was like choice A. I could see right away that the sum would be bigger than 100 just by adding the tens, which equaled 100, and noticing there were ones I hadn't added. **T:** So before you wrote anything down, you did all of that thinking just in your head? **Jackson:** Yep. Then I wrote it down, but I showed my work with partial sums because the way I really did my thinking was too hard to put on paper. **T:** So you actually solved each problem in two ways? **Jackson:** Yep, I guess so!	**T:** *Jackson has a well-developed sense of number and strong estimation skills, which he used to mentally consider the problem. By applying these skills, he found the correct answer. His oral explanation detailed his use of estimation and number sense while his written explanation made use of partial sums. Without chatting with Jackson, I would not have known the strength of his estimation skills and number sense and how he applied them to answer this question.*

Informed Instructional Strategies

Jackson is ready to move on to similar problems with larger numbers. He has a strong command of adding two-digit numbers on paper and mentally. His methods are efficient and accurate. He also shows care in his work: in his verbal and written explanations, he went on to solve choice D "just in case."

Student Work Sample: Mandy

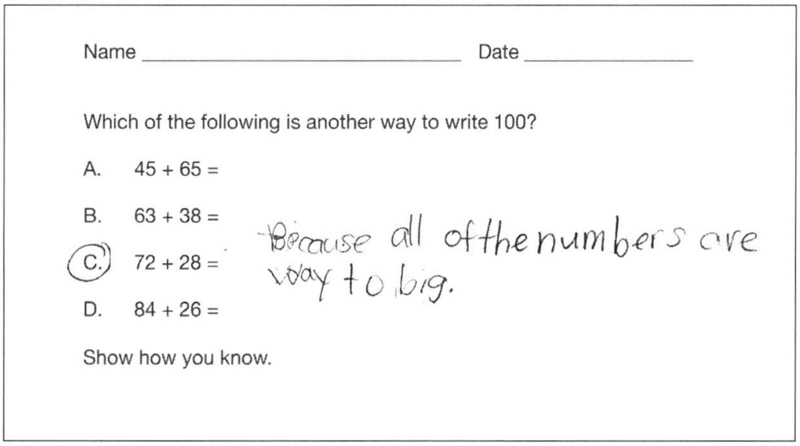

Name ______________________ Date ____________

Which of the following is another way to write 100?

A. 45 + 65 =

B. 63 + 38 =

(C.) 72 + 28 = Because all of the numbers are way to big.

D. 84 + 26 =

Show how you know.

A Conversation with Mandy	Teacher Insights
T: I see you circled choice C. Why did you choose answer C? **Mandy:** Um, I don't really know. Maybe because the other problems seemed like they would be more than one hundred. **T:** What made you think that? **Mandy:** Well, maybe that is wrong. Maybe it should be choice B. Yeah, I think maybe choice B. Can I think about it? **T:** Of course. As you think about it, write down your thoughts so we can talk about them in a few minutes.	**T:** *Mandy did circle the correct answer. But her verbal explanation and what she wrote on her paper indicated that it was essentially a guess. Mandy seemed to have no real basis for her choice. She had a sense that the other three choices would generate sums greater than one hundred, which was correct, but she lacked confidence and clarity about why this was so.*
T: I see you tried to find the sum for sixty-three plus thirty-eight, which is choice B. It looks like you added the tens—sixty plus thirty—and got nine. That doesn't make sense to me. Tell me more. **Mandy:** [Pauses and uses her fingers to confirm that six plus three equals nine.] Well it does because I know that six plus three equals nine. I used my basic facts. **T:** I agree with you that six plus three equals nine. What does the 6 represent in 63? **Mandy:** Maybe sixty? **T:** I agree that the 6 in 63 represents six tens, or sixty. What does the 3 in 38 represent? **Mandy:** I think thirty. **T:** How many tens in thirty? **Mandy:** Three tens are in thirty. Can I correct my work? **T:** Absolutely.	**T:** *Mandy's number sense and understanding of place value are vague. As I watched Mandy correct her work, I noticed that she did not correct the 9 she had written to represent the addition of sixty and thirty. She erased the sum she had written earlier and wrote* 91 *in its place.*
T: I noticed that you didn't change the 9. **Mandy:** That's because six plus three equals nine. **T:** How did you get the sum of ninety-one? **Mandy:** I had the nine and then one more from the eleven makes ninety-one.	**T:** *Mandy's explanation revealed an even deeper weakness in her understanding of place value than I had previously anticipated. Mandy needs to work on number sense and place value before going on with addition.*

Informed Instructional Suggestions

Because Mandy selected the correct answer choice, without further written or verbal explanation, we would have assumed that Mandy understood two-digit addition. We would have missed an important opportunity to better meet her needs. Mandy needs opportunities to strengthen and express her understanding of place value. She needs to use base ten materials to build numbers or take them apart, showing the ones and tens. Using pennies and dimes would be another way to help her develop this knowledge. To help Mandy understand what each of the digits in two-digit numbers represents, we also plan to have her make bean sticks using beans and tongue depressors. Later, when her place-value understanding is better developed, she will be able to use it to solve addition and subtraction problems with numbers containing two or more digits.

Student Work Sample: Billy

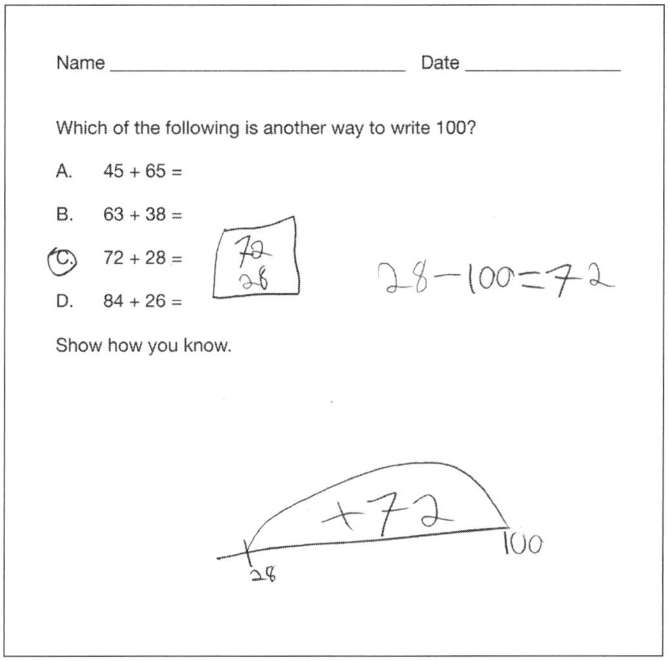
Name ________________ Date ________

Which of the following is another way to write 100?

A. 45 + 65 =

B. 63 + 38 =

C. 72 + 28 = 72 28

D. 84 + 26 =

28 − 100 = 72

Show how you know.

A Conversation with Billy	Teacher Insights
T: I see you wrote on your paper that twenty-eight minus one hundred equals seventy-two. Tell me about your thinking and why that makes sense to you. **Billy:** Well, since I think that 72 and 28 equal 100, I can just turn the numbers around so that 28 minus 100 is 72. It's like a fact family. We learned that last year. You can switch all the numbers around in a fact family.	**T:** *Billy seemed to have some idea that the correct answer was choice C, but his explanation was misguided. The problem he wrote for his proof, 28 – 100 = 72, is incorrect. While Billy has heard of fact families and has most likely tried to make sense of them, he showed confusion and lack of understanding. As a result, he applied his misconceptions in an inappropriate context.*

Informed Instructional Strategies

After a bit of probing, Billy demonstrated he has misunderstandings. Billy needs experiences that will correctly develop his comprehension of fact families. Billy also needs many chances to explore the commutative property. He needs to come to his own understanding that the order of the addends in an addition problem can be changed without affecting the sum, but this is not true with subtraction. The order of the minuend and subtrahend are very important. In a subtraction problem, reversing the order does affect the difference, unless doubles are involved, for example, 4 – 4 = 0. Counters can be used as models to help students see that, for example, 9 – 5 yields a different result than 5 – 9. Number lines could also be helpful to model this.

Student Work Sample: Elaine

Name ______________________ Date ____________

Which of the following is another way to write 100?

A. 45 + 65 = 110

B. 63 + 38 = 100

(C) 72 + 28 = 100

D. 84 + 26 = 110

Show how you know.

It is C. because 72+28=100 and that is how I got it.

45 + 65 = 110; 63 + 38 = 100; 72 + 28 = 100; 84 + 26 = 110

A Conversation with Elaine	Teacher Insights
T: I notice that you didn't choose answer choice A. Convince me that choice A is wrong. **Elaine:** We are supposed to find the problem that equals 100. Choice A equals 110. So because it equals 110, it has to be wrong. **T:** You wrote a little *1* above the 4 when you solved problem A. What does the little 1 mean? **Elaine:** It's just a 1. I added 5 plus 5 and that made 10, so I put down the *0* and carried the 1. Then I added the 1, the 4, and the 6. That made 11. Eleven plus 0 makes 110.	**T:** *Elaine has successfully memorized the standard U.S. algorithm for addition. She was able to apply it to get the correct sum. However, she showed no indication of place-value understanding or number sense. Her last statement, "Eleven plus 0 makes 110," raised my level of concern.*
T: Let's take a look at your figuring for choice B. Please tell me how you solved that problem. **Elaine:** I started by adding three plus eight and that makes ten. Put down the *0* and carry the *1*. Then I added one plus six plus three. That makes ten, so I wrote the *10* at the bottom. Then ten plus zero makes one hundred.	**T:** *Elaine was able to apply the algorithm she memorized, again showing no understanding of place value or the meaning of the steps that she used. This time, she made a computational error: she stated that three plus eight equals ten. Also, she stated that ten plus zero equals one hundred.*
T: You said earlier you were trying to find a problem that equaled one hundred. Didn't you get one hundred for choice B? Why didn't you choose it instead of choice C? **Elaine:** Oh, I guess there are two right answers. I should also circle choice B. **T:** Do you think it would make sense to use a second way of figuring to make sure you found the correct sum? **Elaine:** No, this is the way I do it and I think it's right. Besides, I know there is more than one way to make 100, like 50 plus 50 and 90 plus 10. So I just think there are two right answers.	**T:** *Elaine was right; there is more than one way to make one hundred. I appreciated that she recognized this and was able to give a valid example to make her point. Although Elaine marked the correct answer, and applied the standard U.S. algorithm for addition with reasonable accuracy, she has little understanding. She also stated that she had only one way to add numbers.*

Informed Instructional Suggestions

Elaine marked the correct answer and even showed a correct problem solution. However, she has not actually mastered the mathematics in this type of problem. She needs to learn a second way to solve addition problems. Knowing only one way is limiting. She needs to develop understanding about why the standard U.S. algorithm works as it does. Elaine needs to understand what the 1 she carried actually represents. Elaine indicated in her verbal explanation that she was thinking of all digits in these problems as ones; she did not indicate that sometimes she was adding ones and at other times adding tens. Lastly, it will be important to present Elaine with opportunities to understand that some statements that she made, such as ten plus zero make one hundred, make no sense!

Reassessment

1. Use a similar problem at the same level of difficulty.

   Which of the following is another way to write 100?

   A. 43 + 65 =
   B. 76 + 24 =
   C. 23 + 87 =
   D. 15 + 95 =

   Show how you know.

2. Choose a problem that is similar but slightly more challenging.

   Which of the following is another way to write 200?

   A. 103 + 98 =
   B. 152 + 58 =
   C. 127 + 63 =
   D. 139 + 61 =

   Show how you know.

3. Have students create their own similar problems, asking for other ways to write the sums 100 and 200, and then solve each other's problems.

PROBLEM SIX

Overview

This problem asks students to identify a set of numbers arranged in decreasing order. It is important with a problem such as this that students read the question carefully so as to select the correct order. Also, students must consider all the numbers in each list. This problem requires understanding of place value.

Sample Problem

Which set of numbers is in order from greatest to least?

A. 148, 164, 235, 276
B. 276, 235, 164, 148
C. 276, 164, 235, 148
D. 164, 276, 235, 148

Show how you know.

Possible Student Solution Strategies

- Students systematically determine which numbers are in the correct order.
- Students select the choice that lists the numbers in order from least to greatest rather than greatest to least.
- Students select a choice where there is no particular order to the numbers.

Conversation Starters

- What is this problem asking you to do?
- Does your choice answer the question that was asked?
- How did you think about the problem?
- How can you convince us that your thinking makes sense?
- Create your own problem that is similar to this one.

Student Work Sample: Lani

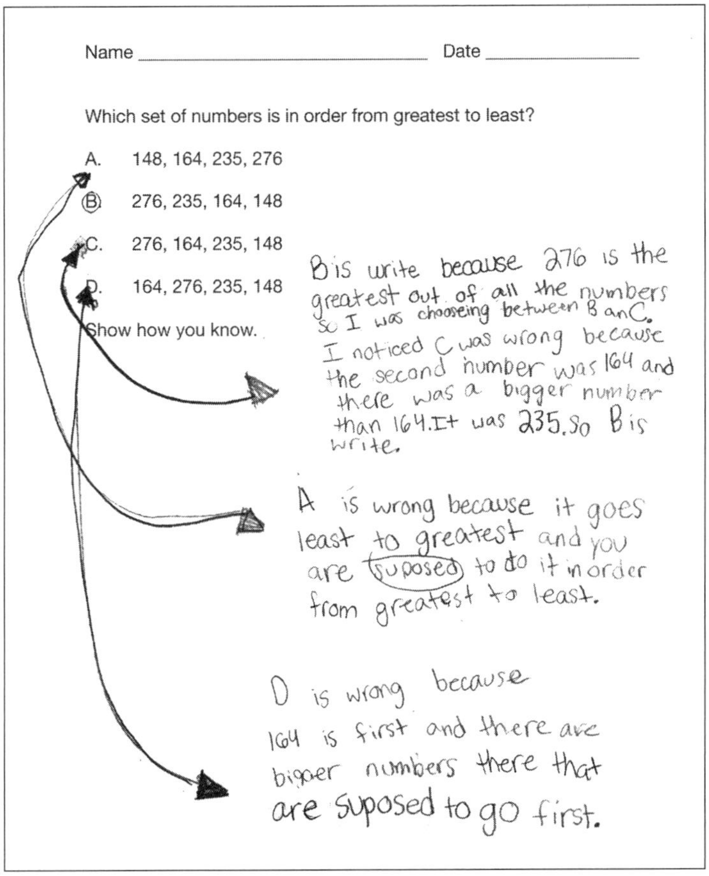

Name ______________________ Date ______________

Which set of numbers is in order from greatest to least?

A. 148, 164, 235, 276

(B) 276, 235, 164, 148

C. 276, 164, 235, 148

D. 164, 276, 235, 148

Show how you know.

B is write because 276 is the greatest out of all the numbers so I was chooseing between B an C. I noticed C was wrong because the second number was 164 and there was a bigger number than 164. It was 235. So B is write.

A is wrong because it goes least to greatest and you are suposed to do it in order from greatest to least.

D is wrong because 164 is first and there are biger numbers there that are suposed to go first.

A Conversation with Lani	Teacher Insights
T: Wow! You did a very clear job of explaining your thinking. It is easy for me to understand your thinking and the process you used.	**T:** *Lani's written explanation was very informative and clearly reflected her strong understanding. Her paper would serve as a good model for other students because of its completeness and clarity.*
T: Because I can see you clearly understand, please create your own problem that is similar to this one. Be sure to include what you think is the correct answer.	**T:** *Asking Lani to write her own problem is a useful, productive way of differentiating instruction for a strong student.*

Informed instructional Suggestions

Because Lani showed strong, clear understanding in her explanation, we plan to give her the opportunity to share her work with the rest of the class. Also, Lani and other students indicating strong comprehension can create and solve each other's similar problems. Finally, Lani is ready to expand her learning to four-digit numbers and beyond.

Student Work Sample: Carla

Name ______________________ Date ____________

Which set of numbers is in order from greatest to least?

A. 148, 164, 235, 276

(B) 276, 235, 164, 148

C. 276, 164, 235, 148

D. 164, 276, 235, 148

Show how you know.

I picked B because all of them were least to greatest exsept B.

A Conversation with Carla	Teacher Insights
T: Carla, I notice that you picked B for your answer. What is the problem asking you to do? **Carla:** It says to put the numbers in order from greatest to least. **T:** Please read what you wrote. **Carla:** "I picked B because, except for B, all of them were least to greatest or mixed up too, but I didn't write that."	**T:** *Carla understood the task. Her written explanation was not as clear as it could have been, but she did a nice job of clearly explaining her thinking aloud.*

Informed Instructional Suggestions

Carla needs to be sure her written explanations are complete and clearly reflect her thinking. Like Lani, she is ready to move on to larger numbers.

Student Work Sample: Sasha

Name ______________________ Date ____________

Which set of numbers is in order from greatest to least?

A. 148, 164, 235, 276

(B.) 276, 235, 164, 148

C. 276, 164, 235, 148

D. 164, 276, 235, 148

Show how you know.

276
235
164
148

A — A is wrong because 2 is not first.

C — C is not right because its first numbers go like this 2,1,2,1.

D — D is not right because its first numbers go like this 1,2,2,1.

A Conversation with Sasha	Teacher Insights
T: Please tell me more about how you thought about this problem. **Sasha:** Um, well I looked at the first number of the numbers and then I decided how to put them in order. **T:** I see in your explanation about choice A that you talk about the number 2. What does the number 2 actually represent? **Sasha:** I'm not sure, it's just the first number. Maybe it means two tens? I just know that last year my teacher said to look at the first numbers. Two of the numbers begin with 2 and two of the numbers begin with 1. So it had to be B.	**T:** *While Sasha was able to get the correct answer, she did so using a misconception. She believes that ordering numbers requires examining only the first digits of the numbers to be ordered. I wondered as I listened to Sasha how she would handle ordering a list of both two-digit and three-digit numbers based on her strategy of looking only at the leading digits.*
T: You said that to put numbers in order, all you had to do was look at the first digit. What about numbers like 21 and 221? Both have 2 as the first digit. **Sasha:** That's easy; I already know that numbers in the 20s are less than numbers in the 200s. **T:** Good, I am glad that is clear for you. However, did your rule work for those two numbers? **Sasha:** Hmm . . . maybe not? The 2 in 21 represents two tens and the 2 in 221 means two hundreds. Is that right?	**T:** *Sasha did use her number sense to answer my question. She was now experiencing disequilibrium, a perfect time for new learning. To further probe her understanding, I decided to give her two three-digit numbers each with the same first digit but different second digits.*
T: What about the numbers 437 and 456? Which is greater? **Sasha:** Well, they both start with 4 in the hundreds place, and that means they are both in the 400s. So then I have to look at the 10s. Four hundred fifty-six has five 10s and 437 has only three 10s. So that means 456 is bigger. **T:** What do you need to do to improve the explanation on your paper? **Sasha:** I need to put that the 2s and 1s stand for hundreds, not just 2 or 1.	**T:** *With some guidance, Sasha was able to expand her understanding of place value and successfully apply it to a new situation.*

Informed Instructional Suggestions

Sasha needs some additional practice with ordering three-digit numbers. Then she will be ready to move to four-digit numbers. A digit's placement within any given number is critical to the value of that number. Sasha's initial written explanation indicated that she was seeing each digit individually rather than as part of a whole number. It will be important to remind Sasha to focus on a digit's placement within a number and what that digit actually represents, as well as to proofread her work to make sure her explanations are complete.

Student Work Sample: Mary

Name ______________________ Date ______________

Which set of numbers is in order from greatest to least?

(A.) 148, 164, 235, 276

B. 276, 235, 164, 148

C. 276, 164, 235, 148

D. 164, 276, 235, 148

Show how you know.

~~164~~ 276 ~~235~~ ~~148~~

148, 164, 235, 276

I think B., C., and D. are wrong because the nembers ar mixed up. I think the reason why they're mixed up is because they're trying to trick me.

A Conversation with Mary	Teacher Insights
T: What is this problem asking you to do? **Mary:** I have to put the numbers in order. **T:** Into what order are you supposed to put them? **Mary:** Greatest to least? Oh no! It tricked me, just like I wrote! I did least to greatest! These problems always trick me!	**T:** *Mary made a very common error. She chose the set of numbers that went from least to greatest.*
T: What is the correct answer? **Mary:** Actually, that's easy. It's B. C and D are all mixed up.	**T:** *Mary was able to select the correct answer and give a brief explanation of why it makes sense. She recognized that choices C and D are mixed up while A is arranged least to greatest.*

Informed instructional Suggestions

We need to remind Mary to read each problem carefully and, perhaps, restate to herself what the problem is asking her to do. Then Mary needs to check her work to be sure that she has answered the question asked. After some additional practice with ordering three-digit numbers and checking to be sure she has answered the question, she will be ready to take on larger numbers.

Reassessment

1. Use a similar problem at the same level of difficulty.

   Which set of numbers is in order from greatest to least?

   A. 356, 281, 345, 269
   B. 281, 269, 345, 356
   C. 356, 345, 281, 269
   D. 345, 356, 281, 269

   Show how you know.

   Which set of numbers is in order from least to greatest?

   A. 245, 381, 256, 369
   B. 381, 369, 256, 245
   C. 256, 245, 381, 369
   D. 245, 256, 369, 381

   Show how you know.

2. Choose a problem that is similar but slightly more challenging.

   Which set of numbers is in order from greatest to least?

   A. 566, 516, 561, 511
   B. 511, 516, 561, 566
   C. 566, 516, 561, 511
   D. 566, 561, 516, 511

   Show how you know.

3. Have students create their own problems.

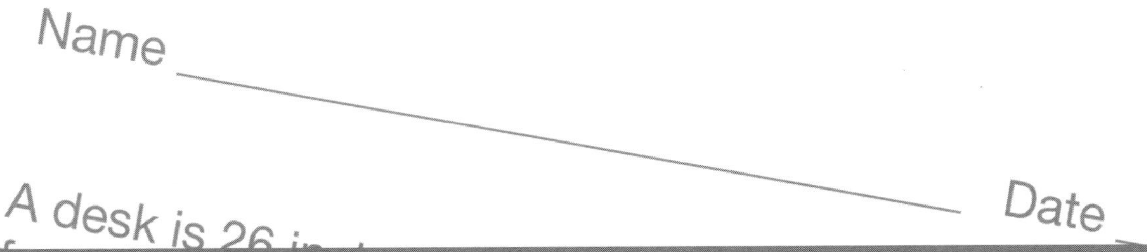

Measurement

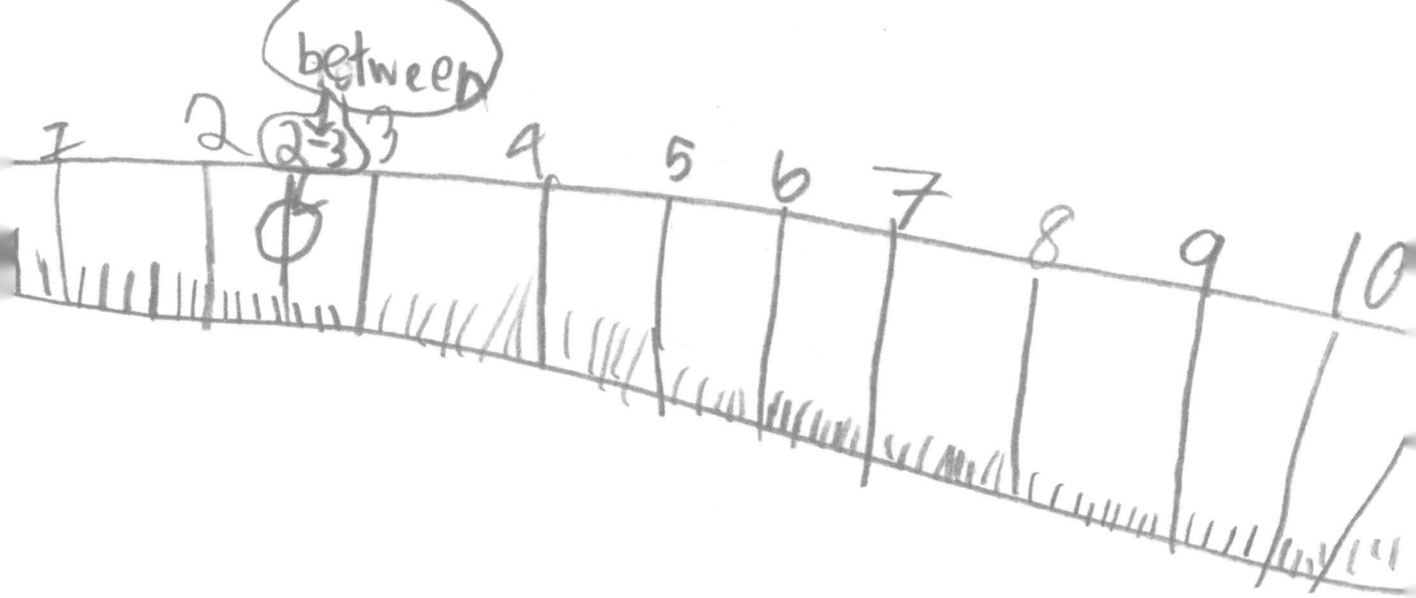

PROBLEM ONE

Overview

This problem is typical of measurement problems found on multiple-choice tests for grades two and three. To solve it, students must use the provided conversion information. Questions such as this often ask students to convert feet to inches, yards to feet, meters to centimeters, quarts to cups, hours to minutes, and so on. Students can use multiplication or repeated addition to compute conversions from larger units to smaller units. It is important to note that conversion from smaller units to larger units involve division.

Sample Problem

One afternoon, Ellen set up a lemonade stand. She sold 6 quarts of lemonade. How many cups did she sell? (1 quart = 4 cups)

A. 10 cups
B. 12 cups
C. 24 cups
D. 6 cups

Show how you know.

Possible Student Solution Strategies

- Students use multiplication to find the total cups of lemonade sold.
- Students find the total cups of lemonade using repeated addition.
- Students make a computational error while attempting to use a multiplication or repeated addition strategy.
- Students fail to use the information provided by the problem—1 quart equals 4 cups—and find an incorrect total.

Conversation Starters

- What information is needed to solve this problem?
- How can multiplication help you solve this problem?
- How could drawing a picture help you answer this question?
- What do you know about quarts and cups?
- What do the numbers you used in your solution represent?
- How could you explain your solution to a younger student?

Student Work Sample: Mallory

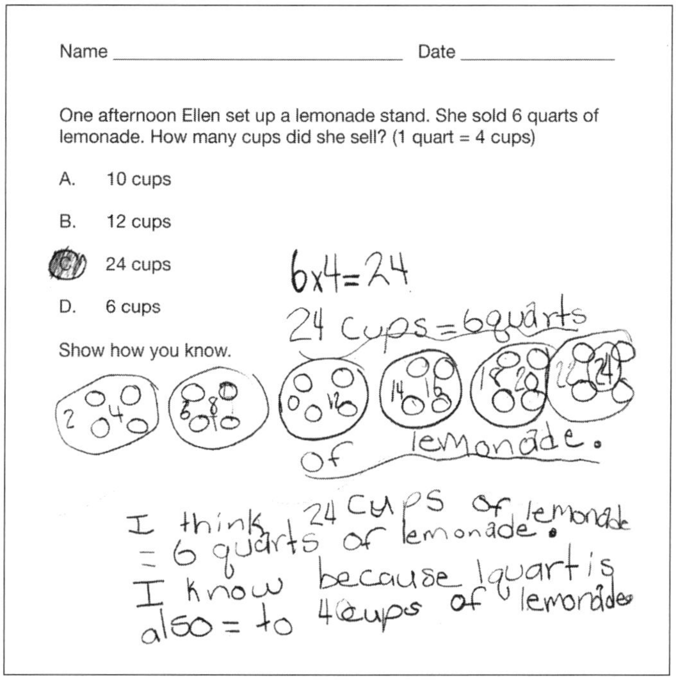
Name ______________________ Date ______________

One afternoon Ellen set up a lemonade stand. She sold 6 quarts of lemonade. How many cups did she sell? (1 quart = 4 cups)

A. 10 cups

B. 12 cups

C. 24 cups

D. 6 cups

Show how you know.

6x4=24
24 cups=6quarts of lemonade.
I think 24 cups of lemonade = 6 quarts of lemonade.
I know because 1quart is also = to 4cups of lemonade

A Conversation with Mallory	Teacher Insights
T: I see you used a picture to show how you solved this problem. Tell me more about how your picture represents the problem. **Mallory:** The problem says 6 quarts of lemonade were sold. I drew six circles because of the number 6. Next it says that each quart is the same amount as 4 cups. So I put 4 cups in each circle. I counted the cups by twos. That made 24 cups. I also wrote $6 \times 4 = 24$ because I drew six groups of 4 cups and that made 24 cups altogether. **T:** How would you explain your thinking to a younger student? **Mallory:** I'd draw a picture just like I did and explain as I was drawing what everything meant.	**T:** *Mallory used the information provided by the problem to effectively find an accurate solution. She was able to link her picture and the numbers she used directly to the problem.*

Informed Instructional Suggestions

Mallory understood what the problem was asking her to do and she had an accurate strategy to find an answer. Next steps for Mallory might be to work on measurement problems requiring other conversions involving multiplication, for example, finding the number of quarts in a given number of gallons or the number of inches in a given number of feet. Then, to provide a challenge, we can introduce Mallory to conversions involving division, for example, finding the number of feet in a given number of inches.

Student Work Sample: Annika

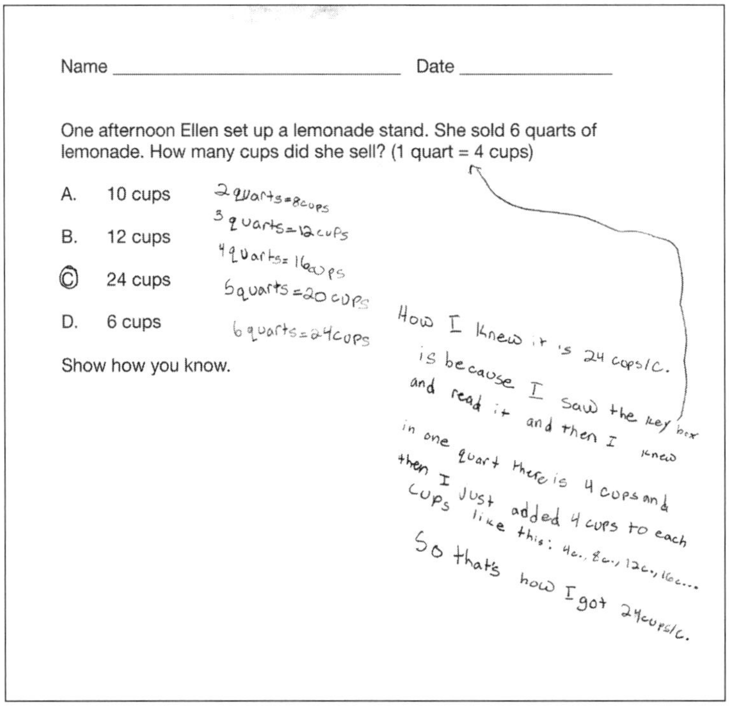
Name ______________________ Date ____________

One afternoon Ellen set up a lemonade stand. She sold 6 quarts of lemonade. How many cups did she sell? (1 quart = 4 cups)

A. 10 cups

B. 12 cups

(C) 24 cups

D. 6 cups

Show how you know.

2 quarts=8cups
3 quarts=12cups
4 quarts=16cups
5 quarts=20cups
6 quarts=24cups

How I knew it's 24 cups/c. is because I saw the key box and read it and then I knew in one quart there is 4 cups and then I just added 4 cups to each cups like this: 4c., 8c., 12c., 16c... So that's how I got 24cups/c.

A Conversation with Annika

T: What information did you need to solve this problem?

Annika: I needed to know how many cups in a quart. There are 4 cups in 1 quart.

T: Why did you need to know the number of cups in a quart?

Annika: Because the problem told me Ellen sold 6 quarts of lemonade. But the question it asked was, How many cups is that? So somehow, I had to have some information to put into my brain to figure that out. The information was that there are 4 cups in a quart.

T: What did you do with that information?

Annika: I made a chart. I put down that 2 quarts is equal to 8 cups because four plus four equals eight. Then every time I added a quart, I added 4 more cups. I stopped when I got to 6 quarts and it was 24 cups. And, yippee, 24 was one of the choices!

T: What would you have done if your answer weren't a choice?

Annika: I would have been sad and maybe tried again or made my best guess.

Teacher Insights

T: *Annika was able to make sense of the problem and was able to use the information provided to accurately find the number of cups in 6 quarts. Both her written and verbal explanations were clear.*

Informed Instructional Suggestions

While Annika has a strategy that worked well for this problem, she needs opportunities to expand her repertoire of strategies by exploring multiplication as a useful tool. Once Annika is comfortable using multiplication as a strategy for converting measurements, she can work on the same types of problems we suggested for Mallory.

Student Work Sample: Donny

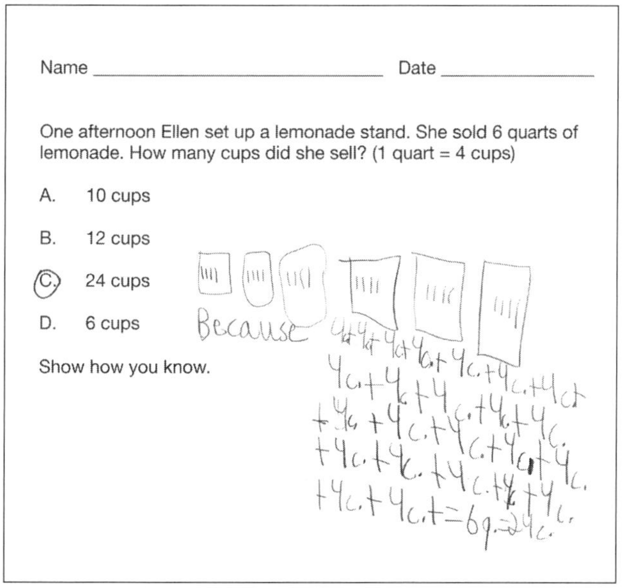
Name ______________________ Date ____________

One afternoon Ellen set up a lemonade stand. She sold 6 quarts of lemonade. How many cups did she sell? (1 quart = 4 cups)

A. 10 cups

B. 12 cups

(C.) 24 cups

D. 6 cups

Show how you know.

A Conversation with Donny	Teacher Insights
T: Tell me about your thinking. **Donny:** I put six boxes on my paper because the problem says there are 6 quarts. Each box is like a quart. Then I put four lines in each box to show that there are 4 cups in each quart, like it says. I counted up the lines and there were twenty-four, so I chose C. Then I wrote *4 cups* twenty-four times. **T:** Hmm, were there six groups of 4 cups, like you drew, or were there twenty-four groups of 4 cups, like your numbers show? **Donny:** I am not too sure. [Donny pauses a few moments to think about this question.] I think one of the parts of my answer is wrong. I think it's all the 4s. Oh yeah, it is, because 6 quarts is six groups of four. Oh no! There are way too many 4s. There should only be six and there are twenty-four.	**T:** *Donny's understanding is fragile and just emerging. He made the correct choice and he showed a correct explanation, but he also included an incorrect explanation on his paper. However, when I asked about his writing, he was able to work through his disequilibrium.*

Informed Instructional Suggestions

Donny needs more experiences with converting quarts to cups along with other conversions such as gallons to quarts, feet to inches, and yards to feet. A variety of concrete, hands-on experiences with these measurements should help him develop a good visual understanding of what they represent.

Student Work Sample: Charlie

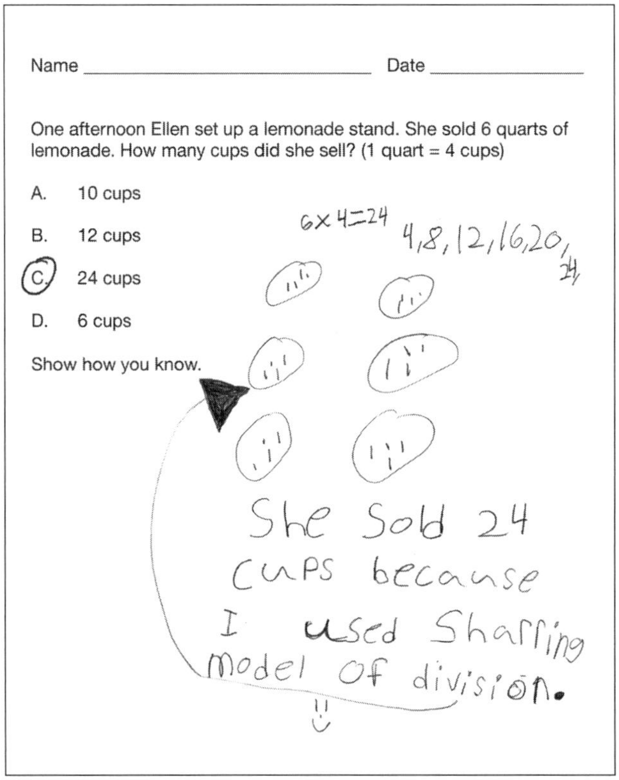
Name ______________________ Date ____________

One afternoon Ellen set up a lemonade stand. She sold 6 quarts of lemonade. How many cups did she sell? (1 quart = 4 cups)

A. 10 cups

B. 12 cups

(C.) 24 cups

D. 6 cups

Show how you know.

A Conversation with Charlie	Teacher Insights
T: I see you drew a picture. How did a picture help you solve this problem? **Charlie:** Each circle is like a quart. And each quart has 4 cups, so I put in four tallies for the cups. Then I counted up the tallies by fours and that made twenty-four. It's the sharing model of division. **T:** How could you use multiplication to help you solve this problem? **Charlie:** [Looking a bit perplexed] Wait a minute. I am not sure if my picture is division or multiplication. I'm confused.	**T:** *Charlie solved the problem correctly. He was able to represent his correct solution with a picture and was able to explain his thinking verbally. However, Charlie is confused about the operations of multiplication and division.*

Informed Instructional Suggestions

Charlie needs additional experiences to deepen his knowledge of multiplication and division and the similarities and differences between these two operations. Hands-on activities involving converting measures such as cups into quarts and quarts into cups and feet into yards and yards into feet would help Charlie develop these understandings.

Student Work Sample: Freddie

Name ______________________ Date ____________

One afternoon Ellen set up a lemonade stand. She sold 6 quarts of lemonade. How many cups did she sell? (1 quart = 4 cups)

A. 10 cups

B. 12 cups

(C) 24 cups

D. 6 cups

I Know that it's C because 6X5=24.

Show how you know.

A Conversation with Freddie	Teacher Insights
T: I see you used multiplication to help you solve this problem. Please tell me more about your thinking. **Freddie:** I used six because there are 6 quarts. Then I multiplied the six by five and it equals twenty-four. **T:** Why did you multiply by five? **Freddie:** Because, uh, I don't know. I just did and it was twenty-four. **T:** How many cups are in a quart? **Freddie:** Maybe five?	**T:** *Freddie made the connection between the 6 in the problem and the multiplication sentence he wrote. Initially he could not explain where he got the 5 in his written explanation until I asked how many cups are in a quart. He responded with uncertainty that maybe there are 5 cups in a quart. Freddie did not seem to use the information stated in the problem, and he believes that six multiplied by five equals twenty-four.*

Informed Instructional Suggestions

Freddie marked the correct answer, but his written explanation and conversation revealed some significant gaps in his understanding. Freddie needs concrete experiences with cups and quarts and the relationship between these two measures. He also needs to work on learning the basic multiplication facts.

Student Work Sample: Tony

Name ______________________ Date ____________

One afternoon Ellen set up a lemonade stand. She sold 6 quarts of lemonade. How many cups did she sell? (1 quart = 4 cups)

A. 10 cups

B. 12 cups

C. 24 cups

(D) 6 cups

Show how you know.

Because She said

A Conversation with Tony	Teacher Insights
T: Tell me what you know about quarts and cups. **Tony:** Well, you can drink milk out of a cup. I don't know about quarts. **T:** The problem gives you some information about cups and quarts. Read the problem and see if you can find the information. **Tony:** The problem says she sold 6 quarts of lemonade. Oh, I see something. It says 1 quart equals 4 cups. I didn't see that before. I just thought maybe a quart and a cup were the same thing, so I wrote that she sold 6 cups. **T:** Can you use the new information to help you solve the problem? **Tony:** I don't think so. I don't know what to do.	**T:** *Tony had no understanding of this problem, as his answer and explanations indicated. He was surprised to discover that there is a difference between cups and quarts.*

Informed Instructional Suggestions

Tony's incorrect multiple-choice answer indicated a weakness but did not show how serious his weakness is. It could have been that he had interpreted the word *cup* using its everyday meaning rather than as a unit of measure. It is important to be aware of words that hold everyday meaning as well as mathematical meaning and provide vocabulary development of these words in both contexts to students. From Tony's written explanation and conversation, it is clear he needs beginning experiences with cups and quarts to help him understand the two measures and the relationship between them. By using cups to fill quart containers with materials such as sand, popcorn, or beans, he will quickly come to see that 4 cups is equal to a quart. With this understanding in place, he will be better prepared to answer questions such as this. He may need basic experiences such as these for other forms of measure as well.

Reassessment

1. Use a similar problem at the same level of difficulty.

   One hot summer day, Sam set up a small plastic swimming pool. He put in 9 quarts of water before he noticed the pool was leaking. How many cups of water did he put in the pool before he saw the leak? (1 quart = 4 cups)

   A. 24 cups
   B. 36 cups
   C. 13 cups
   D. 18 cups

   Show how you know.

2. Choose a problem that is similar but slightly more challenging.

   At the school track meet, Jenny's team drank 20 cups of water. How many quarts did they drink? (1 quart = 4 cups)

   A. 20 quarts
   B. 4 quarts
   C. 5 quarts
   D. 10 quarts

   Show how you know.

PROBLEM TWO

Overview

Students in the second and third grades are often asked to find the area and perimeter of simple polygons on multiple-choice tests. To solve this perimeter problem, students must understand that they have been given the measurement of the perimeter and use that information to find the length of one side of the triangle. This provides a bit of a twist, as students generally are asked to find the sum of all sides to get the perimeter rather than use the perimeter to find a missing length of one side.

Sample Problem

The figure below has a perimeter of 15 centimeters. What is the missing measurement?

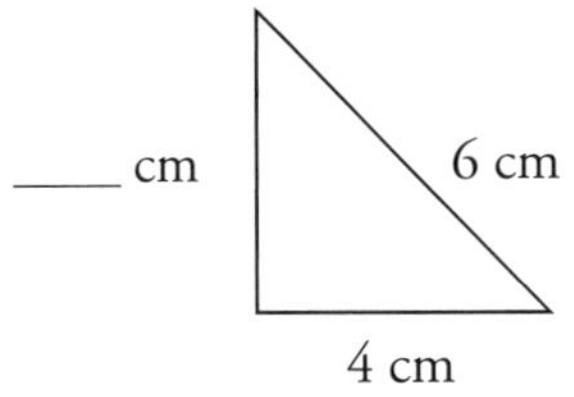

A. 4 centimeters
B. 5 centimeters
C. 6 centimeters
D. 8 centimeters

Show how you know.

Possible Student Solution Strategies

- Students recognize that the sum of the sides of the triangle give the perimeter. Using this knowledge, they add the two known sides. To find the missing measurement, they either subtract the sum of the known sides from fifteen or add a number to the sum of the known sides to equal fifteen.
- Students do not indicate understanding of perimeter and attempt to use a ruler to measure the side with the missing measurement.
- Students do not indicate understanding of perimeter and rely on visual clues to determine the missing measurement.

Conversation Starters

- How did you think about this problem?
- What does perimeter represent?
- Are the measurements shown on this triangle accurate?

Student Work Sample: Pat

Name ______________________ Date ____________

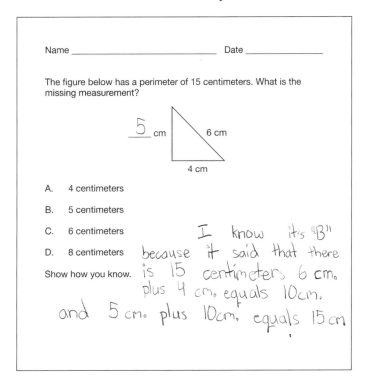

The figure below has a perimeter of 15 centimeters. What is the missing measurement?

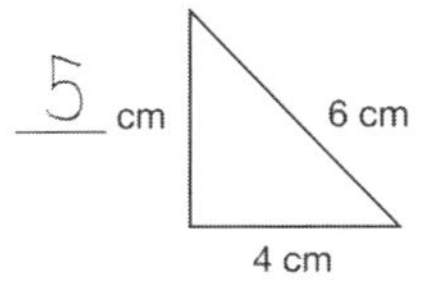

A. 4 centimeters

B. 5 centimeters

C. 6 centimeters

D. 8 centimeters

Show how you know. I know it's "B" because it said that there is 15 centimeters 6 cm. plus 4 cm. equals 10cm. and 5 cm. plus 10cm. equals 15 cm

A Conversation with Pat	Teacher Insights
T: How did you think about this problem? **Pat:** The perimeter is the distance around the outside of the triangle in the picture. So I have to find a perimeter of 15. Two of the sides equal 10 because 6 plus 4 equals 10. If I add 5 more to 10, that will be 15, and that's the perimeter. The answer is 5. **T:** You did a clear job of explaining your thinking.	**T:** *Pat chose the correct answer and his written and verbal explanations demonstrated his strong understanding of perimeter.*

Informed Instructional Suggestions

Pat is ready to create triangles and other polygons and find their perimeters using standard and nonstandard measurement. As an extension, we could provide Pat with given perimeters and ask him to construct (with materials or on paper) polygons with those perimeters.

Student Work Sample: Maria

Name ______________________ Date __________

The figure below has a perimeter of 15 centimeters. What is the missing measurement?

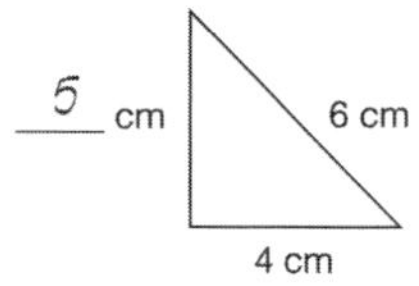

A. 4 centimeters

(B.) 5 centimeters

C. 6 centimeters

D. 8 centimeters

Show how you know.

D.
I think D. is Not right because I measured and D. is impossible to get cause it's too high.

A Conversation with Maria	Teacher Insights
T: I noticed you measured one side of the triangle. Why did you measure? **Maria:** Because I have to find the length of the side of the triangle. **T:** What information does the problem give you? **Maria:** It tells me that one side is 6 centimeters and another side is 4 centimeters. **T:** Does the problem give you any other information? **Maria:** Not really. It says the perimeter is 15 centimeters. **T:** What does *perimeter* mean? **Maria:** *Perimeter* means how far around. **T:** Can you use that information to help you solve the problem? **Maria:** No, I have to measure with the ruler.	**T:** *Although Maria knows a definition of perimeter, she could not apply the definition to help her solve this problem. Instead she reached for a ruler, which is always available to students, convinced that she must use the ruler to measure the side with the missing label. In this case, the labels of the known sides are not true measurements of the figure, so a ruler was not a good option. A student who understands perimeter can efficiently and accurately solve this problem based on the information provided.*
T: What did you find out when you used your ruler to measure the side labeled 6 centimeters? **Maria:** I started off with this side of the ruler [Maria indicates the side with inches], and that wasn't close, so I turned the ruler over [Maria indicates the side with centimeters], and that was closer. So I just figured it was right. **T:** Is there any way you can use the perimeter of 15 to help you? **Maria:** No, I don't think so.	**T:** *Even when Maria saw that the measurements she got when using a ruler didn't match the labels, she persisted in trying to measure to find the missing length.*

Informed Instructional Suggestions

Maria did mark the correct answer to this problem. However, she had no understanding of the information provided and what she was being asked to do. Here again, a correct multiple-choice response masked significant misunderstanding that was revealed in Maria's writing and her verbal explanation. Maria needs many opportunities to learn what perimeter really is and how it is related to the measurements of the sides of polygons. Then she needs support to discover that if she knows the measurements of two sides of a triangle and the perimeter, she can indeed find the missing measurement through computation.

Student Work Sample: Sarah

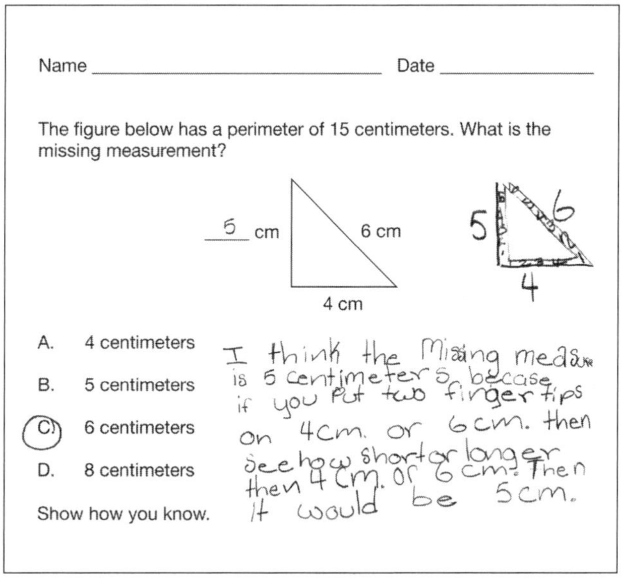

Name ______________________ Date ____________

The figure below has a perimeter of 15 centimeters. What is the missing measurement?

5 cm   6 cm   4 cm   5 6 4

A. 4 centimeters

B. 5 centimeters

(C) 6 centimeters

D. 8 centimeters

Show how you know.

I think the missing measure is 5 centimeters because if you put two finger tips on 4cm. or 6cm. then see how short or longer then 4 cm. or 6 cm. Then it would be 5cm.

A Conversation with Sarah	Teacher Insights
T: How do the measurements you made with your fingers relate to the measurements shown on the triangle? **Sarah:** I could put six fingers on 6 centimeters and four fingers on 4 centimeters and five fingers on the third side. **T:** Was the 6-centimeter side exactly six fingertips? **Sarah:** Nope. It was "about." I was estimating. **T:** What do you know about perimeter? **Sarah:** I don't really know, but maybe it has something to do with the sides.	**T:** *Sarah did not see the usefulness of knowing the perimeter and measurements of two sides when finding a missing side.*

Informed Instructional Suggestions

Sarah marked the correct answer but still lacks understanding. She needs experiences with measuring the sides of triangles and other polygons with mathematical tools and then finding their sum to determine the perimeter. Then she needs opportunities to find the length of a missing side when the other sides and the perimeter are known.

Student Work Sample: Shawna

Name ______________________ Date ____________

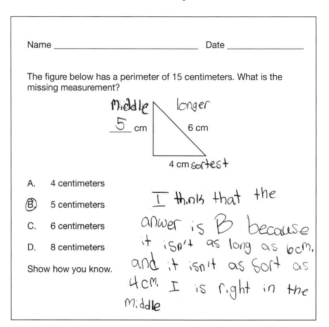

The figure below has a perimeter of 15 centimeters. What is the missing measurement?

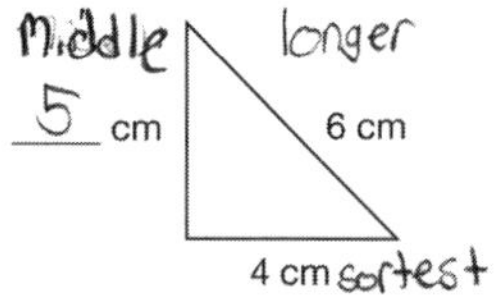

A. 4 centimeters

(B.) 5 centimeters

C. 6 centimeters

D. 8 centimeters

Show how you know.

I thinks that the anwer is B because it isn't as long as 6cm. and it isn't as Sort as 4cm. I is right in the middle

A Conversation with Shawna	Teacher Insights
T: Tell me about your thinking. **Shawna:** I used my eyes and I noticed that the longest side is 6 and the shortest is 4. The side with no number is in the middle. I looked at the answers and the only answer that was in the middle of 4 and 6 is 5. So I chose 5.	**T:** *Shawna used visual clues and logic effectively. But she provided no evidence for what she knows or doesn't know about perimeter.*

Informed Instructional Suggestions

Shawna marked the correct answer and gave a reasonable explanation. However, we don't know what, if anything, Shawna knows about perimeter and its relationship to the sides of polygons. We need to further probe Shawna's understanding to find out what she knows about perimeter and if she can find the measure of one missing side if the perimeter and lengths of other sides are given. If Shawna can do this, then she is ready for activities similar to those suggested for Pat. If this is an area of difficulty, the instructional suggestions made for Maria would also be appropriate for Shawna.

Student Work Sample: AJ

Name ______________________ Date ____________

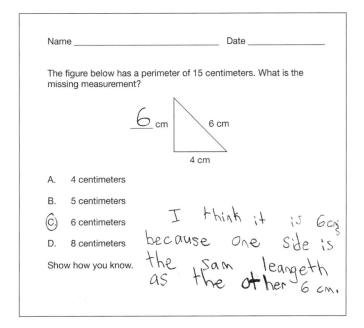

The figure below has a perimeter of 15 centimeters. What is the missing measurement?

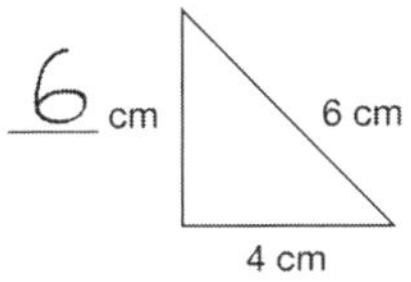

A. 4 centimeters

B. 5 centimeters

(C.) 6 centimeters

D. 8 centimeters

Show how you know. I think it is 6cms because one side is the sam leangeth as the other 6 cm.

A Conversation with AJ	Teacher Insights
T: Why do you think the missing length is 6 centimeters? **AJ:** Because it looks the same. **T:** What information does this problem give you? **AJ:** It gives me the lengths of two sides, and I need to find the third one. **T:** Does it give you any other information? **AJ:** No, that's it. That's why it was so easy.	**T:** *AJ did not recognize all the information provided by the problem. He ignored the perimeter measurement and didn't see its importance to this problem. Also, he used visual clues that misled him.*
T: Please reread the problem aloud. What do you think *perimeter* means? **AJ:** My brain forgot.	**T:** *AJ does not have understanding of perimeter.*

Informed Instructional Suggestions

AJ ignored the information that the perimeter was equal to 15 centimeters. The sum of the sides of the triangle he labeled equaled 16 rather than 15. An important first step would be to help AJ consider all aspects of problems. In addition, like several other students, he needs to develop his understanding of perimeter and its relationship to the sides of polygons.

Reassessment

1. Use a similar problem at the same level of difficulty.

The figure below has a perimeter of 24 ce

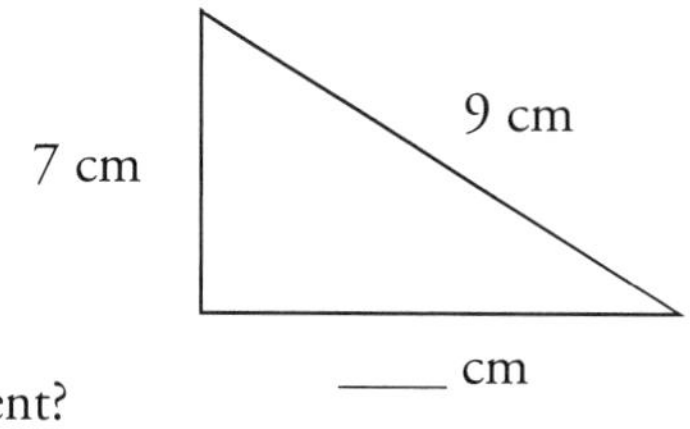

What is the missing measurement?

A. 6 centimeters
B. 7 centimeters
C. 8 centimeters
D. 11 centimeters

Show how you know.

2. Choose a problem that is similar but slightly more challenging.

The figure below has a perimeter of 39 centimeters.

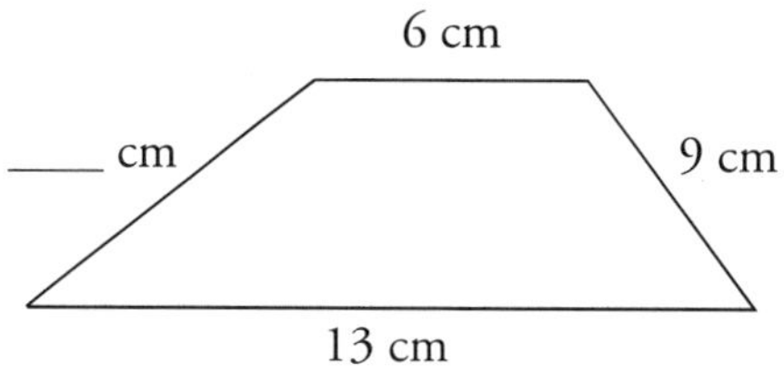

What is the missing measurement?

A. 15 centimeters
B. 11 centimeters
C. 13 centimeters
D. 10 centimeters

Show how you know.

PROBLEM THREE

Overview

This problem asks students to find the area of a polygon, a typical task on multiple-choice tests for students in these grades. Because of the way the polygon is drawn, students can count the area. There is no need to apply a formula, as will be necessary in higher grades. A common error students make is failing to count the two triangles as 1 square unit.

Sample Problem

What is the *best* estimate of the area of this figure?

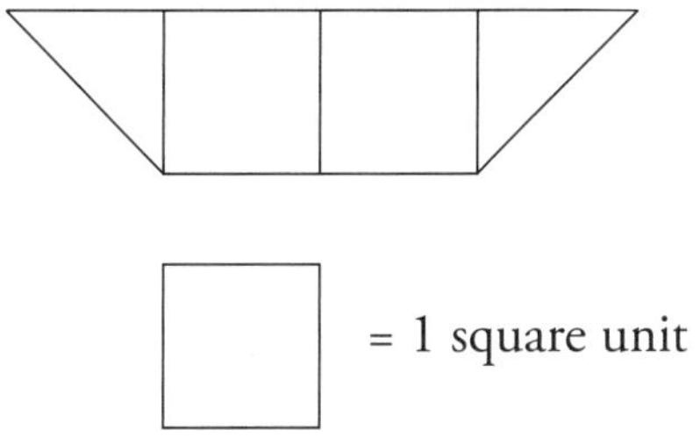

A. 2 square units
B. 3 square units
C. 4 square units
D. 5 square units

Show how you know.

Possible Student Solution Strategies

- Students correctly find the area by counting the squares and combining the two triangles to make a square unit.
- Students do not understand what a square unit is and misapply their ideas to find the area in one of the following ways: they count only the squares, ignoring the triangles, or they try to figure the number of whole squares that would cover the entire figure.
- Students attempt to find the perimeter rather than the area.

Conversation Starters

- How did you think about this problem?
- What do you know about area and how did it help you find a solution to this problem?
- What do you think *square unit* means?
- Why does your answer make sense to you?

Student Work Sample: Bob

Name ______________________ Date ____________

What is the *best* estimate of the area of this figure?

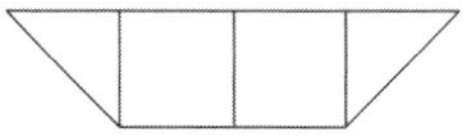

 = 1 square unit

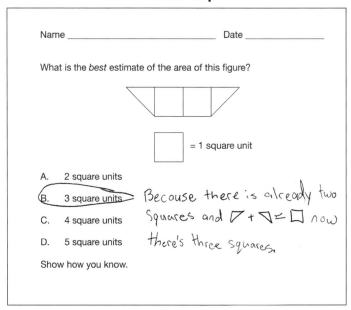

A. 2 square units

B. 3 square units (circled)

C. 4 square units

D. 5 square units

Show how you know.

Because there is already two Squares and ◸ + ◹ = □ now there's three squares.

A Conversation with Bob	Teacher Insights
T: How did you think about this problem? **Bob:** I think the area is 3 square units because there are two squares, so that's one, two. Then there are two triangles. If you turn one of the triangles around, you can put it with the other one and they can make a square. So the triangles are one square. Put that with the other two squares, and that makes 3 square units. **T:** You are telling me that it is OK to put two triangles together to make a square? **Bob:** Yep, and the square they make has to be the same size as the square unit, and I think it will be.	**T:** *Bob's written work indicated he was comfortable with applying his understanding of area. He understood the idea of a square unit and was not confused by the two triangular portions of the polygon. He simply combined them to create another whole unit.*

Informed Instructional Suggestions

Bob is confident and accurate in his application of finding the area for polygons such as the one in this problem. Next steps could include providing him with similar problems that are slightly more complicated, for example, a question about a polygon whose area includes a fraction such as one-half. Also, we could provide Bob with grid paper and let him create his own polygons and try to count the area. For reinforcement, he could do this same activity using geoboards and rubber bands.

Student Work Sample: Jinlee

Name ______________________ Date ____________

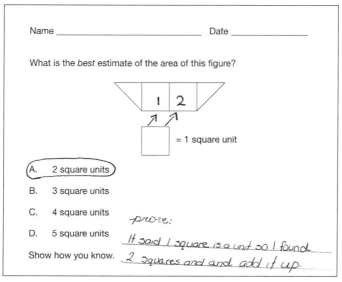

What is the *best* estimate of the area of this figure?

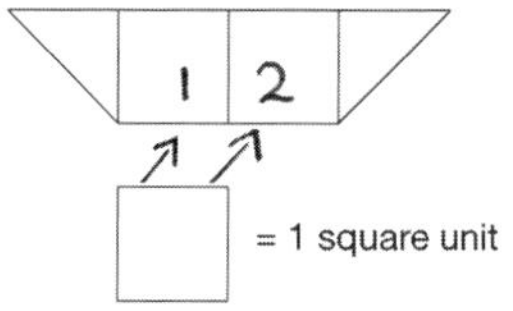

(A. 2 square units) — circled

B. 3 square units

C. 4 square units

D. 5 square units

Show how you know.

prove:
It said 1 square is a unit so I found 2 squares and and add it up.

A Conversation with Jinlee

T: What do you think *square unit* means?

Jinlee: It means something that is a square and is 1 unit.

T: Based on that information, tell me why your answer makes sense to you.

Jinlee: It makes sense because there are two squares in the shape. So that is 2 square units.

T: What about the triangles? Are they a part of the area of the polygon?

Jinlee: Area is what something covers, but the triangles are triangles, not squares, so I didn't count them.

T: Is there a way to rearrange the triangles into a square?

Jinlee: Maybe, but I am not exactly sure.

T: If you could make the two triangles into a square the same size as the square unit, would you count it as another square unit?

Jinlee: Maybe, if the square is the same size, but I don't know; it says square unit.

Teacher Insights

T: *Jinlee marked the wrong answer and she does not understand the concept of square unit. But had she just marked an incorrect answer, I would have known little about her lack of understanding. With Jinlee's written and verbal comments, I can plan next instructional steps in a clear, focused manner to effectively meet her needs.*

Informed Instructional Suggestions

Jinlee stated that area is the space that an object covers. However, Jinlee took the term *square unit* too literally by not realizing that other shapes within a polygon, for example the two triangles in this polygon, can be combined to form squares. A few carefully chosen experiences with counting area in situations such as the one in this problem will help Jinlee understand why all shapes within a polygon need to be combined and included as part of the total area. She could use grid paper or a geoboard to explore area concretely.

Student Work Sample: Melody

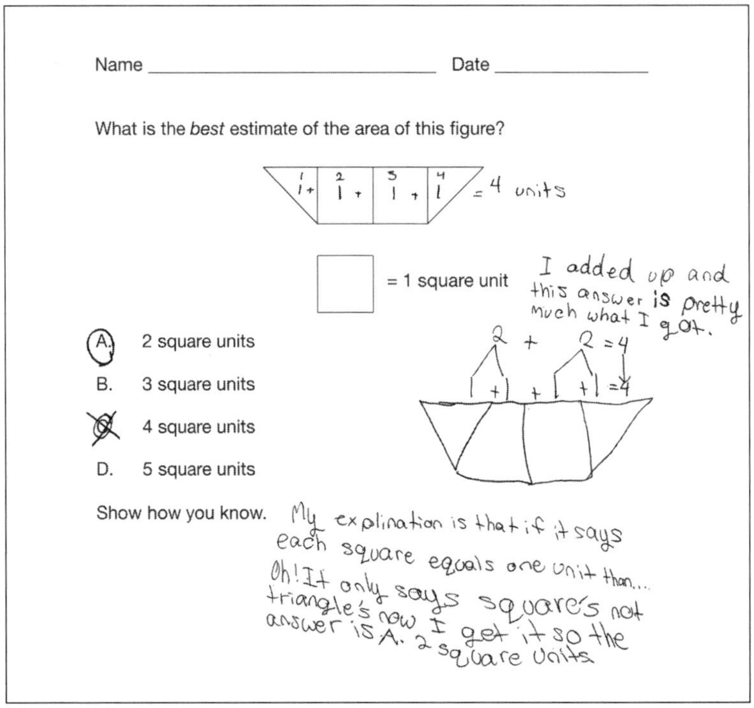
Name ______________________ Date ____________

What is the *best* estimate of the area of this figure?

= 1 square unit

A. 2 square units

B. 3 square units

C. 4 square units

D. 5 square units

Show how you know.

1+ 1+ 1+ 1 = 4 units
I added up and this answer is pretty much what I got.
2 + 2 = 4
1 + 1 + 1 + 1 = 4
My explination is that if it says each square equals one unit than... Oh! It only says square's not triangle's now I get it so the answer is A. 2 square units

A Conversation with Melody

T: I see you started your explanation about why the answer was 4 and then changed your mind and now you think the answer is 2. Why did you change your mind?

Melody: At first I just thought I had to count up how many squares the polygon would cover. I thought it would be four.

T: Do you think the polygon would cover up four complete squares?

Melody: No, that's part of the reason I changed my answer. It says square units, not triangles. There are only two squares, so I picked choice A.

T: Do you think it's OK to ignore the triangles?

Melody: Yes because they are triangles and it says square units.

T: Let's look at the square unit. Do you think there is a way to make that square unit into triangles?

Melody: Yes, you could cut it in half like this. [Melody runs her finger along the diagonal of the square.]

T: Let me be sure I understand you. You are saying that I could make a square into two triangles. [Melody nods.] Is it possible that two triangles could equal a square?

Melody: I am not too sure about that. Maybe?

Teacher Insights

T: *Like Jinlee, Melody marked the incorrect answer, although her thinking differed somewhat from Jinlee's. Melody was willing to entertain the idea that the two triangles in this problem might be arranged into a square that would be congruent with the square unit. Jinlee was much more reluctant to consider this idea. In both cases, asking these students to explain their thinking in writing and through a brief conversation allowed me to determine the appropriate next steps to take.*

Informed Instructional Suggestions

Melody's needs are similar to Jinlee's. She needs opportunities to explore squares to discover that a square can be cut into triangles and that triangles can be combined to form squares. Then she can continue to examine other shapes that can form squares. Like Jinlee, Melody needs to develop an understanding of the term *square unit* and how to determine the area of figures that include spaces that are not square.

Student Work Sample: Janessa

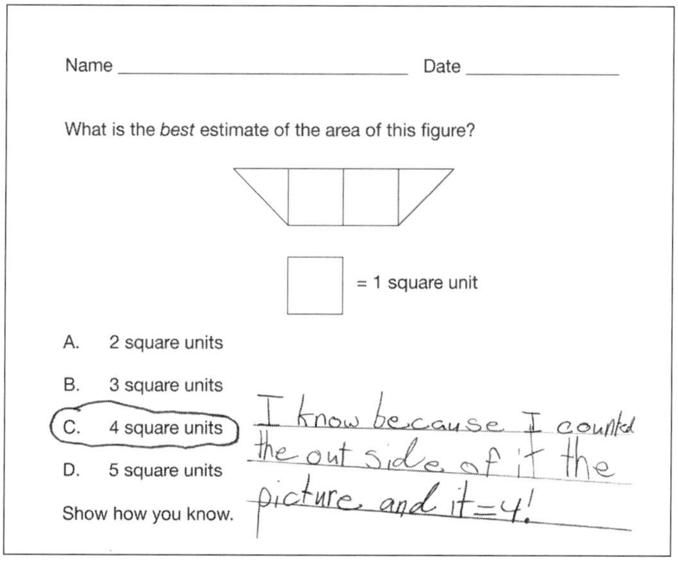
Name ______________________ Date ____________

What is the *best* estimate of the area of this figure?

= 1 square unit

A. 2 square units

B. 3 square units

C. 4 square units

D. 5 square units

Show how you know.

I know because I countd the out side of it the picture and it=4!

A Conversation with Janessa	Teacher Insights
T: What is this problem asking you to do? **Janessa:** Find the area. **T:** What do you think "find the area" means? **Janessa:** It means to count around the outside, like this. [Janessa demonstrates by counting the number of sides on the polygon.] One, two, three, four. The area is 4, so I chose choice C. **T:** Look at the square unit. It says one square equals a square unit. How does your idea compare with what your paper says about what a square unit is? **Janessa:** Oh, that's tricky. Does that mean the whole square is 1? **T:** You got it! That's exactly what it means. **Janessa:** Oops! I don't think the answer is 4 now. I am not sure what it is. It could be 2 or maybe 3, but not 5 I don't think. I don't know.	**T:** *Janessa was in a state of disequilibrium: her beliefs were being challenged and she was ready to consider and learn something new. One of her errors was mixing up the meaning of area and perimeter. She also indicated that she didn't really understand the idea of a unit of measure when she simply counted the sides of the polygon to determine what she understood to be the area.*

Informed Instructional Suggestions

Although Janessa marked the wrong answer on her paper, she provided valuable information about her misunderstandings. It is apparent that she needs experiences to help her clarify what perimeter is and what area is. She also needs opportunities to develop the idea of a unit of measure. Janessa should also work on the activities suggested for Jinlee and Melody.

Student Work Sample: Sumita

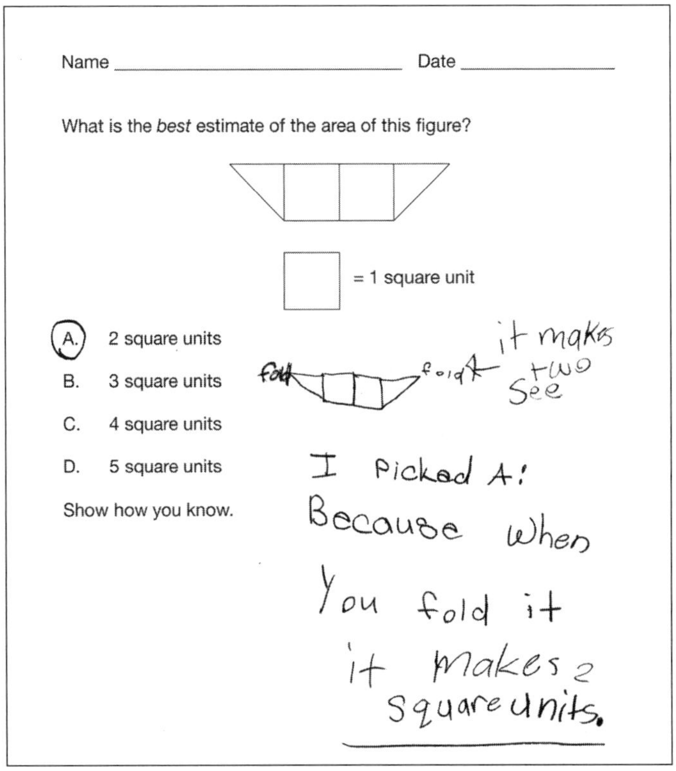
Name ______________________ Date ____________

What is the *best* estimate of the area of this figure?

= 1 square unit

(A.) 2 square units

B. 3 square units

C. 4 square units

D. 5 square units

Show how you know.

A Conversation with Sumita	Teacher Insights
T: I notice that you wrote about folding the polygon to help you think about the answer. Tell me more about this. **Sumita:** I can fold each triangle on top of a square to make it two squares. That's why I chose answer A. **T:** Why did you think you needed to fold the polygon? **Sumita:** I think that because the square unit makes me think I have to fit everything into squares. When I fold the triangles over onto the squares, I can fit it onto 2 square units.	**T:** *Sumita chose an unusual approach in her thinking about this problem. She dealt with the triangles by "folding" each of them on top of another square and then ignoring them. She, like several other students, has an incomplete idea of* square unit.

Informed Instructional Suggestions

Like several of the other students, Sumita needs several concrete activities to further develop her understanding of the meaning of a square unit and how it applies to finding area.

The errors made by students in this class revealed different levels of understanding and different ways they were thinking about this problem. However, most of these students would benefit from a similar series of connected experiences to help them explore and solidify their understanding of square units and how to use this idea to find area. Because these students showed slightly different misunderstandings, it will be important for us to vary our questioning for each of them to help them fill in the holes.

Reassessment

1. Use a similar problem at the same level of difficulty.

   What is the *best* estimate of the area of this figure?

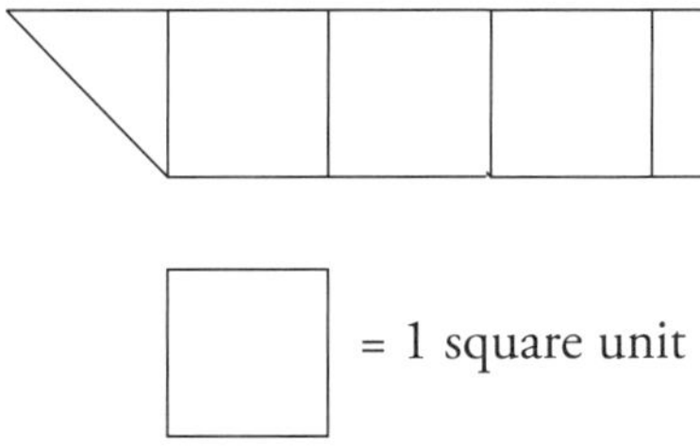

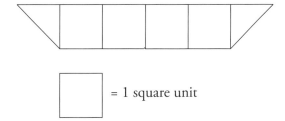

   A. 5 square units
   B. 6 square units
   C. 4 square units
   D. 7 square units

   Show how you know.

2. Choose a problem that is similar but slightly more challenging.

   What is the *best* estimate of the area of this figure?

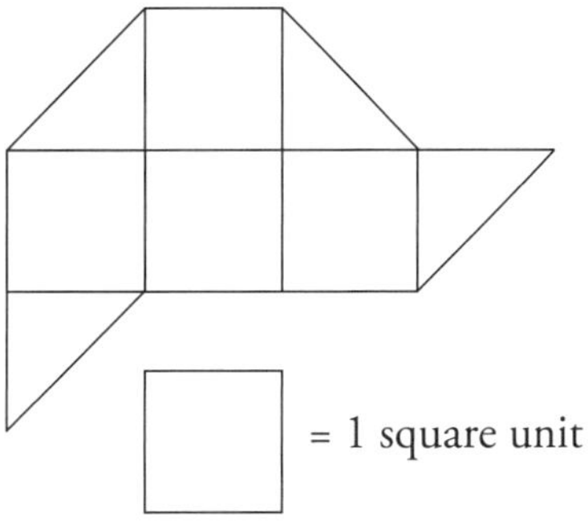

   A. 8 square units
   B. 4 square units
   C. 5 square units
   D. 6 square units

   Show how you know.

PROBLEM FOUR

Overview

This problem asks students to find two equivalent measurements. Students need to know the relationship among kilometers, meters, centimeters, and millimeters. Students who understand these units of measure can quickly eliminate three of the four answers as unreasonable. No conversion or computation is actually required.

Sample Problem

A skate ramp is 60 meters long. Which of these measurements is the same as 60 meters?

A. 6 millimeters
B. 600 kilometers
C. 6 centimeters
D. 6,000 centimeters

Show how you know.

Possible Student Solution Strategies

- Students apply knowledge of equivalent metric measures to convert meters into centimeters.
- Students make a correct guess.
- Students have little or no understanding of the meaning or relationship among metric measures of length.

Conversation Starters

- What do you need to know about metric measurement to correctly solve this problem?
- How are meters, centimeters, millimeters, and kilometers related?
- What is the order of these measurements from smallest to largest?
- Where would you see examples of this measurement in real life?
- Would you measure something long or short with this measurement?

Student Work Sample: Cassy

Name ____________________ Date __________

A skate ramp is 60 meters long. Which of these measurements is the same as 60 meters?

~~A. 6 millimeters~~

~~B. 600 kilometers~~

~~C. 6 centimeters~~

(D.) 6000 centimeters

Show how you know. I think the answer is D because 1 meter is 100 centimeters and 60 meters would be 6000.

A Conversation with Cassy	Teacher Insights
T: What did you know about metric measurement that helped you find the answer to this problem? **Cassy:** I know that 1 meter is equal to 100 centimeters. I know that millimeters are smaller than meters and kilometers are a lot larger than meters. It made sense to change from meters into centimeters, but I suppose we could change it into millimeters, but that would be a huge number of millimeters, and I didn't see any number of millimeters that big. **T:** What did you do to find 6,000 centimeters? **Cassy:** I know 1 meter is equal to 100 centimeters and so 60 would be 6,000. **T:** How do you know that? **Cassy:** Sixty times 100 is 6,000.	**T:** *Cassy had a clear understanding of metric linear measurement and was able to convert meters into centimeters. She was also able to recognize that converting meters into millimeters would produce a very large number, larger than any choice provided. She efficiently applied her knowledge of multiplication of ten and multiples of ten to solve this problem.*

Informed Instructional Suggestions

We can now give Cassy problems involving conversions of other linear metric measurements to be sure she is as fluent with them as she is with meters and centimeters.

Student Work Sample: Felicia

Name ____________________ Date __________

A skate ramp is 60 meters long. Which of these measurements is the same as 60 meters?

A. 6 millimeters

B. 600 kilometers

C. 6 centimeters

(D.) 6000 centimeters

Show how you know.

100×60=6,000
100×10=1,000
100×20=2,000
100×30=3,000
100×40=4,000
100×50=5,000
100×60=6000

A Conversation with Felicia	Teacher Insights
T: Why did you multiply one hundred by sixty? **Felicia:** I did that because there are 100 centimeters in a meter. There are 60 meters, so that is the same as 60 a hundred times. Then I just figured it out by 10 times 100, which is 1,000, so 20 times 100 must be 2,000, and like the rest of what I wrote. **T:** Your thinking makes sense to me.	**T:** *Felicia knows that 100 centimeters equal 1 meter. She used this knowledge along with her knowledge of the relationship of hundreds and thousands to figure out the correct answer.*

Informed Instructional Suggestions

Like Cassy, Felicia is ready to explore other metric measures and conversions. Her strong number sense will support her work with the metric measurement system.

Student Work Sample: Monica

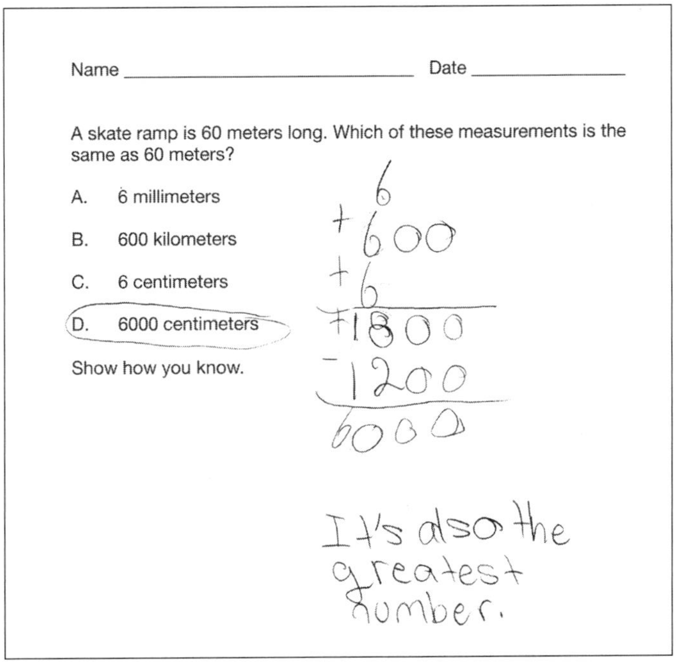

Name ______________________ Date ____________

A skate ramp is 60 meters long. Which of these measurements is the same as 60 meters?

A. 6 millimeters

B. 600 kilometers

C. 6 centimeters

D. 6000 centimeters

Show how you know.

A Conversation with Monica	Teacher Insights
T: Why do you think the answer needs to be "the greatest number"? **Monica:** Because I added them up. I added the first three choices and got 1,800. Then I noticed if I subtracted 1,200, I'd get 6,000, and that is choice D. **T:** OK. That's interesting thinking. Tell me what you mean by "greatest number." **Monica:** I just noticed when I chose it that it was the biggest number.	**T:** *Monica clearly has issues on several levels. First, she is not able to accurately add or subtract. Second, while 6,000 is the greatest number in the answer choices, it does not represent the greatest distance. The greatest distance listed is actually 600 kilometers. Third, she seemed to have no understanding of how to go about solving the problem or performing measurement conversions.*
T: Which is the shortest measurement: centimeters, millimeters, or kilometers? **Monica:** Centimeters? **T:** What is something you might measure with centimeters? **Monica:** I could measure my desk. **T:** Show me about how long you think a centimeter is. **Monica:** About this long? [Monica spreads out her arms to show her idea of a centimeter.]	**T:** *Monica confirmed her lack of understanding of linear metric measurement when she guessed that centimeters were the smallest of the units of measure I mentioned. Monica later correctly responded that she could measure her desk using centimeters, indicating some possible slight understanding. However, her example of the size of a centimeter was way off, revealing more confusion.*

Informed Instructional Suggestions

Hidden behind Monica's correct response was a multitude of misunderstandings, including inability to add and subtract correctly and numerous misconceptions about linear metric measurement. Monica needs help with important concepts in number as well as many hands-on experiences with linear metric measurement. We will also need to guide her with carefully constructed questions to help her make connections among the various measurements. As with most children, it will be important to continue to probe the thinking behind Monica's responses even when they are correct.

Student Work Sample: Jasper

Name ______________________ Date ____________

A skate ramp is 60 meters long. Which of these measurements is the same as 60 meters?

A. 6 millimeters

B. 600 kilometers

C. 6 centimeters

(D.) 6000 centimeters

Show how you know. Today, I make a guess, I chose the most likely selection, D.

A Conversation with Jasper	Teacher Insights
T: I see you wrote that you guessed. I noticed that you chose an answer that was in centimeters. What can you measure in centimeters? **Jasper:** I know that I can measure my foot, my sandwich, my pencil, and stuff like that in centimeters. **T:** Good examples of things you could measure in centimeters. What would make sense to measure in meters? **Jasper:** The track could be measured in meters, or maybe the distance from home base to first base. **T:** Is a kilometer longer or shorter than a meter? **Jasper:** I am not too sure. That's why I ended up guessing. I knew that 6 centimeters was about this long [indicating a reasonably accurate distance using his fingers]. That is way too short for a skate ramp! And I really don't know what a millimeter is. So, 6,000 centimeters is way bigger than 6 centimeters, so I chose it.	**T:** *Jasper has an understanding of centimeters and can apply that knowledge to things he could measure with centimeters. Jasper also has an understanding of things that can be measured using meters. However, as the conversation progressed, it became apparent that Jasper needs help developing knowledge and understanding of kilometers and millimeters.*

Informed Instructional Suggestions

Although Jasper marked the correct choice, he is not proficient in his understanding of linear metric measurement. He has some beginning understanding that he was able to apply to find the correct answer, but he still needs many more experiences to complete and solidify his knowledge. Opportunities to measure common objects using standard tools and then record his findings will allow him to develop his understanding of what the measurements represent. Measuring the same objects using different measurement scales will help him understand the relationships among the units of measurement.

Student Work Sample: Amelia

Name ______________________ Date ____________

A skate ramp is 60 meters long. Which of these measurements is the same as 60 meters?

A. 6 millimeters

(B.) 600 kilometers

C. 6 centimeters

D. 6000 centimeters

Show how you know.

I think it is B. because I think meters are biger then kilometers so thats why I think there needs to be more kilometers so it will equal 60 meters.

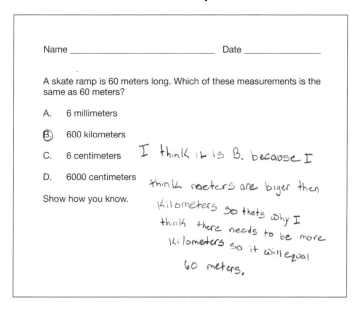

A Conversation with Amelia	Teacher Insights
T: Where do you think you might have seen an example of something that is about a meter long? **Amelia:** My car. **T:** What is something that is about a kilometer? **Amelia:** Your desk.	**T:** *Amelia's responses showed she has little or no understanding of meters and kilometers. She didn't mention centimeters or millimeters, so I will have to probe further to uncover her knowledge of those concepts.*

Informed Instructional Suggestions

Amelia needs to explore millimeters, centimeters, meters, and kilometers through hands-on activities. Once she has experience with these measures, she needs many opportunities to use them and develop understanding of equivalent measures, such as 1 meter and 100 centimeters.

Reassessment

1. Use a similar problem at the same level of difficulty.

   An obstacle course is 75 meters long. Which of these measurements is the same as 75 meters?

   A. 750 kilometers
   B. 7 millimeters
   C. 7,500 centimeters
   D. 750 centimeters

   Show how you know.

2. Choose a problem that is similar but slightly more challenging.

   A pool is 3,000 centimeters long. Which of these measurements is the same as 3,000 centimeters?

   A. 30 meters
   B. 300 centimeters
   C. 30 millimeters
   D. 3 kilometers

   Show how you know.

PROBLEM FIVE

Overview

This problem asks students to apply their knowledge to convert a measurement in inches to an approximate length in feet. Students should be able to either estimate to figure the answer or use computation to solve the problem.

Sample Problem

A desk is 26 inches wide. Which of these best describes the width in feet?

A. less than 1 foot
B. between 1 foot and 2 feet
C. between 2 feet and 3 feet
D. more than 3 feet

Show how you know.

Possible Student Solution Strategies

- Students apply their understanding of inches and feet to accurately solve the problem.
- Students make a real-world connection to help them think about the problem and solve it.
- Students make a guess.
- Students incorrectly apply knowledge of linear measurement.

Conversation Starters

- What do you know about inches and feet?
- What operation did you use to help you figure out your answer?
- Is a ruler necessary to answer this question? Why or why not?
- How would you explain your thinking to a younger student?

Student Work Samples: Mark and Lisa

Name ______________________ Date ____________

A desk is 26 inches wide. Which of these best describes the width in feet?

A. ~~less than 1 foot~~ – 11 in. or lower

B. ~~between 1 foot and 2 feet~~ – 12 in. to 24 in.

(C.) between 2 feet and 3 feet

D. ~~more than 3 feet~~ – 36 in. or higher

Show how you know.

I know it is C because 26 inches is between 24 in. and 36 in.

Name ______________________ Date ____________

A desk is 26 inches wide. Which of these best describes the width in feet?

A. less than 1 foot

B. between 1 foot and 2 feet

(C.) between 2 feet and 3 feet

D. more than 3 feet

Show how you know.

what best discribes the desk is choice C because it can't be choice A because 1 foot is only 12 inches and the desk is 26 so that won't work. Choice B is wrong because 24 inches is 2 feet and the desk is 26 so that is too small. Choice D is also wrong because 3 feet is 36 inches and 26 is smaller than 36 so that is too big. So, Choice C is write because 26 is between 24 and 36.

A Conversation with Mark and Lisa	Teacher Insights
T: Mark and Lisa, I notice that you are finished. Please share your work with each other and see what is similar and what is different about what you did. **Mark:** First I looked at all the choices and thought about what each one meant. **Lisa:** Me too. We did that the same. But you did it mostly with numbers and I did it with lots of words. **Mark:** We both chose choice C. Your words say mostly the same thing as my numbers.	**T:** *Because Mark and Lisa were sitting next to each other and their answers were different ways of saying the same idea, it was beneficial for them to share their work and discover this for themselves.*

Informed Instructional Suggestions

Lisa and Mark wrote clear explanations. They were able to look at each other's ideas and find similarities even though their explanations looked different. Lisa and Mark need other opportunities to estimate and measure objects in their environment and convert the measurements from inches to feet and feet to inches. They could also measure objects at home. Working together to measure objects can help to build skills in cooperation.

Student Work Sample: Romee

Name ______________________ Date ____________

A desk is 26 inches wide. Which of these best describes the width in feet?

A. less than 1 foot

B. between 1 foot and 2 feet

(C) between 2 feet and 3 feet

D. more than 3 feet

Show how you know.

I Know because Ive had a $5.00 foot long at subway allot of times so I Know excacly how long a foot is 12".

A Conversation with Romee	Teacher Insights
T: Tell me about your thinking. It's very interesting. **Romee:** I really love Subway sandwiches, you know, "Five dollar, five dollar foot-long" [singing and demonstrating as in the restaurant's TV commercial]. My dad always makes me get a foot-long and split it with my brother—half for me, half for him. I know how long a foot is. It's 12 inches. Twelve inches and 12 inches is 24 inches. Twenty-six inches is 2 inches longer, so a desk that is 26 inches is more than two foot-long sandwiches, but less than three.	**T:** *Romee has a good visual grasp of the length of a foot through her experiences with Subway sandwiches. She used this real-world experience to correctly solve the problem.*

Informed Instructional Suggestions

Romee's approach was different than those of Lisa and Mark, but she has a clear way of thinking about inches and feet. Romee would benefit from the same activities and experiences that we suggested for Mark and Lisa.

Student Work Sample: Brian

Name ____________________ Date __________

A desk is 26 inches wide. Which of these best describes the width in feet?

A. less than 1 foot

B. between 1 foot and 2 feet

(C.) between 2 feet and 3 feet

D. more than 3 feet

Show how you know.

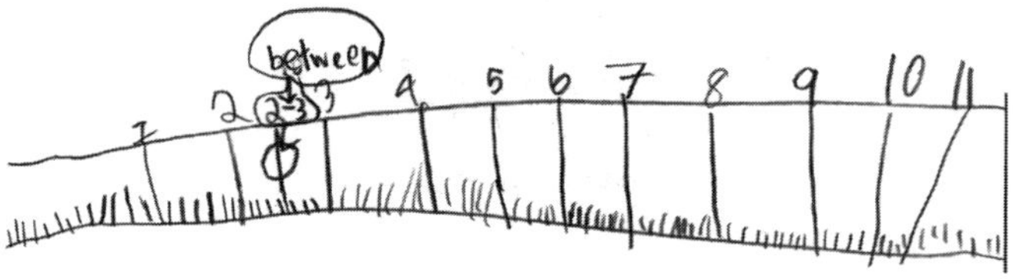

A Conversation with Brian	Teacher Insights
T: It looks like you started to draw a ruler. What made you think a ruler was necessary to solve this problem? **Brian:** I knew the problem was about measuring a desk. So I got out my ruler because you measure with a ruler. I drew it on my paper. **T:** What do you know about inches and feet? **Brian:** I am not too sure. Maybe there are 16 inches in a foot. I tried to count the little lines starting at the end of the ruler, and when I got to twenty-six, it was between 2 and 3.	**T:** *Brian was apparently under the impression that each small line on the ruler indicated 1 inch.*

Informed Instructional Suggestions

Brian's correct choice masked his fragile understanding. He used a misconception and coincidentally produced the correct answer. Brian needs many hands-on experiences with using linear measurement tools to develop his concepts of inches and feet.

Student Work Sample: Tanya

Name ______________________ Date ______________

A desk is 26 inches wide. Which of these best describes the width in feet?

A. less than 1 foot

B. between 1 foot and 2 feet

(C) between 2 feet and 3 feet

D. more than 3 feet

Show how you know.

C is right because 2 feet and 3 feet are kindof in the middle so 26 is mostly in the middle of 2 feet and 3 feet.

A Conversation with Tanya	Teacher Insights
T: What do you know about inches and feet? **Tanya:** You can use a ruler to measure inches and feet. **T:** What else do you know? **Tanya:** Inches are smaller and feet are larger. A ruler is a foot. That's all. **T:** Do you know how many inches in a foot? **Tanya:** I don't think so. I did look at the ruler and it has an 11 on it, so I figured 26 inches is more than two elevens. But it's not three elevens. It's sort of in the middle of two and three elevens.	**T:** *Tanya marked the correct answer, but her understanding is limited. She knows inches are smaller than feet but does not know how many inches are in a foot. She has not had enough experience with a ruler to know that it represents 12 inches.*

Informed Instructional Suggestions

Like Brian, Tanya's correct answer hid large gaps in her knowledge about inches and feet. Her needs are similar to his. Many hands-on, concrete experiences will help Tanya develop an understanding of inches and feet and of measurement tools. Tanya also needs guidance to help make her written answers more clear.

Student Work Sample: Melissa

Name ____________________ Date ____________

A desk is 26 inches wide. Which of these best describes the width in feet?

A. less than 1 foot

B. between 1 foot and 2 feet

C. between 2 feet and 3 feet

D. more than 3 feet

Show how you know.

I know it's C because, 20+6=26 and if you look at the problem you know the anser in gonna be C.

A Conversation with Melissa	Teacher Insights
T: Why did you decompose twenty-six? **Melissa:** I like to decompose numbers. I know a foot is 10 inches. I knew that twenty-six is the same thing as twenty plus six. So I wrote that. Two feet is twenty inches. Twenty-six comes between twenty and thirty.	**T:** *Melissa misapplied her knowledge of the base ten number system to our standard system of measurement.*

Informed Instructional Suggestions

Melissa needs experiences to help her understand that a foot is equivalent to 12 inches rather than 10, and she must learn the distinction between the base ten system and the standard U.S. linear measurement system. As with the other students, she needs many opportunities to measure objects with rulers and other measurement tools to correct her misunderstanding.

Student Work Sample: Sami

Name ______________________ Date ____________

A desk is 26 inches wide. Which of these best describes the width in feet?

A. less than 1 foot

(B.) between 1 foot and 2 feet

C. between 2 feet and 3 feet

D. more than 3 feet

Show how you know.

I think it is B: Because if you look at a real desk then you will know.

A Conversation with Sami	Teacher Insights
T: Tell me more about your thinking. **Sami:** Well, I took out my ruler and measured my desk. It was 23 inches. That's less than 2 feet and more than 1 foot, so I chose B. **T:** What information did the problem give you about the width of the desk? **Sami:** The problem said the desk was 26 inches wide, but the problem was wrong. I measured and the problem was wrong.	**T:** *Sami ignored information in the problem. However, she understands how to measure and the relationship between inches and feet.*

Informed Instructional Suggestions

Clearly Sami understands far more about measurement than the previous three students who marked the correct answer and had limited or no understanding. It is evident from Sami's verbal explanation that she does not need basic concept development. She does need to understand how to effectively use information provided in a problem to answer the question. Sami would benefit from reviewing how to read various problems and determine what they are asking as well as what information she can use from them.

Reassessment

1. Use a similar problem at the same level of difficulty.

   A table is 38 inches long. Which of these best describes the length in feet?

   A. less than 2 feet
   B. more than 4 feet
   C. between 3 feet and 4 feet
   D. between 2 feet and 3 feet

   Show how you know.

2. Choose a problem that is similar but slightly more challenging.

   A bookshelf is between 3 and 4 feet long. Which of these measurements could be its length in inches?

   A. 26 inches
   B. 34 inches
   C. 42 inches
   D. 53 inches

   Show how you know.

PROBLEM SIX

Overview

Students in second and third grade are often called upon to find the perimeter of polygons. Because not all measurements are provided in this problem, it is important that students apply the understanding that opposite sides of rectangles are congruent. Students who do not understand this will typically add the two measurements provided, thus finding only half of the perimeter.

Sample Problem

Sam's bedroom has a perimeter of 64 feet.

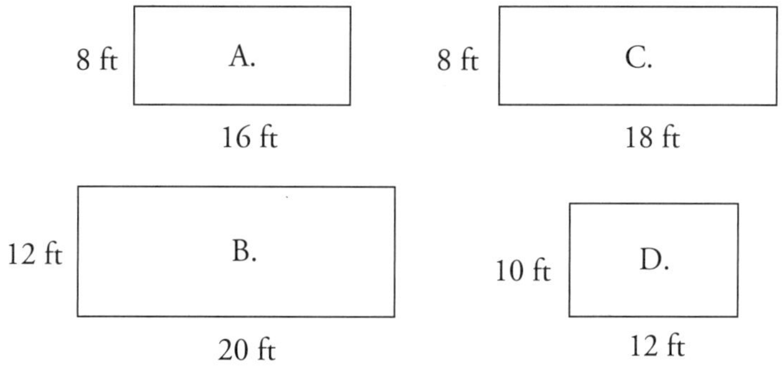

Which rectangle above could represent a room with a perimeter of 64 feet? Circle your answer below.

A. rectangle A
B. rectangle B
C. rectangle C
D. rectangle D

Show how you know.

Possible Student Solution Strategies

- Students include each side of the rectangle in figuring the answer, using addition or multiplication.
- Students figure the perimeter by adding only the labeled sides.
- Students choose their response based solely on the illustration, with little understanding of what the problem is asking.
- Students misunderstand the meaning of *perimeter*.
- Students use only the measurement of one side of the rectangle to figure the perimeter.

Conversation Starters

- What do you know about perimeter?
- What is this problem asking you to do?
- How did you think about this problem?
- What do you need to be careful of in this problem?

Student Work Sample: Lilly

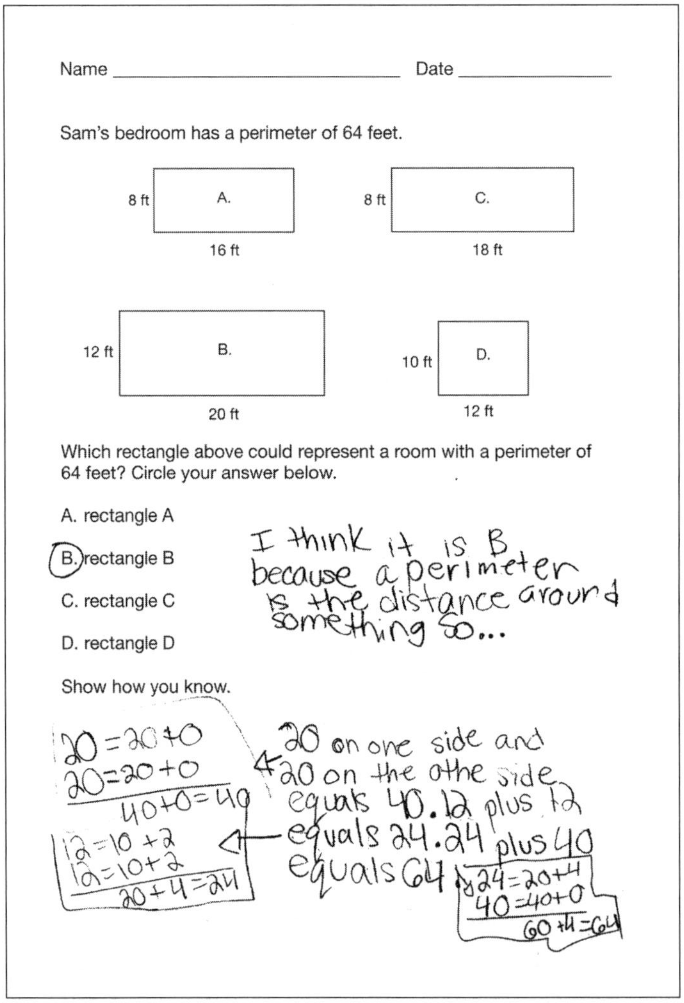
Name ______________________ Date ______________

Sam's bedroom has a perimeter of 64 feet.

Which rectangle above could represent a room with a perimeter of 64 feet? Circle your answer below.

A. rectangle A

(B.) rectangle B

C. rectangle C

D. rectangle D

I think it is B because a perimeter is the distance around something so...

Show how you know.

20 = 20+0
20 = 20+0
40+0 = 40

12 = 10+2
12 = 10+2
20+4 = 24

20 on one side and 20 on the othe side equals 40. 12 plus 12 equals 24. 24 plus 40 equals 64

24 = 20+4
40 = 40+0
60+4 = 64

A Conversation with Lilly	Teacher Insights
T: I appreciate your use and definition of the word *perimeter.* How did it help you think about this problem? **Lilly:** Like I said, perimeter is the distance around something. That means I have to add up all the sides to find out how far it is around. But I noticed that not all of the sides had a number on them. The opposite sides look like they are the same. So, I added 20 plus 20 and got 40. Then I added 12 plus 12 and got 24. Forty plus 24 is 64. **T:** Did you find the perimeter of choice B first? **Lilly:** Yes. **T:** Why did you start with choice B? **Lilly:** Because I looked at the numbers of all the choices and noticed choice B had a 20, and 20 times 2 is 40 and that is getting close to 64. Then I added 12 plus 12 and that is 24. I didn't have to go any farther.	**T:** *Lilly's written explanation indicated a strong understanding of perimeter of rectangles. She used her number sense to help her know where to start.*

Informed Instructional Suggestions

Lilly's understanding is clear enough that she is ready for a slightly different look at perimeter of rectangles. We could provide Lilly with a perimeter and ask her to draw and label different rectangles that could have the given perimeter. We could also teach her more efficient strategies for adding and multiplying, especially for doubles.

Student Work Sample: Callie

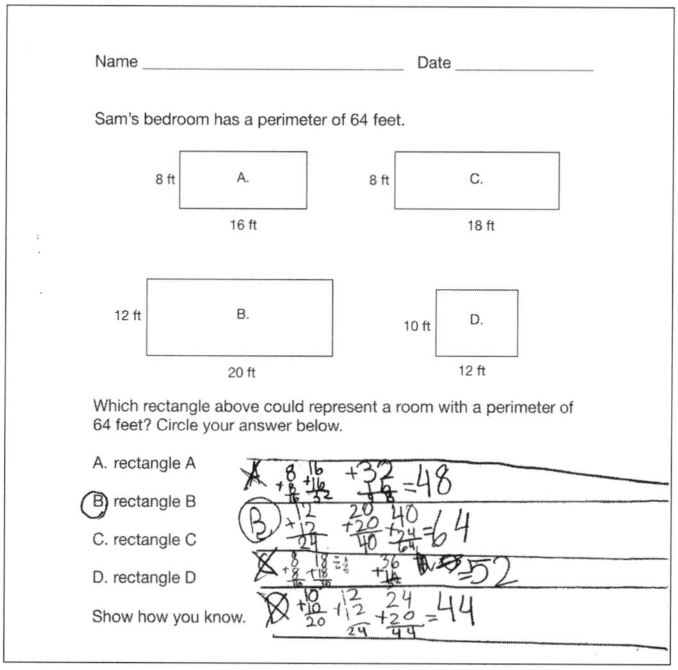
Name ______ Date ______

Sam's bedroom has a perimeter of 64 feet.

Which rectangle above could represent a room with a perimeter of 64 feet? Circle your answer below.

A. rectangle A

B. rectangle B

C. rectangle C

D. rectangle D

Show how you know.

A Conversation with Callie	Teacher Insights
T: I noticed by looking at your figuring that you doubled each of the sides. What do you know about perimeter that caused you to do this? **Callie:** They didn't put all of the numbers on the rectangles. But I knew from looking that opposite sides of the rectangles are the same. So I doubled the sides I knew. I did that for them all. Then I knew choice B was the one that equals 64.	**T:** *Callie has a clear, accurate method of finding the perimeter of a rectangle.*

Informed Instructional Suggestions

After providing Callie with additional practice to reinforce her understanding, we could ask her to write some similar problems for other students to solve.

Student Work Sample: Saree

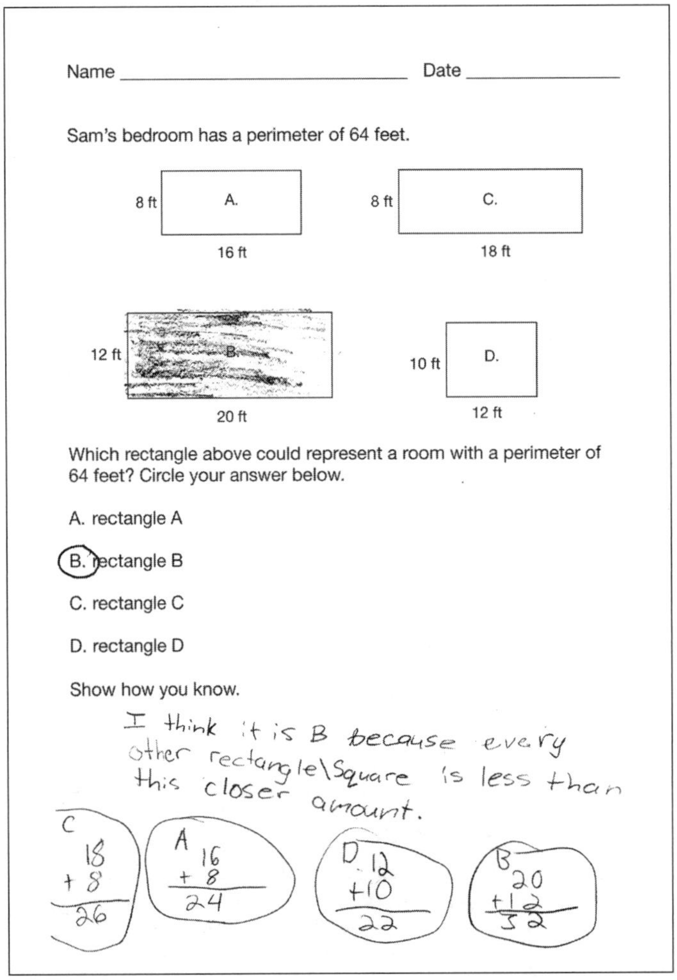

Name ____________________ Date __________

Sam's bedroom has a perimeter of 64 feet.

Which rectangle above could represent a room with a perimeter of 64 feet? Circle your answer below.

A. rectangle A

B. rectangle B

C. rectangle C

D. rectangle D

Show how you know.

I think it is B because every other rectangle\Square is less than this closer amount.

C 18 + 8 = 26

A 16 + 8 = 24

D 12 + 10 = 22

B 20 + 12 = 32

A Conversation with Saree	Teacher Insights
T: What do you know about perimeter? **Saree:** I think it is how far around you have to go. I just added the numbers. And that's how I got my answer. **T:** The perimeter is supposed to be 64 feet, but none of your answers is 64. How do you explain that? **Saree:** Um, well, 32 is closest to 64. **T:** How many sides does each of these rectangles have? **Saree:** Four. **T:** But I see by looking at your work that you only added two sides. What about the other two sides? **Saree:** There were only two sides with numbers, so I added them.	**T:** *While Saree marked the correct answer and was able to give a simplistic definition of perimeter, she was unable to apply her explanation to the rectangles in this problem. She accounted for only the labeled sides of the rectangles in her figuring. She made calculations about all four rectangles, then selected the sum closest to 64 feet. She did not seem concerned that none of her answers was 64 nor that she had accounted for only two sides of each rectangle.*

Informed Instructional Suggestions

Saree has several areas of need. She needs to learn that when figuring the perimeter of a polygon, she has to include all sides. She needs experiences to help her understand that opposite sides of a rectangle are congruent. This understanding would help her easily know what to do when only two dimensions of a rectangle are given. One way to help Saree explore the congruent nature of opposite sides of rectangles would be to ask her to fold several different rectangles in half either vertically or horizontally (not on the diagonal) and explain what she notices. When the rectangles are folded in half, the opposite sides will be laid one on top of the other, and she'll be able to see they are congruent.

Student Work Sample: Cameron

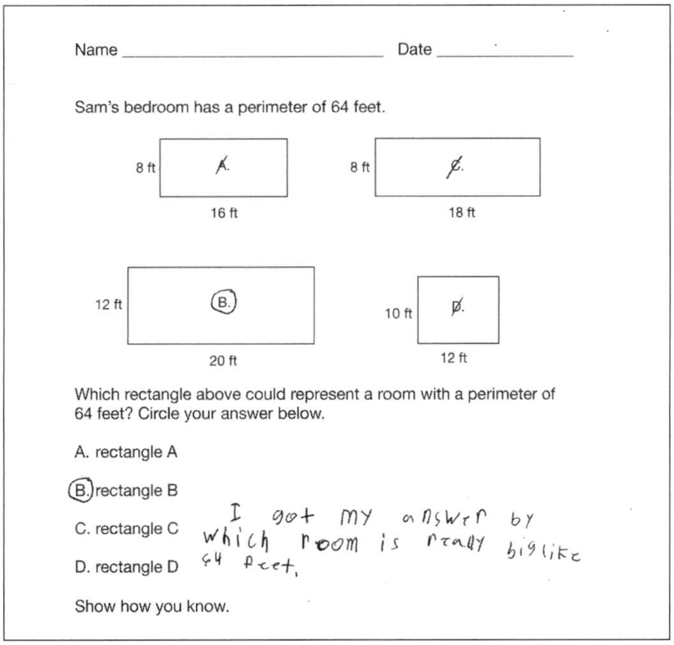
Name ____________ Date ________

Sam's bedroom has a perimeter of 64 feet.

Which rectangle above could represent a room with a perimeter of 64 feet? Circle your answer below.

A. rectangle A

B. rectangle B

C. rectangle C

D. rectangle D

I got my answer by which room is realy biglike 64 feet,

Show how you know.

A Conversation with Cameron	Teacher Insights
T: What is this problem asking you to do? **Cameron:** I have to find the room that is big. **T:** What do you mean by "big"? **Cameron:** Sixty-four feet must be big. **T:** What do you think 64 feet measures in this problem? **Cameron:** I don't know, but I looked at the pictures and B looks like a really big room, so it must be 64.	**T:** *Cameron's explanations indicated he has no understanding of perimeter of rectangles. He had the false assumption that he should look for the largest room to answer the question. He relied on the illustrations to determine which rectangle looked the biggest, paying no attention to the measurements given. While that strategy happened to work for this question, it certainly would not always be successful when dealing with perimeter problems.*

Informed Instructional Suggestions

Cameron needs to develop the concept of perimeter through hands-on experiences with measuring and figuring the perimeters of rectangles and other polygons. Cameron also should explore the properties of rectangles to understand that the opposite sides are congruent; this will allow him to solve similar problems in the future. Finally, he should learn not to rely solely on illustrations in a test, because they might not be accurate.

Student Work Sample: Georgia

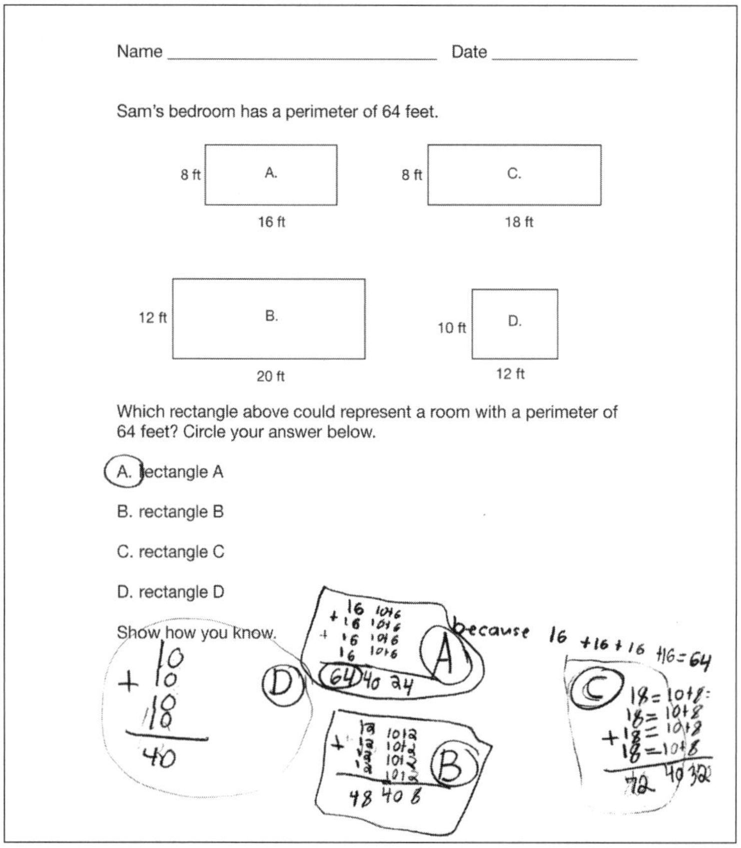

A Conversation with Georgia	Teacher Insights
T: Tell me about your thinking. **Georgia:** *Perimeter* means the distance around something. That means I have to add up the sides. **T:** I see you did that. What do you have to be careful of in this problem? **Georgia:** Some of the numbers are missing. **T:** What did you do about that? **Georgia:** I started with rectangle A. I wrote an 8 on the top because there was no number there and the 8 was on another side. But the sides didn't match. So I erased it. Then I decided to pick a side and add it four times because there are four sides. For rectangle A I chose 16, added it four times, and got 64. That must be right, so I chose A. But I did the others to be sure.	**T:** *Georgia has an understanding of perimeter. She knows that it is the distance around a polygon. She also recognized that some of the measures of the sides were missing in this problem. While her thinking would work for finding the perimeter of a square, it will not work for finding the perimeter of rectangles that are not squares. She did not show an understanding that opposite sides of rectangles are congruent.*

Informed Instructional Suggestions

It will be important to provide Georgia with additional experiences with measuring and calculating the perimeters of rectangles and other polygons. She also needs hands-on opportunities to develop the understanding that opposite sides of rectangles are congruent to further support her ability to solve problems when only two measurements are given. In addition, it would be helpful to reinforce Georgia's understanding that *all* sides of a square are congruent through similar activities.

Student Work Sample: Hope

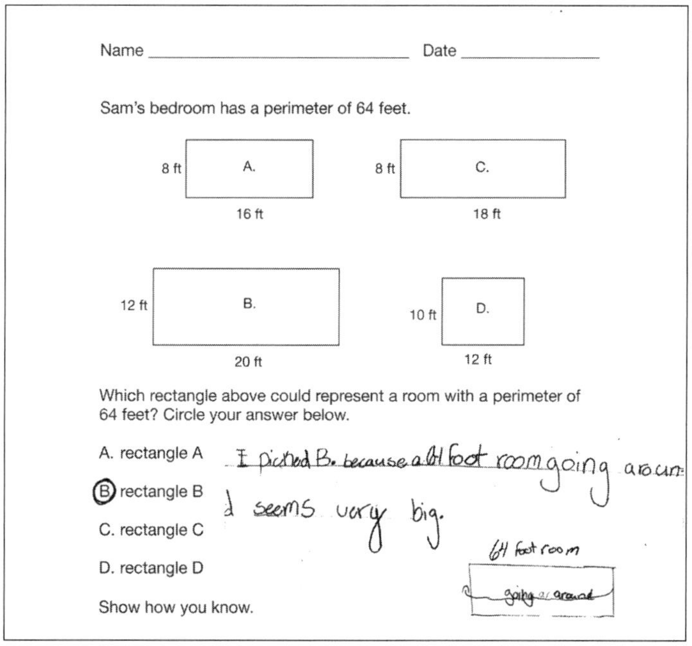
Name ____________ Date ________

Sam's bedroom has a perimeter of 64 feet.

Which rectangle above could represent a room with a perimeter of 64 feet? Circle your answer below.

A. rectangle A

(B) rectangle B

C. rectangle C

D. rectangle D

Show how you know.

A Conversation with Hope	Teacher Insights
T: Hope, tell me about what you know about perimeter. **Hope:** I know it is going around something, sort of like a Hula-hoop except that a Hula-hoop is bigger. I drew my picture to show you. **T:** Your picture tells me a lot about how you are thinking about perimeter. Why do you think there are numbers next to some sides of the rectangles? **Hope:** Oh, I didn't see the numbers. Hmm. I just thought 64 was a big number so I thought B must be the answer.	**T:** *Hope chose the right answer and made her best effort to make sense of this problem. But she has little understanding of perimeter. Her interpretation of what it means to measure around something is flawed and she paid no attention to the measurements shown for the rectangles.*

Informed Instructional Suggestions

Before all else, Hope needs experiences that will develop her conceptual understanding of perimeter. For example, she could walk around the perimeter of such things as the classroom, a four-square court, and the playground to gain a kinesthetic awareness of what perimeter represents. Other ways to develop this understanding include tracing the outlines of rectangles on a page or of her desk. Hope is able to add accurately, so once she has a clear understanding of what perimeter represents, she will be able to efficiently calculate it. Additionally, she will need opportunities to explore the idea that the opposite sides of rectangles are congruent and that all sides of a square are congruent.

Reassessment

1. Use a similar problem at the same level of difficulty.

   The perimeter of a garden is 62 feet.

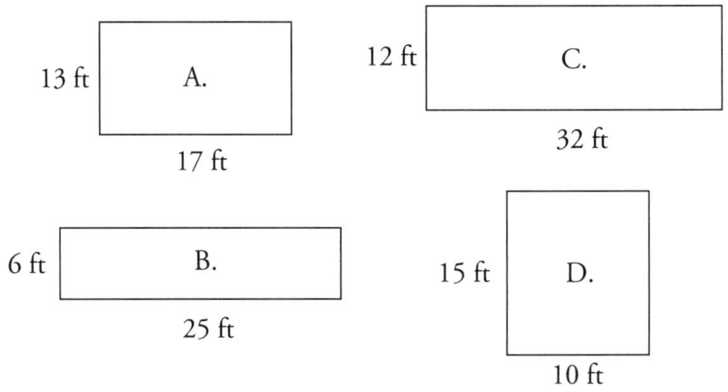

   Which rectangle above could represent a garden with a perimeter of 62 feet? Circle your answer below.

A. rectangle A
B. rectangle B
C. rectangle C
D. rectangle D

Show how you know.

2. Choose a problem that is similar but slightly more challenging. (Note: In the following problem, the perimeter is slightly larger and the measurements of the sides are less-friendly numbers.)

A puppy's play yard has a perimeter of 86 feet.

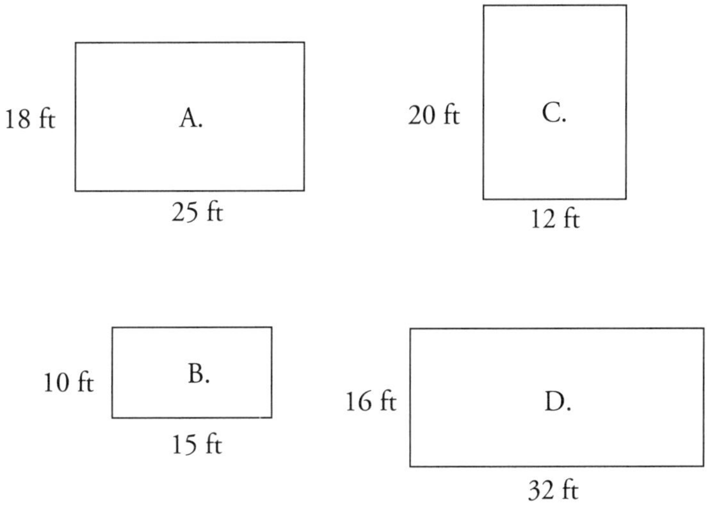

Which rectangle above could represent a play yard with a perimeter of 86 feet? Circle your answer below.

A. rectangle A
B. rectangle B
C. rectangle C
D. rectangle D

Show how you know.

Algebra

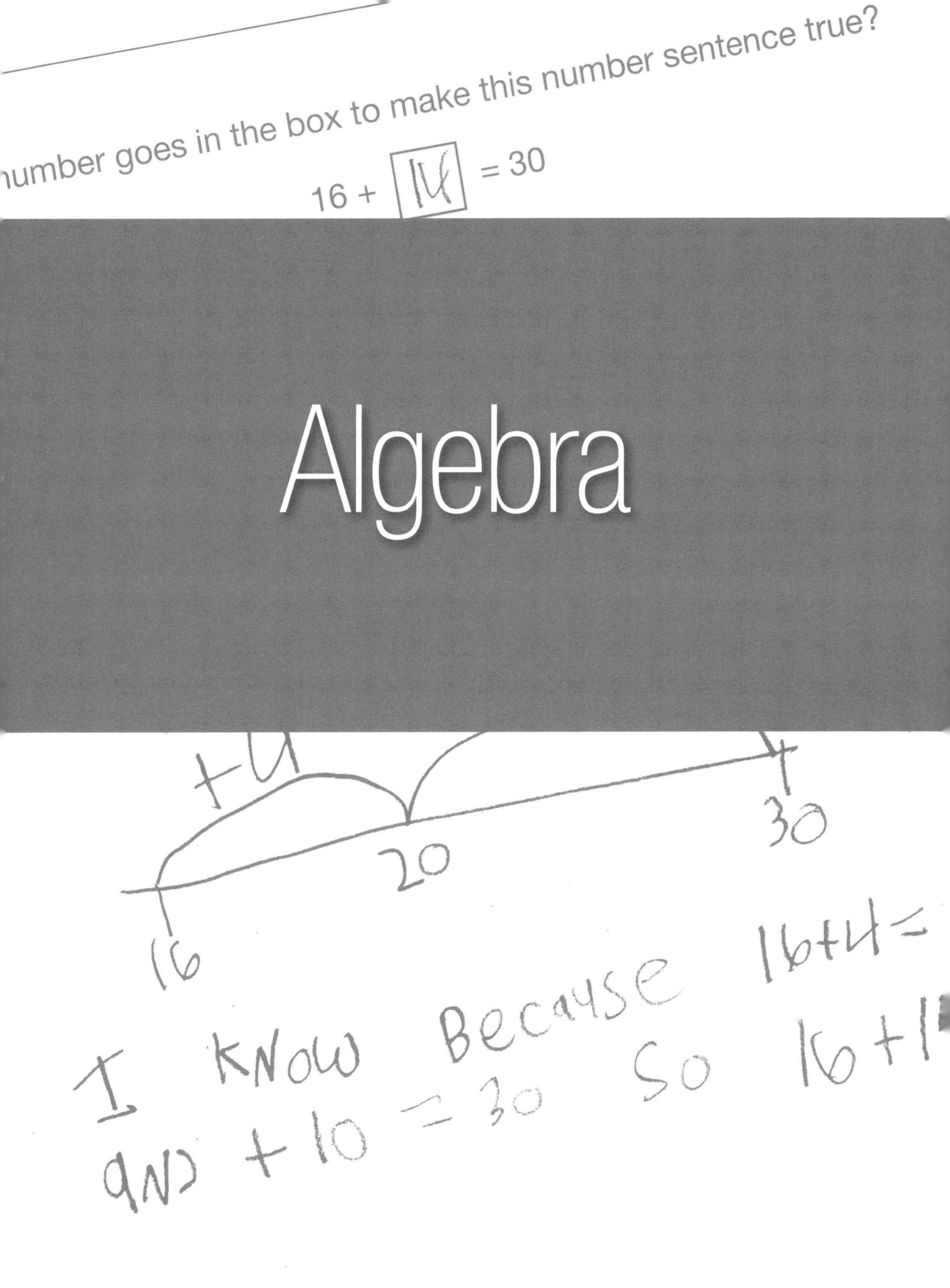

number goes in the box to make this number sentence true?
16 + 14 = 30
+4
20
30
16
I know Because 16+4=
So 16+1

PROBLEM ONE

Overview

Equivalence is key to this problem and an important idea in algebra. Many young children think the equal sign indicates an action when in reality it indicates a relationship. No computation is actually required to find the solution in this sample question. In this case, if 13 is on both sides of the equation and 7 is on one side and a box is on the other, the only possible number that can correctly complete the equation is 7. Students who do not understand equality often find the sum of the first two addends to fill in the box and complete the equation.

Sample Problem

What number goes in the box to make this number sentence true?

$$13 + 7 = \square + 13$$

A. 13
B. 6
C. 7
D. 20

Show how you know.

Possible Student Solution Strategies

- Students recognize that the equal sign indicates an equivalent relationship between two quantities and apply this knowledge to find the variable.
- Students recognize and apply the commutative property of addition and realize that 13 + 7 equals 7 + 13.
- Students add the addends on the left side of the equation to find the sum and then find the difference of that sum and the known addend on the right side of the equation to find the variable.
- Students add thirteen and seven to find the sum of twenty and use this sum as the variable, not recognizing the meaning of the equal sign.
- Students subtract seven from thirteen to get six.

Conversation Starters

- What do you think the equal sign means?
- Why does your answer make sense?
- Why doesn't one of the other answers make sense?
- Does the equal sign mean to do something or does it show a relationship? How do you know?
- How could someone get the answer of twenty? Why doesn't it make sense?
- If you switch the order of the addends in any addition problem, will it change the sum? How do you know?

Student Work Sample: Tommy

Name ______________________ Date ____________

What number goes in the box to make this number sentence true?

13 + 7 = [7] + 13

20 20

A. 13

B. 6

(C.) 7

D. 20

Show how you know.

I know that it is 7. beacause the left side of the equasion equals 20. So the right side has equal 20 and 13+7=20.

A Conversation with Tommy	Teacher Insights
T: Tell me about what you think the equal sign means. **Tommy:** I know that it means whatever is on one side of the equal sign is the same amount as what is on the other side of the equal sign. **T:** How did your understanding help you with this problem? **Tommy:** I figured out the left side of the problem first because it had both numbers. I added thirteen plus seven and it is twenty. I know that the thirteen plus the missing number has to be twenty. I started with thirteen and counted up to twenty, and it was seven. The missing number is seven.	**T:** *Tommy used his understanding of the meaning of the equal sign to help him find the missing addend. Rather than use the commutative property of addition to find the missing addend, he used a counting-on strategy.*

Informed Instructional Suggestions

Tommy's strategy worked well for these small numbers. Next, Tommy needs experiences that will help him see the usefulness of the commutative property of addition for quickly solving this type of problem, especially when larger numbers are involved.

Student Work Sample: Leslie

Name ______________________ Date ____________

What number goes in the box to make this number sentence true?

13 + 7 = ☐ + 13

A. 13

B. 6

(C.) 7

D. 20

Show how you know.

It is just the same number problem fliped around. (I call it a fliparoony)

A Conversation with Leslie	Teacher Insights
T: Why does your answer make sense? **Leslie:** When you add, you can add the numbers in any order and it will still be the same answer. For example, 2 plus 3 equals 5; so does 3 plus 2. It's the same; the numbers are just flipped. **T:** Why doesn't the answer of twenty make sense? **Leslie:** I think if you add 13 and 7 you get 20. But there's more. The problem says that 13 plus 7 is equal to some number plus 13. Both sides have to equal the same amount. If you add 20 to 13 that's 33, and 13 plus 7 does not equal 33. Both sides of the equal sign have to equal the same amount.	**T:** *Leslie was able to use her knowledge and understanding of both the equal sign and the commutative property of addition to accurately solve this problem.*

Informed Instructional Suggestions

Leslie's understanding appears to be strong. Exploration of larger numbers in similar equations would be a good next step for her. We could also challenge her to solve similar problems using other operations. In addition, Leslie would benefit from formal exploration of the commutative property, including the appropriate vocabulary.

Student Work Sample: Taryn

Name ______________________ Date ____________

What number goes in the box to make this number sentence true?

13 + 7 = □ + 13

7 − 13 = □

A. 13

B. 6

(C.) 7

D. 20

Show how you know.

grapes + apples = apple+grapes because 7+13 = □ = 7 wich is right because if you subtritc you'll get 7.

A Conversation with Taryn	Teacher Insights
T: I noticed that you wrote about apples and grapes. Tell me more about your thinking. **Taryn:** I don't really know. It just seems like if you have some apples and some grapes, it's like having some grapes and some apples. **T:** How does your thinking relate to this problem? **Taryn:** It seems like if you have two things, it doesn't matter which order you put them in, so maybe the order of seven and thirteen doesn't matter. It was a guess mostly.	**T:** *Taryn had an intuitive sense of a strategy that could be used to solve this problem. However, she admitted to guessing and the rest of her written work indicated confusion.*

Informed Instructional Suggestions

Taryn had a basic intuition about how to approach the problem, but she guessed. Taryn's understanding could be further developed through careful questioning. She could also verify her assumption and develop it into mathematical understanding through the use of two different colors of cubes or some other objects. For example, she could make a train of five red cubes and three yellow cubes, then make a train of three yellow cubes and five red cubes, and verify that in fact they are the same length and each is composed of the same numbers, although the order of the two colors is different in each of the trains. Instead of building trains, she could apply this same idea to creating groups, for example, a group of five brown beans and three white beans and a group of three white beans and five white beans.

Student Work Sample: Beth

Name ____________________ Date ____________

What number goes in the box to make this number sentence true?

13 + 7 = ☐ + 13

A. 13

B. 6

(C.) 7

D. 20

Show how you know.

7+13 it is the same thing. because 13+7☐=13 is inposible.

A Conversation with Beth	Teacher Insights
T: I see you marked choice C. Why does that make sense to you? **Beth:** I chose it because thirteen plus seven plus box equals thirteen doesn't make sense. It's impossible. **T:** You wrote on your paper that seven plus thirteen is the same thing. What did you mean by that? **Beth:** Well, it's the same thing because the other way I wrote it is impossible. **T:** Do you think that thirteen plus seven is equal to seven plus thirteen? **Beth:** No, I don't really think so.	**T:** *Beth marked the correct answer, but she indicated fragile understanding of the problem. When pressed to explain her writing, she had difficulty. When asked if thirteen plus seven is equal to seven plus thirteen, Beth indicated confusion.*

Informed Instructional Suggestions

Beth's multiple-choice response might have led to the belief she had mastered the skills necessary to solve this problem. However, she clearly needs more experience with this type of problem. The same instructional suggestions we made for Taryn would be helpful to Beth as well.

Student Work Sample: Keith

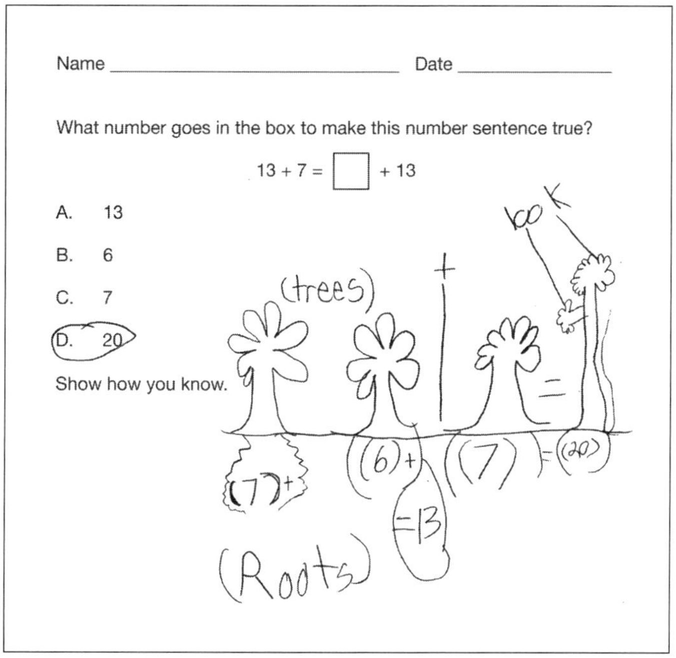

A Conversation with Keith	Teacher Insights
T: Tell me about the picture you drew and how it helped you solve this problem. **Keith:** I drew trees. First I drew a tree with seven branches and another tree with six branches because I know that seven plus six equals thirteen. Then I made a third tree with seven branches and counted all the branches and it equaled twenty branches. I chose choice D because it is twenty. **T:** What about this 13 that comes after the box? **Keith:** I don't know about that. **T:** What does the equal sign mean to you? **Keith:** I have to find the answer. I have to add and find out how much.	**T:** *Keith does not understand that the equal sign indicates a relationship rather than an action. As a result, he added the first two addends to find the sum and considered the problem to be complete. He ignored the 13 on the right side of the equation.*

Informed Instructional Suggestions

The first step for Keith is to help him understand that the equal sign is a relational symbol rather than a verb. The equal sign indicates that both sides of an equation are equivalent. After Keith has a firm grasp of this idea, it would be appropriate to follow the same strategies we suggested for Taryn.

Reassessment

1. Use a similar problem at the same level of difficulty.

   What number goes in the box to make this number sentence true?

   $$16 + 5 = \square + 16$$

   A. 11
   B. 21
   C. 16
   D. 5

   Show how you know.

2. Choose a problem that is similar but slightly more challenging.

   What number goes in the box to make this number sentence true?

   $$\square + 32 = 32 + 13$$

   A. 35
   B. 13
   C. 77
   D. 32

   Show how you know.

PROBLEM TWO

Overview

Missing-addend problems are very commonly found on mathematics assessments and in textbooks. They require children to demonstrate understanding of the equal sign. The equal sign indicates a relationship between the two quantities on either side of it. Children who do not understand this will often add the two numbers together to find the number that goes in the box.

Sample Problem

What number goes in the box to make this number sentence true?

$$16 + \square = 30$$

A. 14
B. 4
C. 46
D. 24

Show how you know.

Possible Student Solution Strategies

- Students add a number to sixteen to equal thirty.
- Students subtract sixteen from thirty to find the missing addend.
- Students show a lack of understanding of the meaning of the equal sign by adding the addend of sixteen to the sum of thirty to get the sum of forty-six.
- Students add a number to sixteen to get to the next ten, which is twenty rather than thirty.

Conversation Starters

- How did you think about the problem?
- What ideas have you learned before that were helpful to you in solving this problem?
- Is your answer reasonable? Why or why not?
- Use manipulatives to check your answer.
- Draw a picture or diagram to show your thinking. How does this prove your answer?

Student Work Sample: Tate

Name ____________________ Date ____________

What number goes in the box to make this number sentence true?

16 + [14] = 30

(A.) 14

B. 4

C. 46

D. 24

Show how you know.

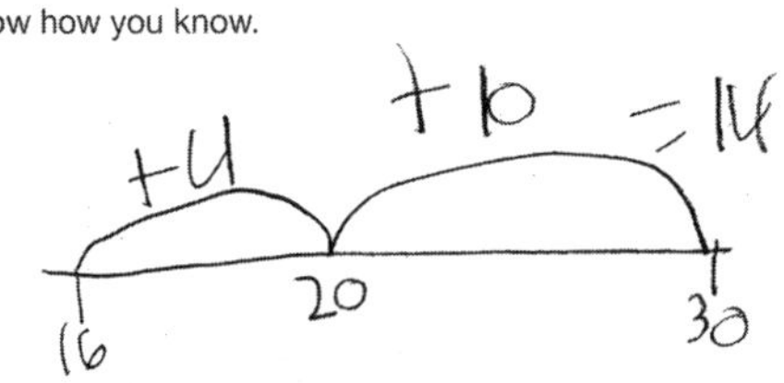

I know because 16+4=20 and +10=30 so 16+14=30.

A Conversation with Tate	Teacher Insights
T: I see you were able to clearly prove your answer by using a number line. What is a second way to use the number line to prove your answer? **Tate:** Well, instead of adding four first, I could add ten, which would get me to twenty-six. Then I could add four to get to thirty. Ten plus four is still fourteen. It makes no difference in which order it goes.	**T:** *Tate has clear understanding of how to find a missing addend.*

Informed Instructional Suggestions

Next, Tate needs opportunities to apply his understanding to three-digit numbers.

Student Work Sample: Rick

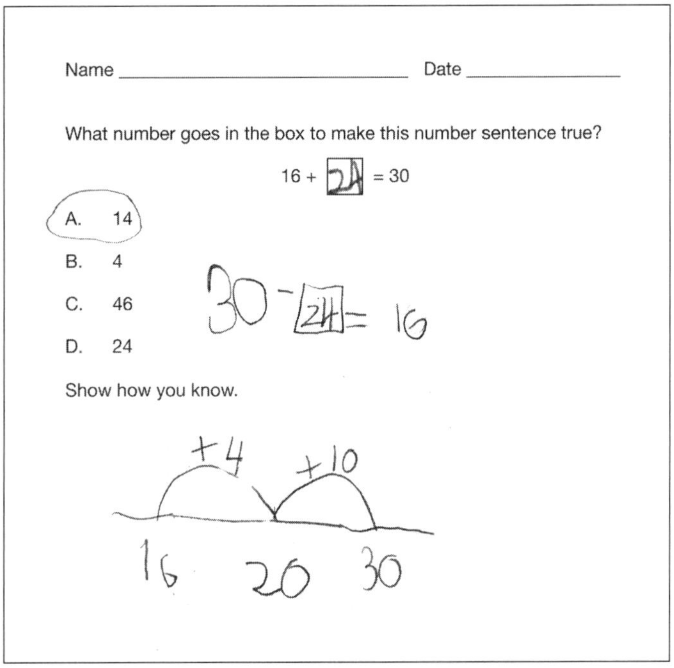
Name ______________________ Date ____________

What number goes in the box to make this number sentence true?

16 + [24] = 30

A. 14

B. 4

C. 46

D. 24

30 − [24] = 16

Show how you know.

A Conversation with Rick	Teacher Insights
T: What ideas have you learned before that were helpful to you in solving this problem? **Rick:** I learned about number lines and I used one in this problem. I started with 16 and added 4 to get to 20 and then I added 10 more and got to 30. Ten plus 4 is 14. **T:** Tell me about the number sentence you wrote: *30 – 24 = 16.* **Rick:** Subtraction is the opposite of addition, so I decided to also solve it with subtraction. To find what goes in the box I did 30 minus 16. In my brain I borrowed a 1 from the 3 and then did 10 minus 6 to get the 4. Then I did 3 minus 1 and got 2. So the answer has to be 24. I wrote *24* in the box.	**T:** *Rick initially solved the problem correctly. When he attempted to solve the problem a second way, he used an appropriate strategy but he misused the subtraction algorithm and did not indicate understanding of place value or number sense.*

Informed Instructional Suggestions

There are a couple of things that would be helpful to Rick. First, he needs to develop awareness that conflicting answers indicate an error. Along with this, he also needs to acquire strategies for what to do when this situation arises. Second, Rick needs to learn a more accurate strategy to solve subtraction problems. It would also be appropriate to help him understand the role of place value and number sense in checking the reasonableness of his answers.

Student Work Sample: Margi

Name ______________________ Date ____________

What number goes in the box to make this number sentence true?

16 + ☐ = 30

(A.) 14

B. 4

C. 46

D. 24

Show how you know.

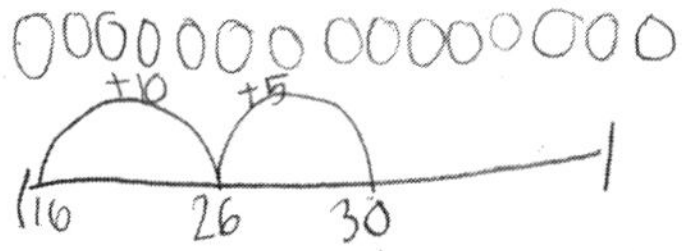

A Conversation with Margi	Teacher Insights
T: I see you used a picture. How does it help prove your answer? **Margi:** Well, I started with a number line. I added ten to sixteen to get twenty-six. Then I added five more to make thirty. Ten plus five makes fifteen. So, I drew ten circles and five circles to show my thinking. I have fifteen circles. **T:** I see you circled choice A, fourteen. **Margi:** I know. I did that because it was the answer that was closest to fifteen. It makes sense to me. **T:** Which number, fourteen or fifteen, when added to sixteen makes thirty? **Margi:** Fifteen.	**T:** Margi marked the correct answer and had an appropriate strategy. However, her computation was incorrect and did not match any of the answer choices. Margi seemed unconcerned by this and selected the answer choice closest to her answer.

Informed Instructional Suggestions

Margi needs to understand that when an answer she has calculated does not match an answer choice, it most likely indicates she has made an error. In this situation, she should recalculate. Margi also needs experiences to help her improve her accuracy with addition.

Student Work Sample: Conner

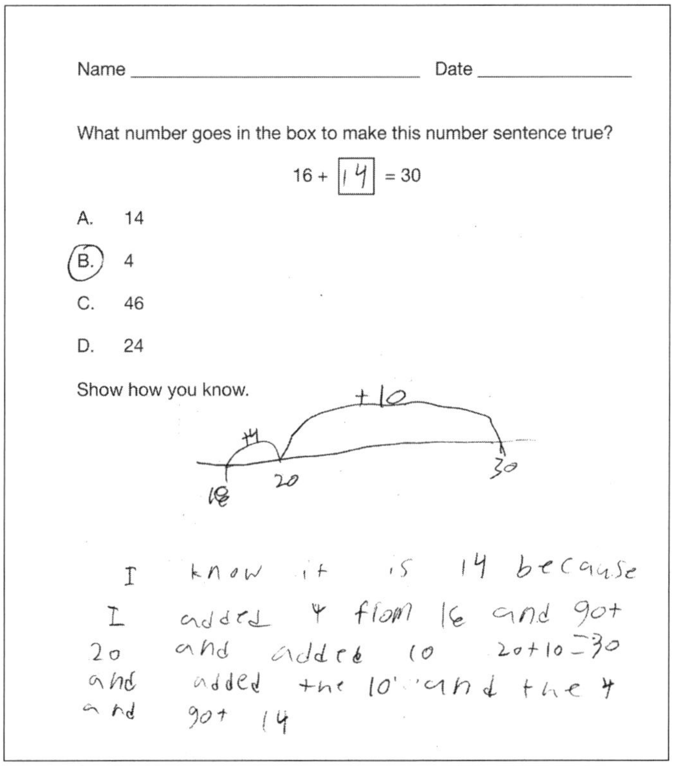
Name ______________________ Date ____________

What number goes in the box to make this number sentence true?

16 + [14] = 30

A. 14

(B.) 4

C. 46

D. 24

Show how you know.

I know it is 14 because I added 4 from 16 and got 20 and added 10 20+10=30 and added the 10 and the 4 and got 14

A Conversation with Conner	Teacher Insights
T: The answer you chose, choice B, doesn't match your solution. Tell me about this. **Conner:** Hmm, I thought I chose fourteen. Oops! Can I change it? It should be choice A. I really know the answer is fourteen. I showed you on my paper.	**T:** *Conner's wrong answer was the result of an error, not a misunderstanding or lack of understanding.*

Informed Instructional Suggestions

Had Conner's multiple-choice selection been the only evidence of his understanding, we would have assumed he was unable to solve this problem. As a result, he might have spent his time doing needless remediation of a skill he actually knew. Both his written and verbal explanations indicated strong understanding and provided better information for planning appropriate further instruction. Conner is ready to apply his understanding to three-digit numbers.

Student Work Sample: JB

Name ______________________ Date ____________

What number goes in the box to make this number sentence true?

16 + [4] = 30

A. 14

(B. 4) (circled)

C. 46

D. 24

I know it is 4 Beacuse I coved the 10 in 16 and add 4+6 =10.

Show how you know.

A Conversation with JB	Teacher Insights
T: I notice you chose four as your answer. Please show your thinking using cubes to check your answer. What do you think you should do first? **JB:** I should count out sixteen cubes. **T:** Why do you think you should start by counting out sixteen cubes? **JB:** Because I see 16 is the first number in the problem. **T:** I see you have counted out sixteen cubes. What will you do next? **JB:** I am going to add four more cubes because I am trying to get to the next ten. Now I have twenty [pausing in a confused manner]. **T:** Look at the problem. How many should you have? **JB:** Oops, I should have thirty. I was only thinking about making tens. So when I added four more, I got to twenty and I really need to get to thirty. That would be four and then ten more. So that's fourteen, not four.	**T:** *Initially JB had partial understanding of a solution that would ultimately work. When solving the problem with cubes using his strategy, he quickly realized his error.*

Informed Instructional Suggestions

JB needs more experience with missing addends. Using manipulatives and small numbers will strengthen his understanding. Also, we should ask JB to state the goal of a problem before he begins to solve it in order to help him clarify his understanding of the task.

Reassessment

1. Use a similar problem at the same level of difficulty.

   What number goes in the box to make this number sentence true?

   $\square + 23 = 40$

   A. 7
   B. 63
   C. 27
   D. 17

   Show how you know.

2. Choose a problem that is similar but slightly more challenging. (Note: In the following problem, the numbers are larger and less friendly. Finding a missing addend for a sum of 97 is considerably more difficult than finding the missing addend for a sum of 40.)

   What number goes in the box to make this number sentence true?

   $54 + \square = 97$

   A. 43
   B. 151
   C. 40
   D. 44

   Show how you know.

3. Choose a problem that is similar but has more challenging numbers.

   What number goes in the box to make this number sentence true?

   $\square + 374 = 575$

   A. 200
   B. 949
   C. 201
   D. 102

   Show how you know.

PROBLEM THREE

Overview

This problem asks students to "translate" a word problem into a number sentence. This requires that students can read the problem and understand clearly what it is asking. For some young children this is quite a challenge. The missing addend in the problem presents a further challenge for most children. Problems like this can be difficult for children, but if we present them in a meaningful context, giving students manipulatives and opportunities to explore the concepts, they develop an understanding and are successful with them.

Sample Problem

Angelo had 20 pennies. He found some more. Now he has 43. Which number sentence could be used to figure out how many pennies he found?

A. $20 + \square = 43$
B. $20 + 43 = \square$
C. $\square - 43 = 20$
D. $\square - 20 = 43$

Show how you know.

Possible Student Solution Strategies

- Students recognize that they could figure the number of missing pennies by adding a number to twenty to get forty-three.
- Students make a correct choice based on little or no understanding.
- Students misunderstand the problem and believe the situation requires adding twenty to forty-three.

Conversation Starters

- What kind of mathematics do you need to solve this problem?
- What do you know about this problem? What do you need to find out?
- How can you convince us that your ideas make sense?
- How would you explain your thinking to a younger student?

Student Work Sample: Carolyn

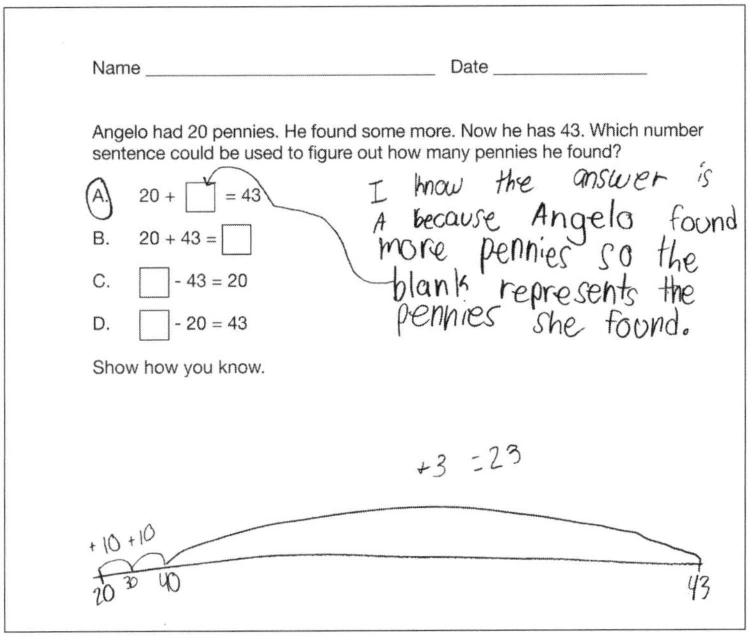
Name ______________________ Date ____________

Angelo had 20 pennies. He found some more. Now he has 43. Which number sentence could be used to figure out how many pennies he found?

(A.) 20 + ☐ = 43

B. 20 + 43 = ☐

C. ☐ - 43 = 20

D. ☐ - 20 = 43

I know the answer is A because Angelo found more pennies so the blank represents the pennies she found.

Show how you know.

+3 =23

+10 +10

20 30 40 43

A Conversation with Carolyn	Teacher Insights
T: What mathematics did you use to help you solve this problem? **Carolyn:** I used addition and I showed it on a number line. The problem says Angelo started out with twenty pennies and ended up with forty-three. So I made a number line and started with twenty. Then I jumped ten and that was thirty. I jumped ten again and that was forty. I only needed to jump three more and I landed on forty-three. So I jumped twenty-three. That's how many pennies that Angelo got. **T:** I notice that the space between 30 and 40 is smaller than the space between 40 and 43. Please tell me about that. **Carolyn:** First I drew the line, then I put a *20* and a *43* on the line. I made two small spaces when I added the two tens, then noticed I had a big space to go to get to forty-three. I know that ten is bigger than three and the space for ten should be bigger than the space for three.	**T:** *Finding a missing addend was not difficult for Carolyn in this context. She was able to solve the problem accurately and with confidence. When asked about the spacing on her number line, she showed understanding.*

Informed Instructional Suggestions

Carolyn is ready for further exploration with missing-addend problems that involve larger numbers. Also, she would benefit from working with other operations. Then we could ask Carolyn to create and solve her own similar problems.

Student Work Sample: Lori

Name ______________________ Date ______________

Angelo had 20 pennies. He found some more. Now he has 43. Which number sentence could be used to figure out how many pennies he found?

(A.) 20 + ☐ = 43

B. 20 + 43 = ☐

C. ☐ - 43 = 20

D. ☐ - 20 = 43

Show how you know.

Choice A is right because Angelo had 20 pennies write? So the first number in the number sentence should be 20. Now that narrows it down to A and B. Angelo found more right. So it has to be a addition problem. It is still a and b. Now he has 43 means that it has to be a missing number sentence. so it is A!

A Conversation with Lori	Teacher Insights
T: What do you know about this problem? What do you need to find out? **Lori:** I know Angelo started with twenty pennies and he ended with forty-three. I have to figure out how many were added to twenty to make forty-three. **T:** How did you use that information to help you solve the problem? **Lori:** Well, I know that choices C and D can't be right because they are subtraction and I know that something was added to twenty to get to forty-three. I also know that twenty should be the first number in the number sentence because he started with twenty pennies. That gets rid of C and D, too. It has to be a missing-number sentence because he added some pennies to twenty to get forty-three, so it has to be choice A. Besides, choice B would mean that he added twenty pennies to forty-three pennies and that would be sixty-three pennies. He didn't have sixty-three pennies, right?	**T:** *Lori understood this problem and is ready for similar but more challenging problems.*

Informed Instructional Suggestions

Lori's needs are similar to those of Carolyn. She is ready to extend her learning.

Student Work Sample: Randy

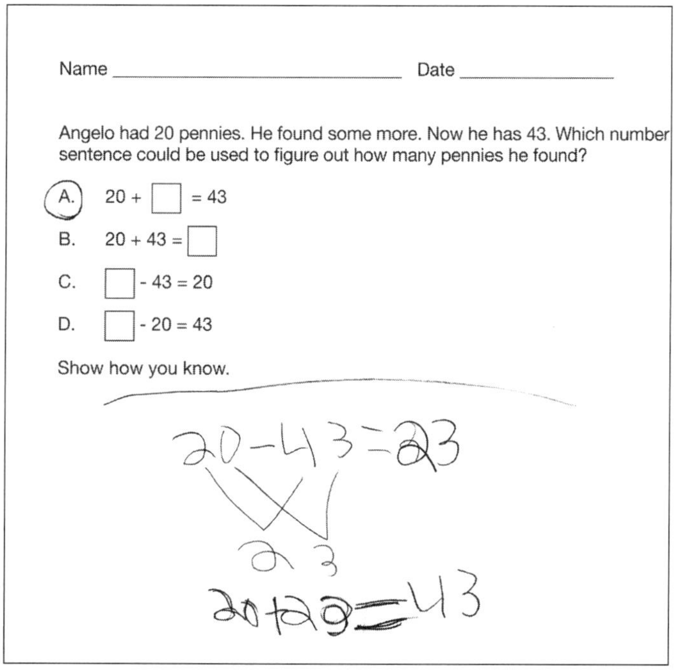
Name ____________________ Date ____________

Angelo had 20 pennies. He found some more. Now he has 43. Which number sentence could be used to figure out how many pennies he found?

A. 20 + ☐ = 43

B. 20 + 43 = ☐

C. ☐ - 43 = 20

D. ☐ - 20 = 43

Show how you know.

A Conversation with Randy	Teacher Insights
T: Randy, what kind of mathematics is needed to solve this problem? **Randy:** Addition and subtraction. I showed it right here. [Randy points to the writing on his paper.] **T:** Please tell me more about your thinking. **Randy:** First I subtracted twenty minus forty-three and got twenty-three. Then added to check my answer and I was right! **T:** What is it about the problem that made you decide to subtract? **Randy:** I wanted to find the difference between twenty and forty-three because that's how many pennies Angelo got.	**T:** *Randy's thinking was fundamentally correct. However, he incorrectly represented the subtraction problem that could be used to find the missing addend.*

Informed Instructional Suggestions

Randy has a successful strategy for finding missing addends. But he needs to work on correctly representing subtraction situations as well as opportunities to develop an understanding that subtracting a larger number from a smaller number results in a negative number.

Student Work Sample: Jayden

Name ______________________ Date ____________

Angelo had 20 pennies. He found some more. Now he has 43. Which number sentence could be used to figure out how many pennies he found?

(A.) 20 + ☐ = 43

B. 20 + 43 = ☐

C. ☐ - 43 = 20

D. ☐ - 20 = 43

Show how you know.

I thinkits A because it said he found 20 pennies and he found some more well didnt we want to know what it is.

A Conversation with Jayden	Teacher Insights
T: Please tell me about your thinking. **Jayden:** I guessed A. The problem said something about twenty pennies and choice A has a 20 at the beginning of it. It made sense to me. It's my best guess. **T:** How would you explain this problem to a younger student? **Jayden:** Um, I'm not too sure. Someone had twenty pennies and then forty-three. **T:** What does the problem want you to find out? **Jayden:** How many pennies in all?	**T:** *Jayden selected the correct answer but seemed to have weak understanding of what the problem was asking or how to solve it. She stated that she made a guess. When asked how she might explain the problem to a younger child, she was able to repeat the information in the problem but did not grasp what the problem was asking.*

Instructional Suggestions

Jayden needs hands-on experiences with finding missing addends. For example, Jayden could build a train using twelve blue cubes. Next, she could add yellow cubes to find out how many more would be needed to make a train of twenty. Counting the yellow cubes would provide the missing addend. Finally, she would need to record a number sentence to represent what she did: she could write *12* + ☐ = *20* and then record an *8* in the box.

Student Work Sample: Robbie

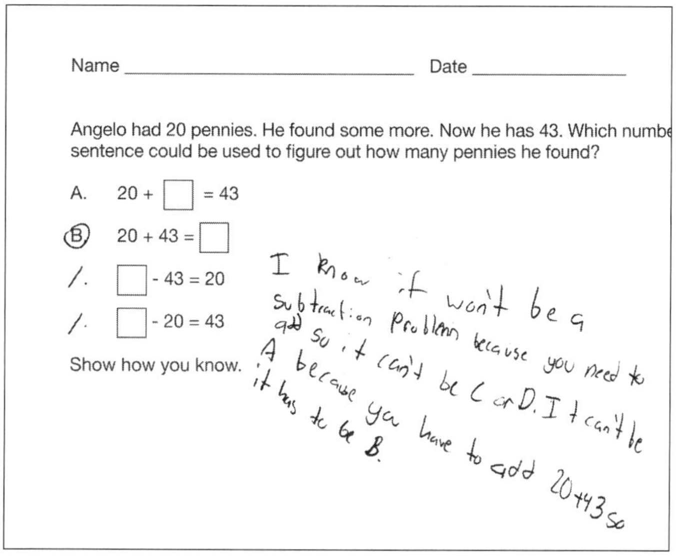
Name ______________________ Date ____________

Angelo had 20 pennies. He found some more. Now he has 43. Which number sentence could be used to figure out how many pennies he found?

A. 20 + ☐ = 43

(B) 20 + 43 = ☐

/. ☐ - 43 = 20

/. ☐ - 20 = 43

Show how you know. I know it won't be a subtraction problem because you need to add so it can't be C or D. It can't be A because you have to add 20+43 so it has to be B.

A Conversation with Robbie	Teacher Insights
T: What is this problem asking you to do? **Robbie:** I am supposed to find out how many pennies Angelo has. He has twenty and then he gets forty-three more. **T:** Please reread the problem and show me where the problem says to do that. **Robbie:** Oh no! It says Angelo had twenty pennies and then he got some more and now he has forty-three. I'm supposed to find out how many he found, not how many he had altogether. **T:** Knowing this, what should you do to solve the problem? **Robbie:** I should start with twenty and then figure out how many more to make forty-three. I think the right choice is really choice A. The box in choice A would be the number of pennies that Angelo found to make forty-three.	**T:** *Robbie misunderstood the problem. Once he was asked to reread the problem, he quickly made sense of it and was able to pick out the correct choice.*

Informed Instructional Suggestions

Robbie's incorrect response, choice B, and his written explanation indicated he did not understand missing-addend situations. However, when Robbie was asked to reread the problem, he quickly caught his error and was able to explain the correct answer verbally, showing his understanding. Robbie needs to develop the habit of rereading problems to ensure he understands what he is being asked to do. If Robbie hadn't had the opportunity to verbally explain his thinking, we would likely have made incorrect assumptions about his understanding and had him spend time on activities that weren't necessary for him.

Reassessment

1. Use a similar problem at the same level of difficulty.

   Alana had 34 pennies. She found some more. Now she has 57. Which number sentence could be used to figure out how many pennies she found?

   A. $\square - 34 = 57$
   B. $\square - 57 = 34$
   C. $57 + 34 = \square$
   D. $34 + \square = 57$

   Show how you know.

2. Choose a problem that is similar but slightly more challenging.

   Morgan had 123 shells. Morgan went to the beach and found some more. Now he has 151 shells. Which number sentence could be used to figure out how many shells he found?

   A. $123 + \square = 151$
   B. $123 + 151 = \square$
   C. $\square - 123 = 151$
   D. $\square - 151 = 123$

   Show how you know.

PROBLEM FOUR

Overview

Students need to know the number of inches in a foot to correctly solve this problem. Problems like this are often found on multiple-choice tests. A student who knows that there are 12 inches in a foot and clearly understands that problems involving equal groups can be solved with multiplication or repeated addition will be able to solve this problem with relative ease.

Sample Problem

Which of the following could be used to find out how many inches are in 4 feet?

A. 4×12
B. $12 \div 4$
C. $4 + 12$
D. $12 - 4$

Show how you know.

Possible Student Solution Strategies

- Students use multiplication or repeated addition to accurately find the number of inches in 4 feet.
- Students use their reasoning about converting inches to feet to eliminate the incorrect choices.
- Students make a correct guess.
- Students believe the situation requires using an operation other than multiplication or repeated addition and arrive at an incorrect choice.
- Students do not understand the process of converting one measurement to another.

Conversation Starters

- What is this problem asking you do?
- What do you know about inches and feet?
- How can knowing about the relationship between inches and feet help you solve this problem?
- How would you explain how to solve this problem to a younger student?
- Why doesn't choice B make sense?
- How can you convince us that your solution makes sense?
- What pattern were you able to use to help you solve this problem?

Student Work Sample: Jasmine

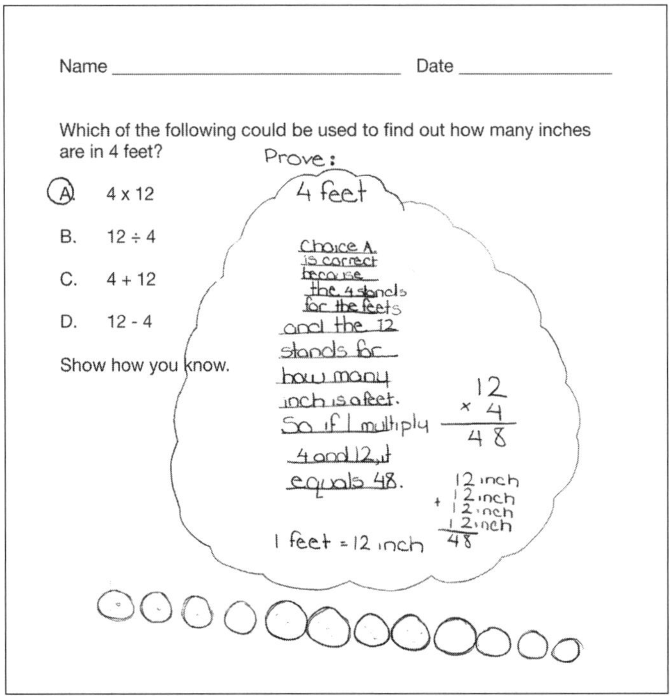
Name ______________________ Date ____________

Which of the following could be used to find out how many inches are in 4 feet?

(A) 4 x 12

B. 12 ÷ 4

C. 4 + 12

D. 12 - 4

Show how you know.

Prove:

4 feet

Choice A. is correct because the 4 stands for the feets and the 12 stands for how many inch is a feet. So if I multiply 4 and 12, it equals 48.

12
× 4
48

12 inch
+ 12 inch
12 inch
12 inch
48

1 feet = 12 inch

A Conversation with Jasmine	Teacher Insights
T: Tell me what you know about inches and feet. **Jasmine:** I know that there are 12 inches in 1 foot. Or you could think of it as 1 foot is equal to 12 inches. **T:** How did knowing about the relationship between inches and feet help you solve the problem? **Jasmine:** Because there are 12 inches in a foot, I multiplied the 4 feets by 12 inches. That is 48. There are 48 inches in 4 feets. I also added twelve four times to check. Then, just to be sure, I drew twelve circles and counted them four times and it was forty-eight. **T:** Which of your three ways do you think would be most helpful to a younger student? **Jasmine:** Probably the way when I drew twelve circles and counted them four times. I'd tell the kid that there are 12 inches in a foot, and the circles are like the inches, there are twelve of them. Then you have to count the circles four times because there are 4 feets. As long as the little kid could count, I think he or she could figure it out.	**T:** *Jasmine is comfortable applying her knowledge of inches and feet. She was able to use three strategies to correctly figure the number of inches in 4 feet. She was also able to consider and suggest which of her strategies might be most helpful to a younger student and explain her reasoning for her opinion.*

Informed Instructional Suggestions

Jasmine is ready to explore other units of measurement and their relationships, such as inches and yards, cups and quarts, and centimeters and meters. She is also ready to explore converting inches into feet, which requires repeated subtraction or division. Use of concrete, hands-on experiences will solidify her conceptual understanding.

Student Work Sample: Bernardo

Name ______________________ Date ____________

Which of the following could be used to find out how many inches are in 4 feet?

A. 4 x 12

B. 12 ÷ 4

C. 4 + 12

D. 12 - 4

Show how you know.

Because with 12÷4=3 and I know that's not right. And 4+12=16 and I know that's not right because that's only 4 inches over 2 feet. And I know 12-4 isn't right because 12-4=8 and that's not even a foot. So A. has to be right.

A Conversation with Bernardo	Teacher Insights
T: How does your answer choice make sense? **Bernardo:** I know that there are 12 inches in a foot. There are 4 feet and that's like four groups of 12. So I can add 12 four times and that will give me the answer. Twelve plus 12 is 24, and 12 more is 36 and 12 more is 48. **T:** Your explanation helps me better understand your thinking. Tell me more about what you wrote on your paper. **Bernardo:** I explained why B, C, and D don't make sense. Twelve divided by 4 is 3 and that just isn't right because 3 inches isn't even close to a foot and there are 4 feet. Four plus 12 is 16 and that's more than a foot, but only 4 inches more. The last one is 12 minus 4 and that's 8, and that's less than a foot, too. The only good answer has to be choice A.	**T:** *Bernardo correctly applied his knowledge of inches and feet. He also verified his thinking by considering and explaining why the other three choices made no sense in light of his understanding.*

Informed Instructional Suggestions

Like Jasmine, Bernardo is ready to explore other units of measurement and possibly measurement situations involving larger numbers.

Student Work Sample: Teri

Name ________________ Date ________

Which of the following could be used to find out how many inches are in 4 feet?

(A.) 4 x 12

B. 12 ÷ 4

C. 4 + 12

D. 12 - 4

Show how you know.

I Picked A. because if you Want to find out how many inches in a feet istead of division, addition, or Subtraction. And thats how I got my answere.

A Conversation with Teri	Teacher Insights
T: Tell me more about your thinking. **Teri:** I don't really know exactly. I know there is a 4 and a 12 in the problem and my choices were to multiply, divide, add, or subtract. Multiplying seemed right, so I chose A. **T:** Tell me what you know about inches and feet. **Teri:** I know you can measure things with them. Inches are smaller and feet are larger. **T:** How many inches are in a foot? **Teri:** Maybe 10 or so?	**T:** *Teri marked the correct answer but has weak understanding of inches and feet, as well as what the problem was asking her to do. Essentially, she made a lucky guess.*

Informed Instructional Suggestions

Teri's weak conceptual understanding was revealed through her written and verbal explanations. Teri needs hands-on, concrete experiences to help her develop understanding of inches and feet and how they are related. She needs to learn that there are 12 inches in 1 foot or that 1 foot is equal to 12 inches.

Student Work Sample: Malia

Name ______________________ Date ____________

Which of the following could be used to find out how many inches are in 4 feet?

(A.) 4 x 12

B. 12 ÷ 4

C. 4 + 12

D. 12 - 4

Show how you know.

I picked Choice A because maybe 4 feet has 48 inches.

A Conversation with Malia	Teacher Insights
T: You said that maybe 4 feet has 48 inches. What made you think that? **Malia:** I am not exactly sure, but I know that there are about 12 inches in a foot so I think 4 feet has to be more than 12. I don't really know how much more. Maybe the answer could be choice C because that one is more than twelve, like choice A. The other two are less than twelve. I know that there has to be a 4 and a 12 in the number sentence because there is a 4 and a 12 in the word part.	**T:** *Malia thinks a foot is "about 12 inches" and she knew that more than 1 foot was involved in this problem. Using this reasoning, she eliminated choice B and choice D, recognizing they were less than twelve. Beyond that, Malia guessed that the correct answer was choice A.*

Informed Instructional Suggestions

If we had only Malia's multiple-choice answer to go on, we would have assumed she understood how to convert feet into inches. But her written and verbal explanations showed that she needs concrete, hands-on measurement experiences to help her approach and solve problems such as this one with understanding and accuracy.

Student Work Sample: Becky

Name ______________________ Date ______________

Which of the following could be used to find out how many inches are in 4 feet?

A. 4 x 12

B. 12 ÷ 4 (circled)

C. 4 + 12

D. 12 - 4

Show how you know.

I think its division because it has no remainders so thats why I think its divison

A Conversation with Becky	Teacher Insights
T: What do you know about feet and inches that could help you solve this problem? **Becky:** There are feet and inches on a ruler. Inches are smaller than feet. I think there are 12 inches in a foot. **T:** Why does your solution make sense? **Becky:** Well, I have to divide the inches into 4 feet. So that would be 12 divided by 4. That equals 3. I did it on my paper. I drew four circles and used tallies for the inches and I divided up the twelve so there were three in each circle. They all have the same amount and there are no leftovers.	**T:** *Becky is confused about the relationship between inches and feet. As a result, she divided twelve by four rather than multiplying twelve by four. Because she does not understand the relationship between inches and feet, she was unable to correctly represent this word problem with an equation.*

Informed Instructional Suggestions

Becky, like the previous students, needs to develop her conceptual understanding of inches and feet before trying to convert one to the other.

Student Work Sample: Steve

Name ______________________ Date ____________

Which of the following could be used to find out how many inches are in 4 feet?

A. 4 x 12

B. 12 ÷ 4

C. 4 + 12

D. 12 - 4

Show how you know.

none of these It's none of these becouse the problem is to find how many inches in for feet, not divide, subtract, add, mutiply.

A Conversation with Steve	Teacher Insights
T: You have a very interesting answer, Steve. I see that you think none of the choices is correct. Please tell me more about that. **Steve:** I'm supposed to find out how many inches in 4 feet, not multiply, add, subtract, or divide. None of those answers have anything to do with what I'm supposed to figure out. **T:** What do you plan to do to figure out the number of inches in 4 feet? **Steve:** I'll get a ruler and measure 4 feet. **T:** How will that help you figure the number of inches in 4 feet? **Steve:** [Shrugging] I don't know.	**T:** *Steve lacks a conceptual understanding of measurement. He also does not grasp an important algebraic idea—that words can be represented symbolically using numbers and number sentences. Steve did not see this connection in the problem. Rather, he saw measurement as disconnected from computation.*

Informed Instructional Suggestions

Steve needs the same hands-on, concrete experiences we suggested for other students. He also needs to learn how numbers and equations can represent words and sentences; therefore, he should spend time working with word problems and representing them with equations.

Reassessment

1. Use a similar problem at the same level of difficulty.

   Which of the following could be used to find out how many inches are in 5 feet?

   A. $5 + 12$
   B. $12 - 5$
   C. 5×12
   D. $12 \div 5$

   Show how you know.

2. Choose a problem that is similar but slightly more challenging (one that uses bigger numbers, for example).

   Which of the following could be used to find out how many inches are in 11 feet?

   A. 11×12
   B. $12 - 11$
   C. $11 + 12$
   D. $12 \div 11$

   Show how you know.

PROBLEM FIVE

Overview

To solve this problem, students need to have knowledge of relational symbols (<, >, and =) and multiplication facts. This type of question is often found on standardized multiple-choice tests but generally reveals little about a student's understanding or misconceptions. Children commonly make the mistake of selecting an answer that makes both sides of the equation equal.

Sample Problem

What number could go in the blank to make this number sentence true?

$$8 \times 6 < 3 \times \_\_\_\_\_$$

A. 17
B. 16
C. 11
D. 14

Show how you know.

Possible Student Solution Strategies

- Students correctly solve the multiplication involved in this problem and show knowledge of relational symbols.
- Students are able to correctly solve the multiplication involved but misunderstand the relational symbols and choose the wrong answer.
- Students make an error in multiplication.
- Students make a guess.
- Students add rather than multiply.

Conversation Starters

- What do you know about this problem? What do you need to find out?

Student Work Sample: Eliza

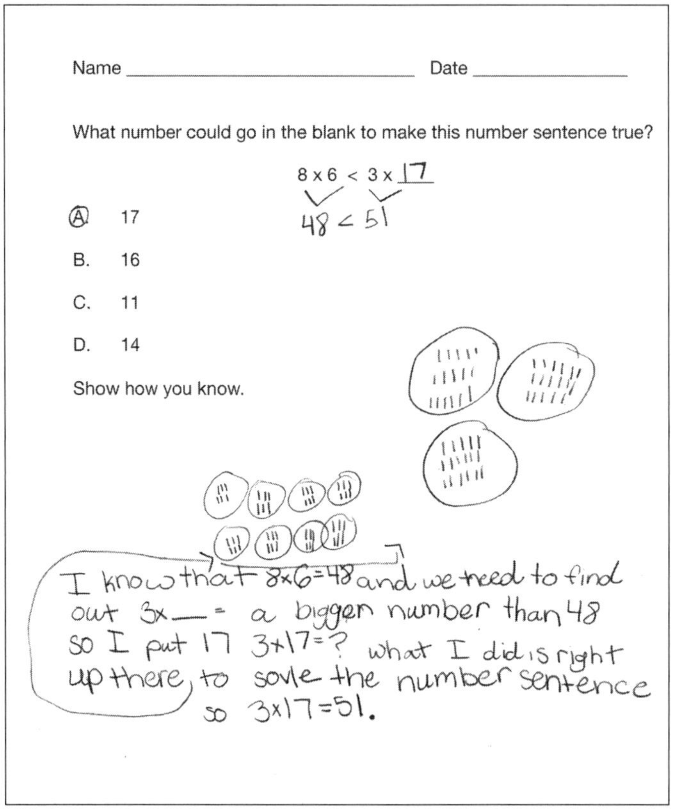
Name ______________________ Date ______________

What number could go in the blank to make this number sentence true?

8 x 6 < 3 x 17

48 < 51

(A) 17

B. 16

C. 11

D. 14

Show how you know.

I know that 8x6=48 and we need to find out 3x___ = a biggen number than 48 so I put 17 3x17=? what I did is right up there, to sovle the number sentence so 3x17=51.

A Conversation with Eliza	Teacher Insights
T: Eliza, you have so clearly communicated your thinking! Tell me about it. **Eliza:** First I figured out eight times six. I drew eight circles with six tally marks. I counted them up by skip-counting and it was forty-eight. I looked where the equal sign should be and it wasn't there. Instead it was a "less than" sign. I knew that forty-eight was less than something because of that sign! I tried seventeen first because it was the first choice. I drew three circles with seventeen tallies in each one. I counted them up and got fifty-one. It was hard because there were a lot of little tallies. Next time I will put them in fives! Fifty-one is greater than forty-eight. So that's my answer. Finished!	**T:** *Eliza has a strategy to accurately solve a multiplication fact. She commented that her solution process is not terribly efficient for larger numbers and stated a better plan for the next time she solves a similar problem. She understands relational symbols and applied her knowledge correctly.*

Informed Instructional Suggestions

Because Eliza noticed that her strategy for multiplying eight by six was a bit cumbersome for figuring three times seventeen, she's ready to work on finding more-efficient strategies for multiplication. Because she knows how to decompose numbers, she could use partial products to solve problems like 3 × 17.

$$\begin{array}{rcr} 17 & = & 10 + 7 \\ \underline{\times 3} & & \underline{\times 3} \\ 3 \times 7 & & = 21 \\ 3 \times 10 & & \underline{= 30} \\ & & 51 \end{array}$$

Student Work Sample: Salina

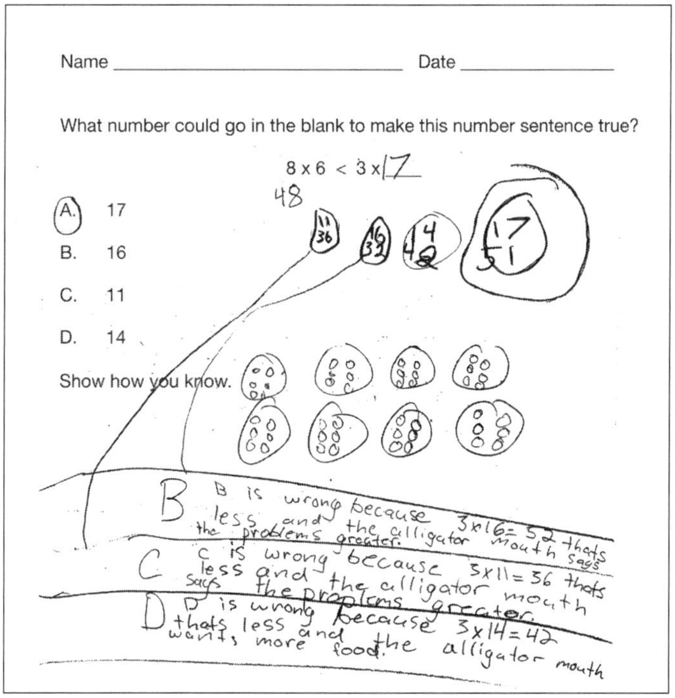
Name ______________________ Date ____________

What number could go in the blank to make this number sentence true?

8 x 6 < 3 x 17
48

(A.) 17
B. 16
C. 11
D. 14

Show how you know.

B is wrong because 3x16=52 thats less and the alligator mouth says the problems greater.
C is wrong because 3x11=36 thats less and the alligator mouth says the problems greater.
D is wrong because 3x14=42 thats less and the alligator mouth wants more food.

A Conversation with Salina	Teacher Insights
T: I see you picked choice A. What was your thinking? **Salina:** I knew how to figure out eight times six. I drew eight big circles and put six little circles inside each big circle. I counted them up and it was forty-eight. Then I saw the alligator mouth. My old teacher told me that the alligator mouth eats the problem that is greater because the alligator wants more food.	**T:** *I had more than one area of concern about Salina's work. The first issue was the alligator analogy. Although Salina did not confuse this analogy, some children interpret it incorrectly, stating that the larger number eats the smaller number and therefore the mouth opens toward the smaller number. (See the discussion of Jim's paper on page 127.) Building number sense and frequently using the relational symbols will better serve students in the long run than teaching a disconnected analogy. The second concern was that some of Salina's multiplication was incorrect.*

Informed Instructional Suggestions

Salina needs many opportunities to practice multiplying two-digit numbers by one-digit numbers. It would also be useful to provide Salina with several concrete experiences to help her fully understand the relational symbols so that she is not dependent on the alligator analogy.

Student Work Sample: Sally

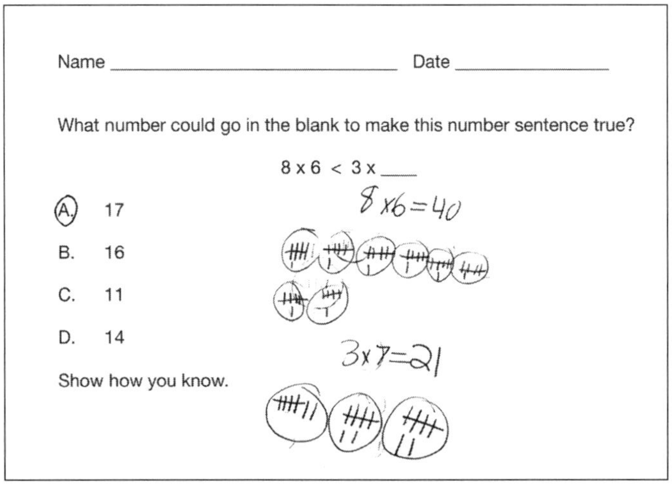
Name ______________________ Date ____________

What number could go in the blank to make this number sentence true?

8 x 6 < 3 x ____

(A.) 17

B. 16

C. 11

D. 14

Show how you know.

A Conversation with Sally	Teacher Insights
T: What do you know about this problem? What do you need to find out? **Sally:** I have to figure out eight times six and then three times something and then compare them. **T:** I can see you drew eight circles with six tallies in each. Why did that make sense to you? **Sally:** Well, the multiplication problem in words means eight groups of six. I drew circles to show the eight groups and put six tallies in each because the problem told me to. **T:** Please count the tally marks again. **Sally:** Uh oh, I must have made a mistake. One, two, three . . .	**T:** *Sally indicated her understanding of the multiplication sentence 8 × 6. When asked to recount, she recognized that she had made an error. It's always important to ask students to double-check correct answers as well as those with errors. This practice deepens students' overall understanding; even when their answers are right, they often uncover misunderstandings or new insights. Sally was able to count the tally marks correctly the second time.*
T: Sally, tell me about the three times seven. **Sally:** Well, first I tried to do three groups of seventeen. I erased it. Three times seven was easier, so I did that instead. **T:** Why did that make sense to you to multiply three times seven instead of three times seventeen? **Sally:** I saw the 7 in the ones place of 17 so I did that, and multiplied three times seven. I didn't know what to do with the 1 in the tens place.	**T:** *Sally was struggling to use what she knew to help her to solve three times seventeen, but her understanding was too weak to carry her through the process.*

Informed Instructional Suggestions

Sally got the right answer. Her work indicated emerging but flawed thinking. Relying only on her multiple-choice answer with no written explanation or conversation would have masked Sally's real need. Sally needs additional work on basic multiplication in order to be efficient and accurate in her figuring. Once she becomes more accurate with basic facts such as 8 × 6, she needs to move to multiplying two-digit numbers by one-digit numbers. She already has some intuitive understanding of how to solve this type of problem using the partial product method. Repeated addition would have also been an effective strategy for this problem.

Student Work Sample: Jim

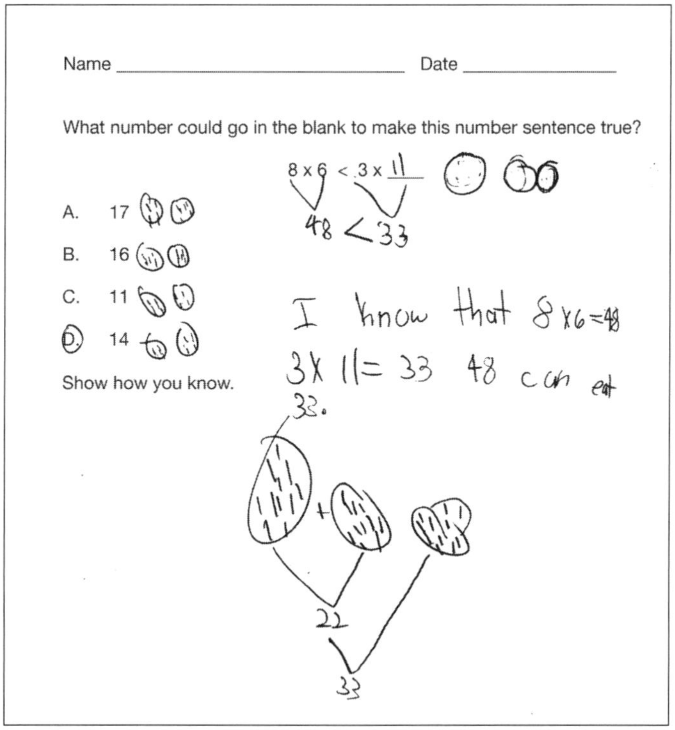
Name ______________________ Date ____________

What number could go in the blank to make this number sentence true?

8 x 6 < 3 x 11

48 < 33

A. 17

B. 16

C. 11

D. 14

Show how you know.

I know that 8 x 6 = 48 3 x 11 = 33 48 can eat 33.

22

33

A Conversation with Jim	Teacher Insights
T: Jim, tell me about what you mean by "Forty-eight can eat thirty-three." **Jim:** Forty-eight is the bigger number, so the alligator can eat thirty-three. The alligator is big and always eats the little numbers.	**T:** *Jim's understanding is confused and backward because of his misinterpretation of the alligator analogy. His idea that the big alligator opens his mouth to eat the little number is flawed in the world of mathematics but makes sense in the real world of alligators.*

Informed Instructional Suggestions

The first order of business for Jim is to help him unlearn the alligator analogy and replace his flawed learning with concrete mathematical experiences that he can represent using the "greater than," "less than," and "equal to" symbols meaningfully. It will be critical to provide immediate feedback for these experiences to correct his misconceptions.

Student Work Sample: Jordan

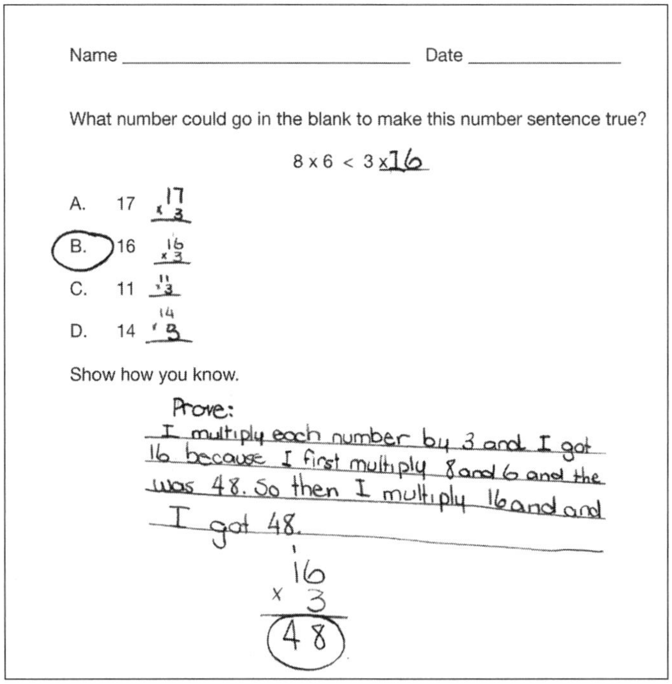
Name ______________________ Date ____________

What number could go in the blank to make this number sentence true?

8 x 6 < 3 x 16

A. 17

B. 16

C. 11

D. 14

Show how you know.

Prove:
I multiply each number by 3 and I got 16 because I first multiply 8 and 6 and the was 48. So then I multiply 16 and and I got 48.

16 × 3 = 48

A Conversation with Jordan	Teacher Insights
T: What is this problem asking you to do? **Jordan:** I have to find a number that I can multiply by three to make forty-eight. **T:** What is it in this problem that tells you that three times some number must equal forty-eight? **Jordan:** It's right here. Eight times six equals forty-eight. I memorized it! I figured out sixteen times three equals forty-eight. So the answer has to be choice B, sixteen. **T:** Why do you think this "less than" sign is in the problem? **Jordan:** Hmm, I don't really know.	**T:** *Jordan has a proficient method of figuring products. However, she did not indicate understanding of relational symbols. Consequently she selected a wrong answer.*

Informed Instructional Suggestions

Jordan needs hands-on experiences involving the meaning and application of relational symbols, as well as practice with reading problems carefully.

Student Work Sample: Caren

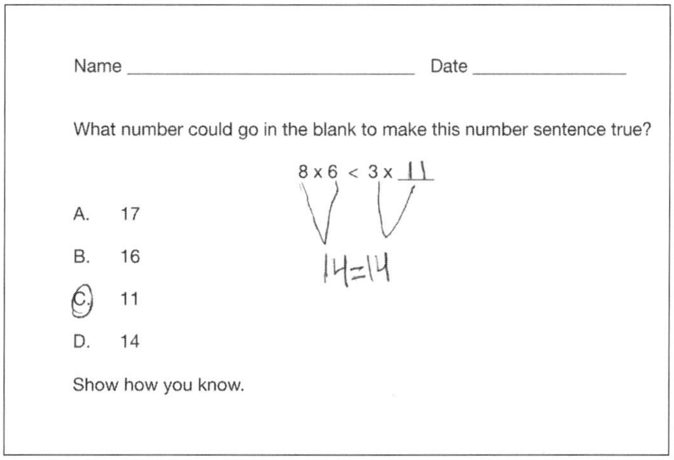
Name ______________________ Date ____________

What number could go in the blank to make this number sentence true?

8 x 6 < 3 x 11

A. 17

B. 16

(C.) 11

D. 14

14=14

Show how you know.

A Conversation with Caren	Teacher Insights
T: Please tell me about what you think this problem is asking you to do. **Caren:** I need to add eight plus six. Eight plus six is fourteen. Then I need to add three plus a number that also equals fourteen. Well, three plus eleven equals fourteen. Done!	**T:** *Caren misread or misunderstood more than just the relational symbol. She also misinterpreted the operational symbol and added rather than multiplied. Her error led her to one of the incorrect answer choices.*

Informed Instructional Suggestions

Caren can add and she can find a missing addend. Next, we need to further examine her failure to correctly recognize the operational symbol by giving her additional work requiring her to identify and act on various operational symbols. Then, she needs to move into work with relational symbols.

Reassessment

1. Use a similar problem at the same level of difficulty.

   What number could go in the blank to make this number sentence true?

   $$7 \times 8 < 4 \times \_\_\_\_\_$$

A. 11
B. 14
C. 13
D. 15

Show how you know.

What number could go in the blank to make this number sentence true?

$$\_\_\_\_\_ \times 8 < 7 \times 6$$

A. 7
B. 8
C. 5
D. 6

Show how you know.

2. Choose a problem that is similar but slightly more challenging (one that uses bigger numbers, for example).

   What number could go in the blank to make this number sentence true?

$$9 \times 9 > \_\_\_\_\_ \times 13$$

   A. 8
   B. 10
   C. 6
   D. 7

   Show how you know.

PROBLEM SIX

Overview

To solve this problem successfully, students need to be able to recognize the commutative property of multiplication. For students who can apply their understanding of the commutative property of multiplication, this is a simple question requiring no computation. For those who don't understand that the order of factors does not change the product, this problem becomes quite difficult, even inappropriate for young children.

Sample Problem

If $8 \times 11 \times 12 = 1{,}056$, then what is $11 \times 8 \times 12$?

A. 88
B. 100
C. 132
D. 1,056

Show how you know.

Possible Student Solution Strategies

- Students use the commutative property to correctly solve the problem.
- Students attempt to solve the problem using multiplication.
- Students use an inappropriate operation or approach to solve the problem.

Conversation Starters

- You did not use computation. What other knowledge did you use to solve this problem?
- Was it necessary to use multiplication to solve this problem? Why or why not?

Student Work Samples: Carly and Lennie

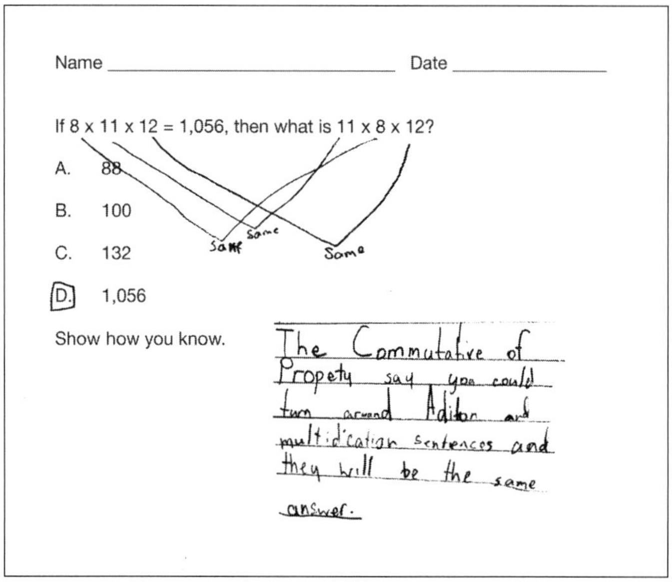
Name ______________________ Date ____________

If 8 x 11 x 12 = 1,056, then what is 11 x 8 x 12?

A. 88

B. 100

C. 132

D. 1,056

Show how you know.

Same
Same
Same
The Commutative of Propety say you could turn around Aditon and multidication sentences and they will be the same answer.

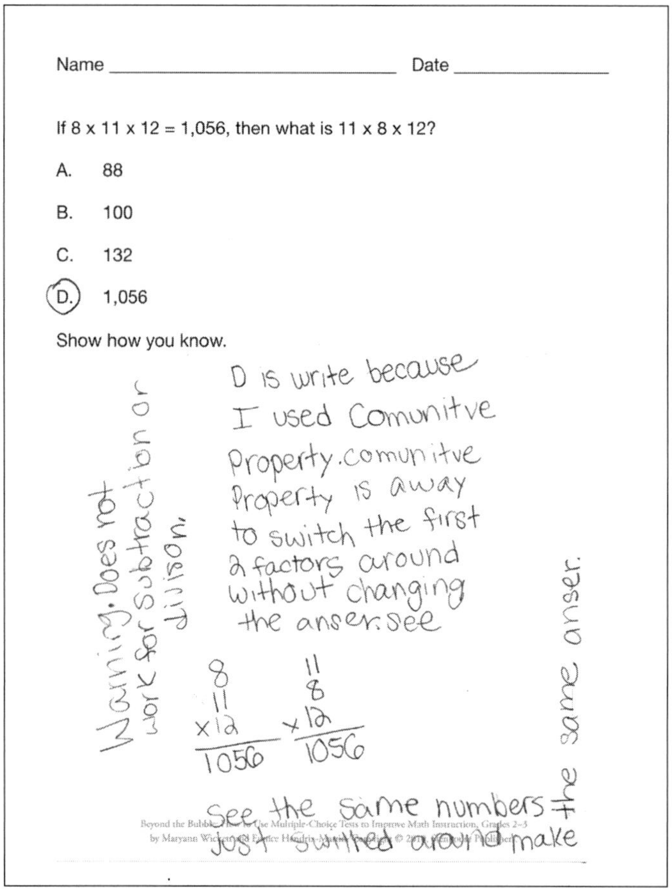
Name ______________________ Date ____________

If 8 x 11 x 12 = 1,056, then what is 11 x 8 x 12?

A. 88

B. 100

C. 132

D. 1,056

D is write because I used Comunitve Property. comunitve Property is away to switch the first 2 factors around without changing the anser. see

See the same numbers just switted around make the same anser.

Show how you know.

A Conversation with Carly and Lennie	Teacher Insights
T: Please share your thinking with each other. First, one of you should explain your solution while the other listens. Then you can change roles. **Carly:** I did the commutative property. **T:** Carly, please explain what the commutative property is. **Carly:** It means that you can turn around multiplication and addition sentences and they will still be the same. **T:** What do you mean by "the same"? **Carly:** The answer won't change, just the order of the other numbers. **Lennie:** Hey, I got that. I even put a warning. It won't work with subtraction or division! I showed that you could change the order of the numbers like this. [Lennie points to her paper.] **Carly:** I guess we agree on that!	**T:** *Because Carly and Lennie showed clear understanding, I asked them to share and listen to each other's responses. This builds good communication skills and respect for one another. Both students indicated understanding and knowledge of the commutative property in their written and oral explanations and were able to easily and accurately apply it to this situation.*

Informed Instructional Suggestions

We can provide these students with a few more similar problems to solve to firmly establish their comfort and fluency with the application of the commutative property. Then it would be useful to give Lennie and Carly the opportunity to work with students whose understanding is not as clear. This will benefit Lennie and Carly as they explain and model their understanding for others and provide support for students who need additional time and practice.

Student Work Samples: Jay and Tami

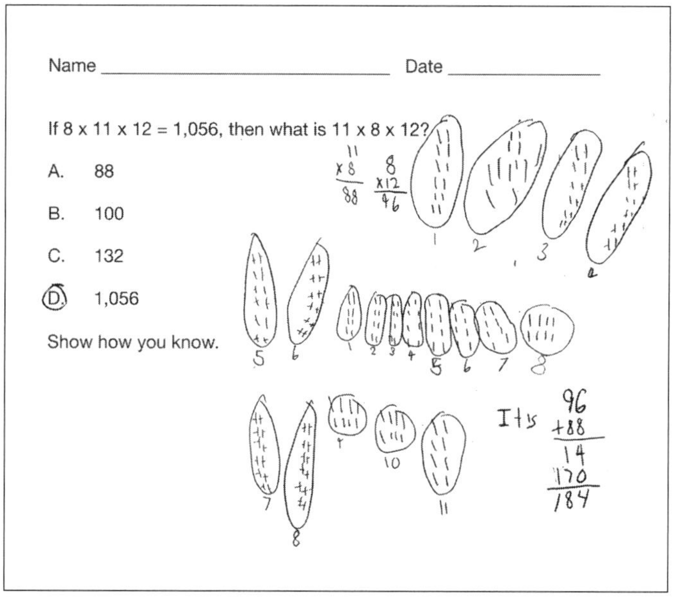
Name ______________________ Date ____________

If 8 x 11 x 12 = 1,056, then what is 11 x 8 x 12?

A. 88

B. 100

C. 132

(D.) 1,056

Show how you know.

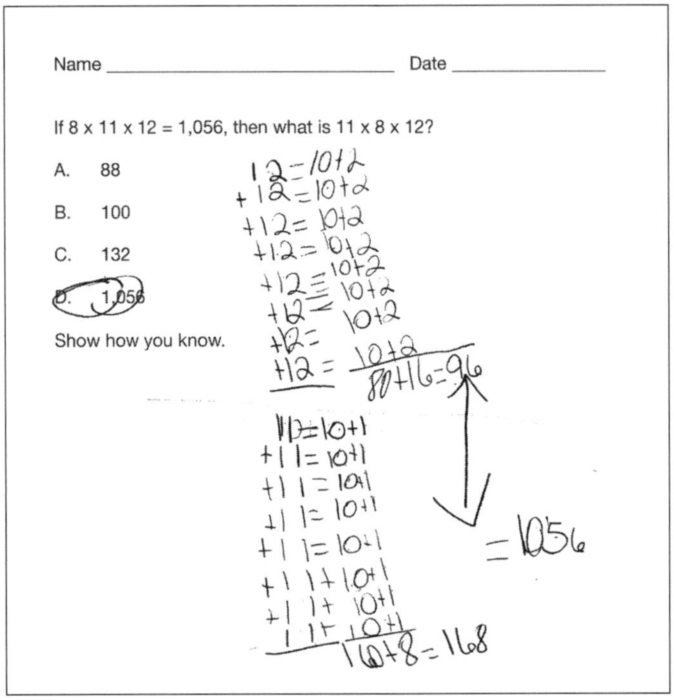
Name ______________________ Date ____________

If 8 x 11 x 12 = 1,056, then what is 11 x 8 x 12?

A. 88

B. 100

C. 132

D. 1,056

Show how you know.

A Conversation with Jay and Tami	Teacher Insights
T: Jay and Tami, please take a few moments to share your solutions with each other. As you are sharing, please look and listen carefully to see what is the same and what is different about your solutions. **Jay:** First I saw that I had to multiply eleven times eight. So I drew eleven circles with eight tally marks in each one. I got eighty-eight. **Tami:** I did that with numbers, but I did it second. First I did 8 times 12, then I did 8 times 11. Next I added up 8 times 12 and added the 80 to the tens from 8 times 11 and got 160. We both got 96 for 8 times 12. Oh, I just noticed something! I forgot to add the 16 from my first problem to the second problem. Oops! **Jay:** We sort of did the same thing, only we showed it differently. You used numbers and I used pictures. **T:** As I look at both of your papers, I notice you both chose 1,056, but the multiplication problems you solved are not close to 1,056. Why did you choose that answer? **Jay:** Because when I added the multiplication answers, I got 184. That wasn't a choice, and A, B, and C were smaller. The only choice left was D. I chose it. **Tami:** I did the same thing, only my answer was 168, but I forgot to add 16. If I had added it right, I would have gotten 184.	**T:** *Jay and Tami both have strategies to accurately solve multiplication problems. However, multiplication computation was not required for this problem. They appeared to be unaware of the commutative property of multiplication and how it can be applied to solve problems such as this one.*

Informed Instructional Suggestions

Both Jay and Tami marked the correct answer choice but had weak understanding of how to approach this problem. Both students used multiplication but with only partial success, although no computation was needed. These students need opportunities to build their understanding of the commutative property of multiplication and how to apply it to solve problems of this nature.

Student Work Sample: Molly

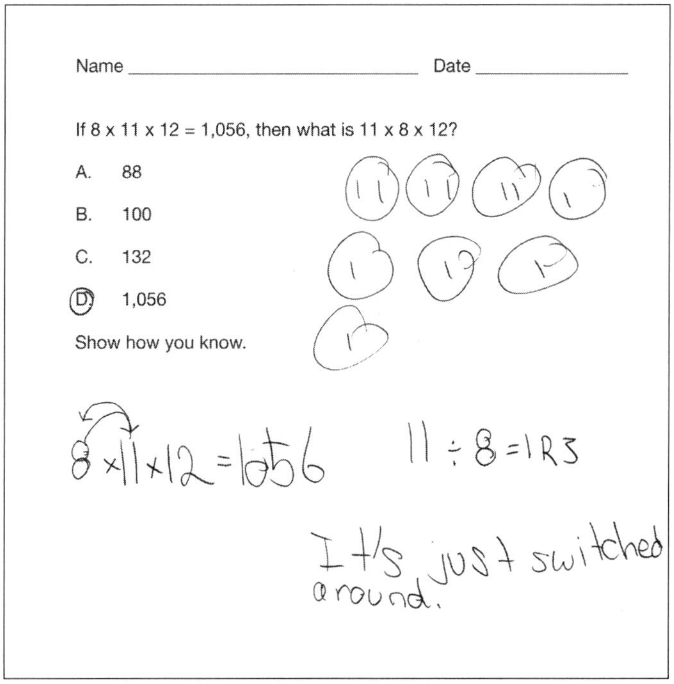

Name ______________________ Date ____________

If 8 x 11 x 12 = 1,056, then what is 11 x 8 x 12?

A. 88

B. 100

C. 132

(D) 1,056

Show how you know.

8 x 11 x 12 = 1056   11 ÷ 8 = 1 R3

It's just switched around.

A Conversation with Molly	Teacher Insights
T: Tell me about your thinking. Was it necessary to use multiplication to solve this problem? **Molly:** No, I didn't have to use multiplication. I used division. I switched the first two numbers in eight times eleven to make the division problem eleven divided by eight. It works that way. I got one remainder three. I drew the picture. It didn't work when I tried eight divided by eleven. **T:** If you got the answer of one remainder three, why did you circle choice D? **Molly:** Because the problem said the answer was 1,056.	**T:** *Although Molly selected the correct answer, she showed no understanding. She changed the problem from multiplication to division and misapplied the commutative property to get a division problem she believed "worked."*

Informed Instructional Suggestions

Molly does not understand the concept being tested by this question. She needs experiences with the commutative property of multiplication using two single-digit factors. She needs to see and understand, for example, that 3 × 4 is equivalent to 4 × 3. To establish this understanding, she can draw three circles and place four tally marks in each and then draw four circles each with three tally marks in each. In either case, the total number of tally marks is twelve. She can also establish this understanding by creating three rows of four tiles and then four rows of three tiles and again discover the totals are the same.

Also, Molly needs hands-on activities that will help her see that division is not commutative and that problems such as eight divided by eleven do "work" (i.e., are solvable).

Student Work Sample: Brianna

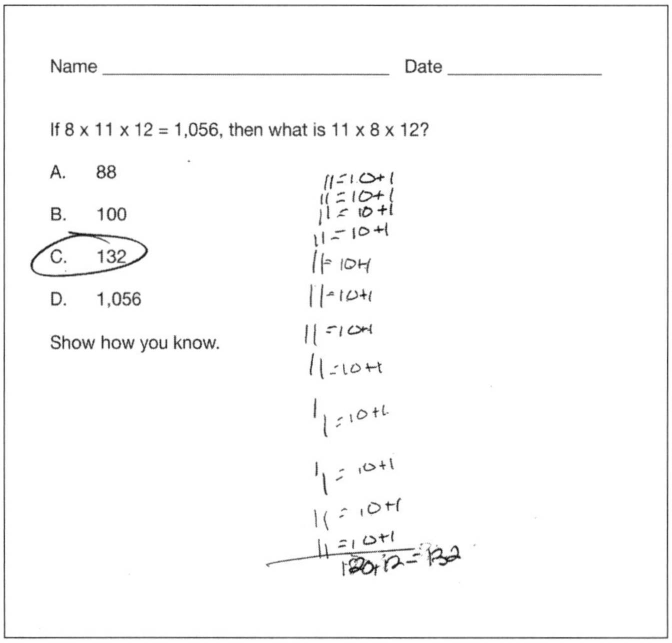
Name ______________________ Date ____________

If 8 x 11 x 12 = 1,056, then what is 11 x 8 x 12?

A. 88

B. 100

C. 132

D. 1,056

Show how you know.

11=10+1
11=10+1
11=10+1
11=10+1
11=10+1
11=10+1
11=10+1
11=10+1
11=10+1
11=10+1
11=10+1
11=10+1
120+12=132

A Conversation with Brianna	Teacher Insights
T: Tell me about your thinking. **Brianna:** Well, I just added 11 twelve times and I got 132. The answer was there, so I circled it.	**T:** *Brianna indicated no awareness of the commutative property or how it could be applied to this question. She saw that the problem involved multiplication and used what she knew about using repeated addition to solve multiplication problems to figure part of this problem.*

Informed Instruction Suggestions

Brianna's needs are similar to Molly's. She should begin with concrete materials or drawings and then move to the abstraction of numbers.

Reassessment

1. Use a similar problem at the same level of difficulty.

   If 6 × 10 × 12 = 720, then what is 12 × 10 × 6?

   A. 120
   B. 72
   C. 720
   D. 1,720

   Show how you know.

2. Choose a problem that is similar but slightly more challenging (one that uses bigger numbers, for example).

   If 9 × 12 × 14 = 1,512, then what is 12 × 14 × 9?

   A. 1,080
   B. 1,800
   C. 1,512
   D. 268

Show how you know.

Date
this solid shape?
made this wooden shape. What two common figure

Geometry

I know it is C because a cone
like this:
this:
and a cylinder
and put them together
you get this
and that
how I got my two shapes.

PROBLEM ONE

Overview

A big idea of geometry for grades two and three is that two-dimensional shapes can be put together or taken apart to form new 2-D shapes. This is a typical multiple-choice question intended to check children's understanding of this notion.

Sample Problem

Which two shapes can be put together to make a square?

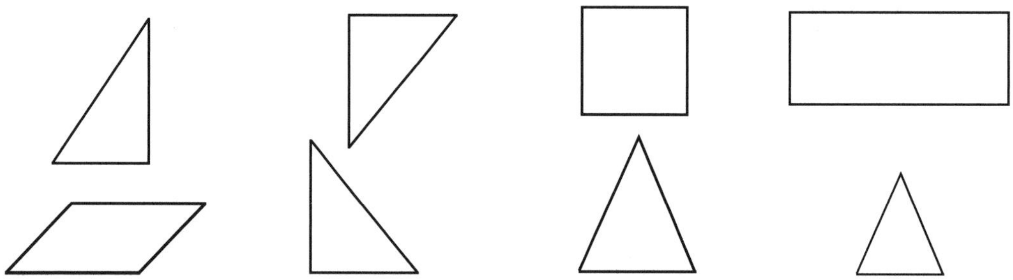

A. B. C. D.

Show how you know.

Possible Student Solution Strategies

- Students draw the pairs of polygons shown for each of the answer choices in an attempt to create a square.
- Students apply the idea that two triangles can make a square in certain cases.
- Students recognize that some of the polygon pairs cannot be arranged into a single polygon with two pairs of congruent parallel sides and four right angles.

Conversation Starters

- Do two triangles always make a square? How do you know?
- What did you do to help you select your answer?
- What did you have to do to show that the two triangles make a square?
- Is there a different polygon that can be created by putting the two triangles together?
- What kind of angles (corners) do all squares have? How do the triangles make those corners when you put them together?
- Is there another way to make a square with two polygons that aren't triangles?
- Can all squares be cut into two triangles? How do you know?
- Why didn't you pick choice C [or one of the other choices not selected]?

Student Work Sample: Beatriz

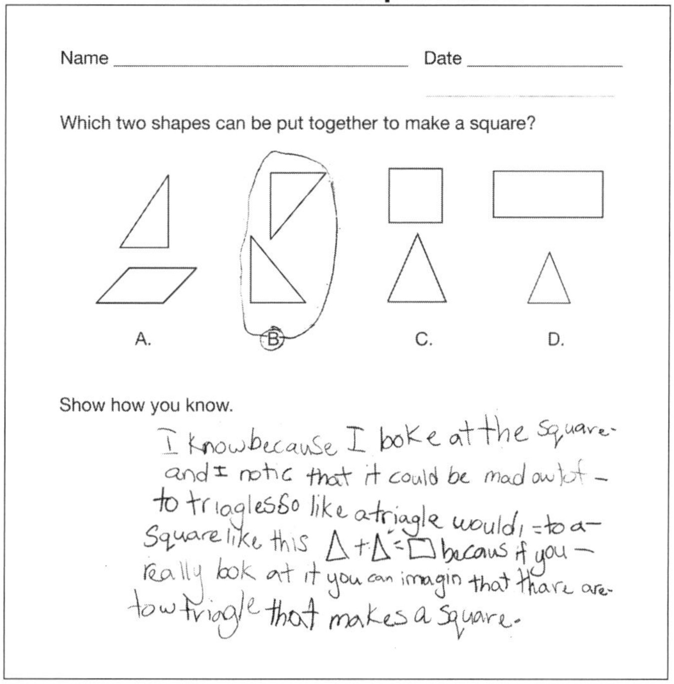
Name ______________________ Date ______________

Which two shapes can be put together to make a square?

A. B. C. D.

Show how you know.

I know because I loke at the square and I notic that it could be mad out of to triagles so like a triagle would = to a square like this Δ+Δ=□ becaus if you really look at it you can imagin that thare are tow triagle that makes a square.

A Conversation with Beatriz	Teacher Insights
T: What did you do to help you select choice B? **Beatriz:** I looked at the square in choice C really hard and thought in my head that it could be made out of two triangles. **T:** What makes a square a square? **Beatriz:** It has to have four sides that are the same and four square corners. But I didn't know it could come from two triangles! That's amazing, I think. **T:** Do you think you could make a square out of four triangles? **Beatriz:** Oh . . . I don't know about that. Maybe? Maybe not? **T:** Can you make any two triangles into a square? **Beatriz:** No. I don't think so, but I'm not sure. My brain will have to think about that.	**T:** *Beatriz seems to have a good foundational understanding of the attributes of squares, enabling her to visualize and consider new possibilities.*

Informed Instructional Suggestions

Beatriz is aware of basic attributes of squares, such as that they have four congruent sides and four right angles ("square corners"), but she needs the opportunity to continue to explore ideas about squares and triangles. For example, Beatriz would benefit from cutting apart squares and making squares from triangles and other polygons. She also needs activities that will help her further develop her geometry vocabulary.

Student Work Sample: Juan

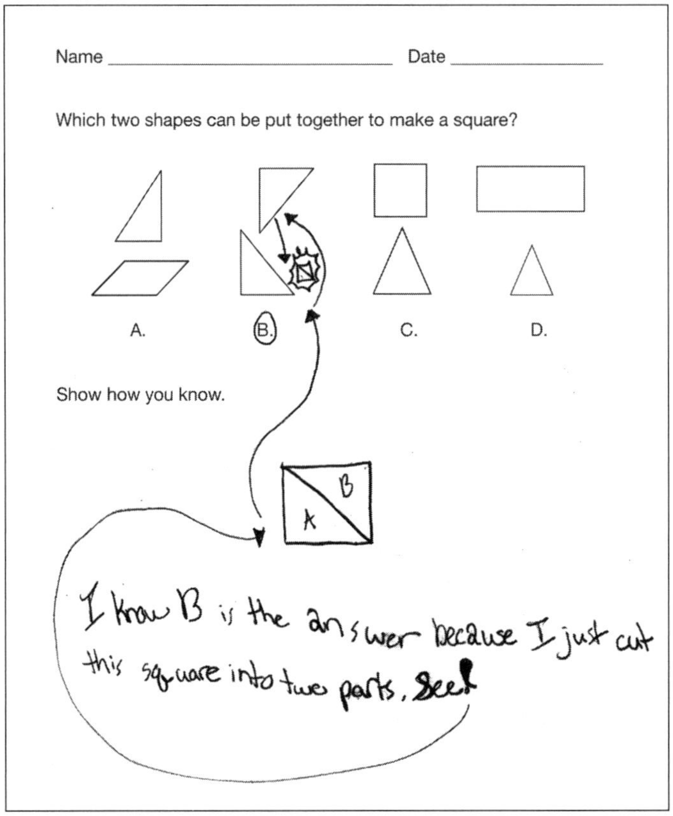
Name ______ Date ______
Which two shapes can be put together to make a square?
A.
B.
C.
D.
Show how you know.
B
A
I know B is the answer because I just cut this square into two parts, see!

A Conversation with Juan	Teacher Insights
T: I see you solved this problem by drawing a picture to show a square cut into two triangles. Can all squares be cut into two triangles? **Juan:** Yes, but you have to cut them across like this. [Juan uses his finger to show the diagonals.] **T:** Can you put any two triangles together to make a square? **Juan:** Yes, because it worked on this problem.	**T:** *Juan had a good strategy to solve this problem; however, he does have a misconception that needs to be addressed. It's not correct that any two triangles can be arranged into a square.*

Informed Instructional Suggestions

As a next step, Juan could explore when triangles do and do not make squares. We should create experiences that also encourage him to develop his geometry vocabulary. Juan's exploration will reinforce and expand his understanding of squares.

Student Work Sample: Gary

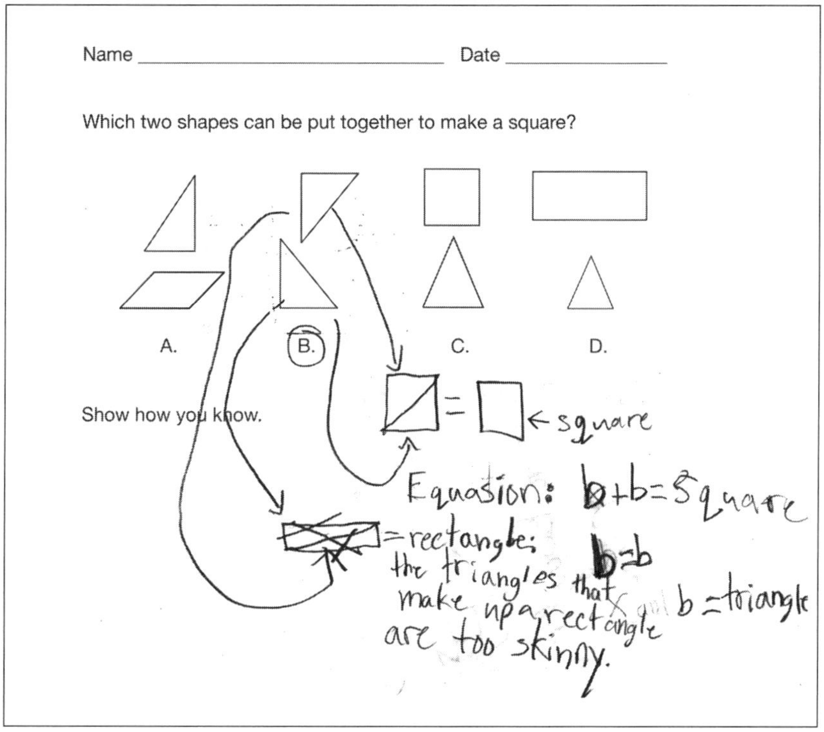

Name ______________________ Date ____________

Which two shapes can be put together to make a square?

A. B. C. D.

Show how you know.

= ← square
Equasion: b+b=square
=rectangle;
the triangles that make up a rectangle are too skinny.
b=b
b=triangle

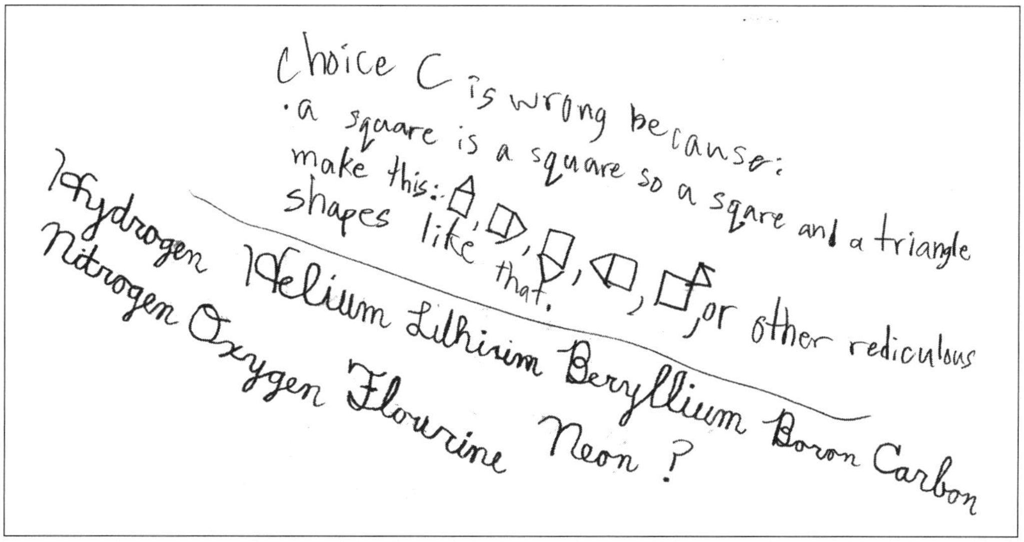

choice C is wrong because:
·a square is a square so a sqare and a triangle make this: , , , , , or other rediculous shapes like that.
Hydrogen Helium Lithium Beryllium Boron Carbon
Nitrogen Oxygen Flourine Neon ?

A Conversation with Gary	Teacher Insights
T: Gary, please tell me about your equations. **Gary:** Well, I noticed that each of the triangles in choice B were the same, so I wrote b = b because the triangles are the same and I wrote b = triangle. [Gary points to his paper to emphasize and clarify his thinking.] Then I wrote b + b = square. I drew a picture to show you, too. **T:** What makes a square a square? **Gary:** Um, I'm not so sure. Maybe it's that they have two triangles in them. They have four sides and four angles. It looks a certain way that I can't describe.	**T:** *Gary has a strong understanding of number and enjoys thinking about equations, as demonstrated in his initial written explanation (see page 143, top). While Gary's understanding and quickness with number are unusually strong, he has only surface understanding in many other areas of mathematics, such as geometry. He has only vague ideas about "squareness" and he was unable to clearly explain the unique attributes that make a square a square.*
T: On the back of your paper, please show how you would explain to someone else why choice C is not correct.	**T:** *Gary's response provided no further insight to his understanding (see page 143, bottom). When I suggested he elaborate, he chose to list the elements of the periodic table in order of their weight. This is an important reminder to tease out and close gaps in the understanding of extremely capable students. Without the written explanations and discussion, I would have assumed Gary knew more than he did.*

Informed Instructional Suggestions

Gary's instructional needs are similar to Beatriz's and Juan's. However, Gary will need additional opportunities and challenges to test his conjectures. For example, we could ask him to find triangles that make squares and those that don't, and compare the attributes of both. He could also investigate whether squares can be made from three, four, five, and six triangles. Gary could then explore other polygons that can be used to create squares, or how to cut squares to make other polygons, noting the shapes of the pieces he cuts to create new polygons. As with Beatriz and Juan, we must encourage Gary to use the language of geometry to describe his thinking.

Student Work Sample: Matty

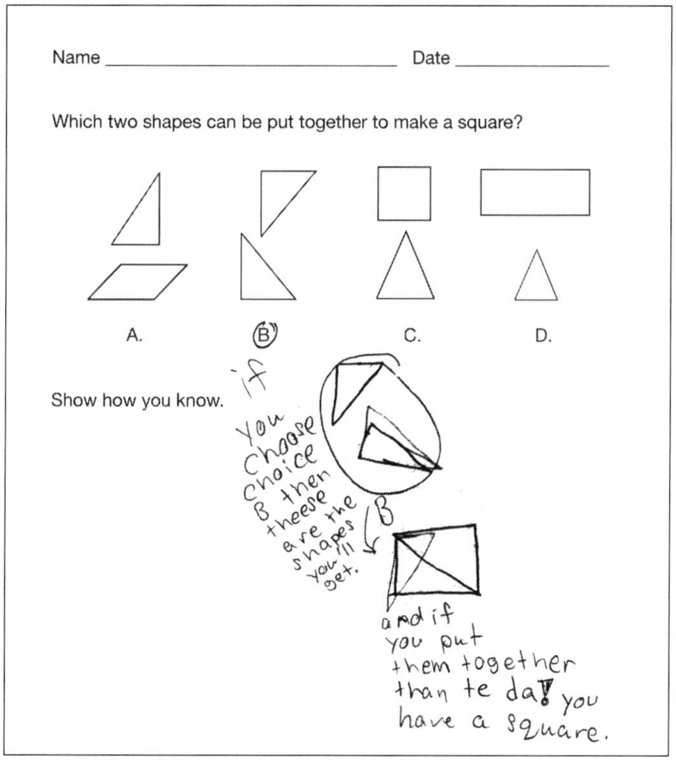
Name ______ Date ______
Which two shapes can be put together to make a square?
A.
B.
C.
D.
Show how you know.
if you choose choice B then theese are the shapes you'll get.
B
and if you put them together than te da! you have a square.

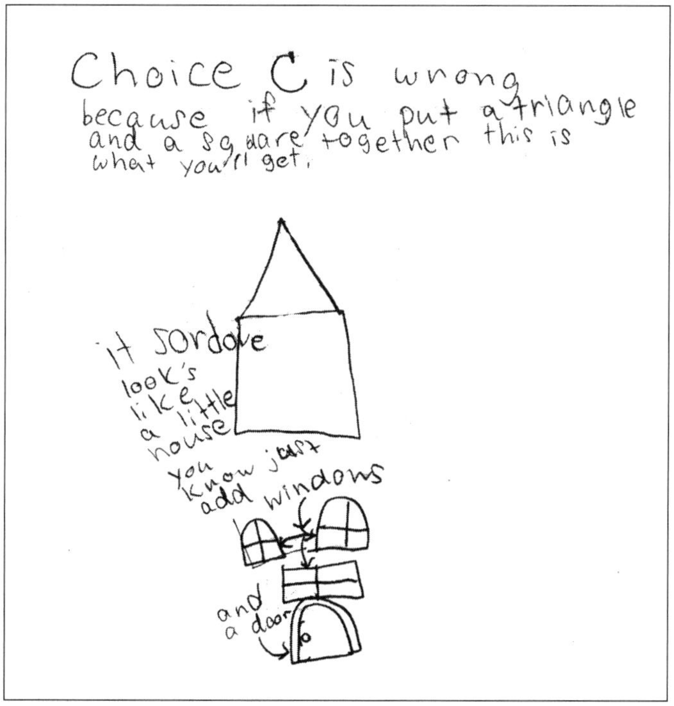
Choice C is wrong because if you put a triangle and a square together this is what you'll get.
it sordove look's like a little house
you know just add windows
and a door

A Conversation with Matty	Teacher Insights
T: Tell me how you knew that the two triangles would make a square. **Matty:** I could see it in my brain and then I drew it on my paper. **T:** What makes a square a square? **Matty:** It has four equal sides and four square corners. **T:** I notice you picked choice B rather than choice C. Please write about your thinking on the back of your paper and I will be back in just a few moments and we can talk about it.	**T:** *Matty seemed confident in her responses and was able to give a simple, correct definition of a square. Instead of having her write about why her thinking made sense, I asked her to write about something that might not have made sense to her.*
T: I see you put the square and triangle together to make a house (see page 145, bottom). **Matty:** Yep, and I showed you that I can add windows and a door, too. **T:** Do you know the name for the polygon you just drew? **Matty:** Only that it is a house. **T:** Is there another way to arrange the triangle and square? **Matty:** I'm thinking. I think I can see in my brain a square ice-cream cone. It's the house turned upside down. The triangle is the cone part and the square is the ice cream.	**T:** *Matty is able to visualize well. She has a beginning vocabulary but needs further experiences to develop her knowledge of geometric shapes, their relationship to one another, and the relevant vocabulary.*

Informed Instructional Suggestions

All students in these classes got this question correct. But by asking them to write and talk about their thinking, we were able to establish where to begin instruction that would be meaningful for each individual. In Matty's case, work on further developing and applying her knowledge of the vocabulary of geometry is indicated. This can be done as she works through hands-on experiences and describes them using appropriate vocabulary. In addition, posting a vocabulary list with pictures when possible will help Matty (and all students) to use words related to geometry.

Reassessment

1. Use a similar problem at the same level of difficulty.

   Which two shapes can you put together to make a parallelogram?

A. 

B. 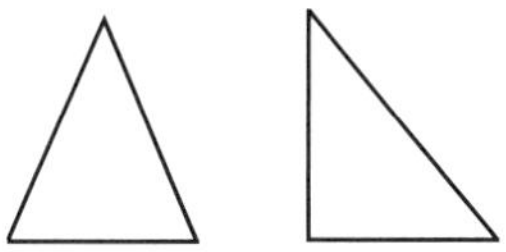

C. 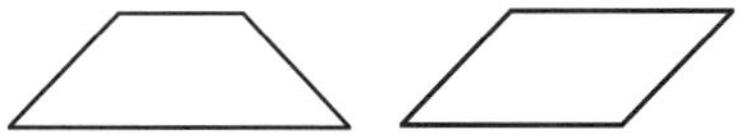

D. 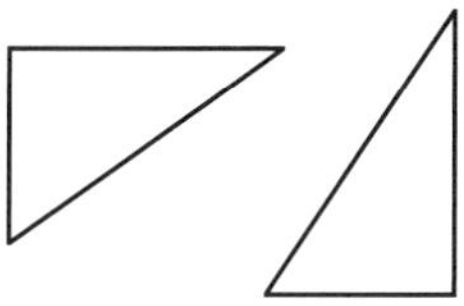

Show how you know.

2. Choose a problem that is similar but slightly more challenging.

Which three shapes can you put together to make a rectangle?

A. 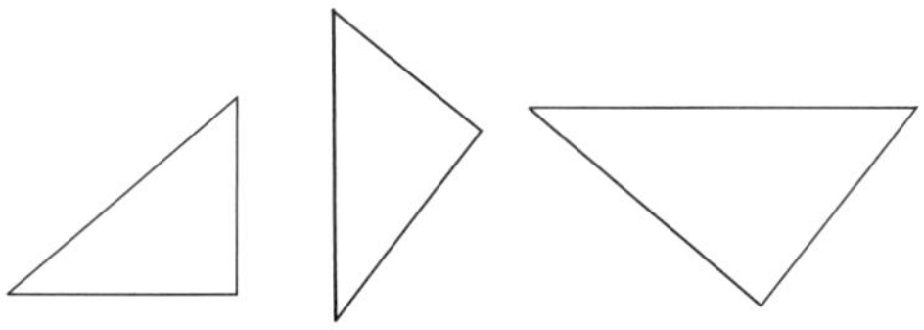

B. 

C. 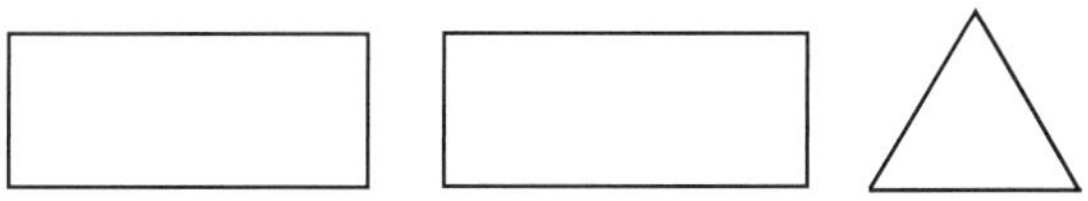

D. 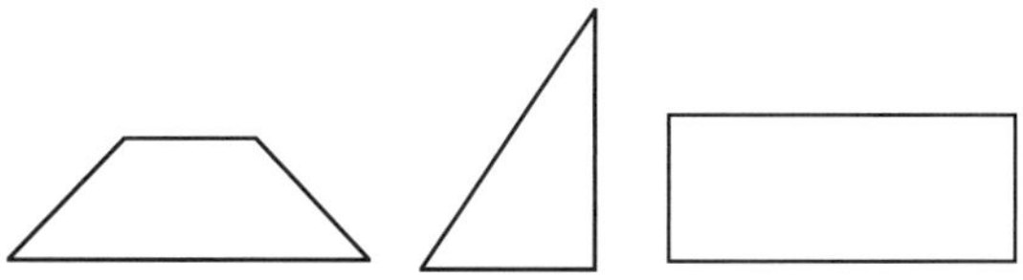

Show how you know.

PROBLEM TWO

Overview

The study of geometry in grades two and three is grounded heavily in vocabulary. This type of question tests students' knowledge of vocabulary relating to three-dimensional geometry: *faces*, *edges*, and *vertex* (*vertices*).

Sample Problem

Which figure has exactly six faces?

A. 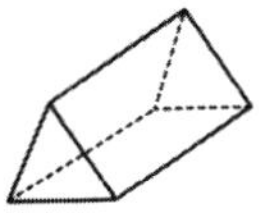

B. 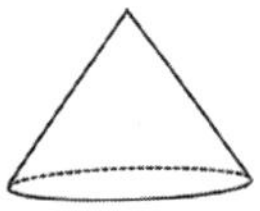

C. 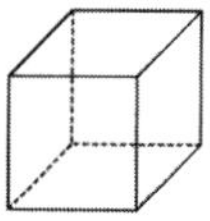

D. 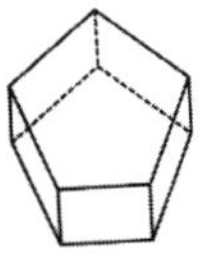

Show how you know.

Possible Student Solution Strategies

- Students are able to correctly explain that a cube has six faces.
- Students count the faces of each choice to determine which has six faces.
- Students connect the various polyhedra with real-life objects in order to determine the number of faces and which has six faces.
- Students identify and count parts of the polyhedra other than faces (i.e., vertices or edges).
- Students miscount the faces.

Conversation Starters

- What is a face?
- What kinds of figures are shown?
- How would you help a younger child figure the number of faces on a polyhedron?
- Why are some lines in the drawings dotted rather than solid?

Student Work Sample: Ellie

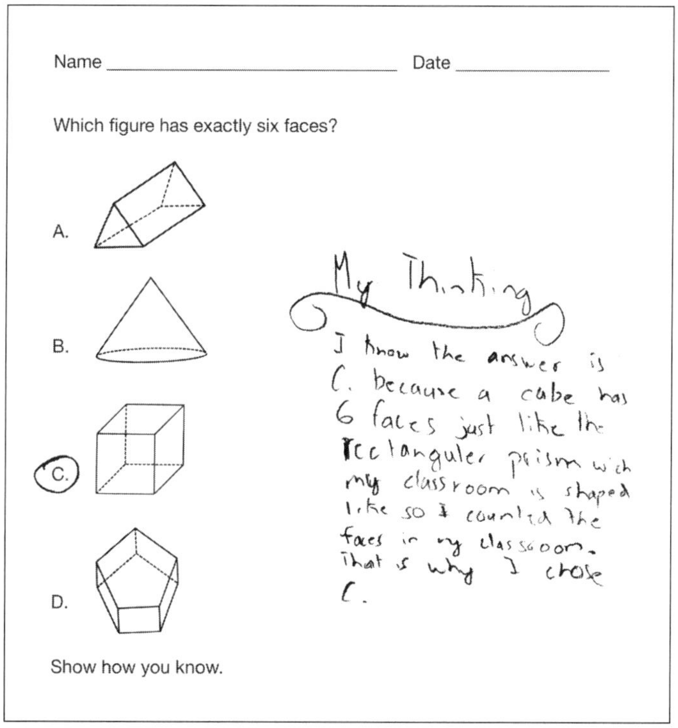

Name ______________________ Date ______________

Which figure has exactly six faces?

A.

B.

(C.)

D.

My Thinking

I know the answer is C. because a cube has 6 faces just like the rectanguler prism wich my classroom is shaped like so I counted the faces in my classroom. That is why I chose C.

Show how you know.

A Conversation with Ellie

T: What is a face, Ellie?

Ellie: It is a flat surface.

T: How many faces does the picture in choice A have?

Ellie: Five.

T: Tell me about your thinking on this problem.

Ellie: I know that a cube is a special kind of rectangular prism. They're the same thing except that all of a cube's faces are equal. I know that our classroom is a rectangular prism, so I just counted all the faces of our classroom. Because I am inside our classroom, I can see all the faces and there are six, so I chose choice C, which is a cube.

T: Nice connection, Ellie.

Teacher Insights

T: *Ellie was able to connect her understanding of cubes and rectangular prisms to reality to solve this problem. She understands what cubes and rectangular prisms are in addition to understanding what a face is.*

Informed Instructional Suggestions

Ellie is ready to continue to explore and learn about 3-D geometry at a higher level, especially visualizing what happens when composing and decomposing 3-D figures. Her next experiences should reinforce vocabulary and connections to the real world.

Student Work Sample: Pablo

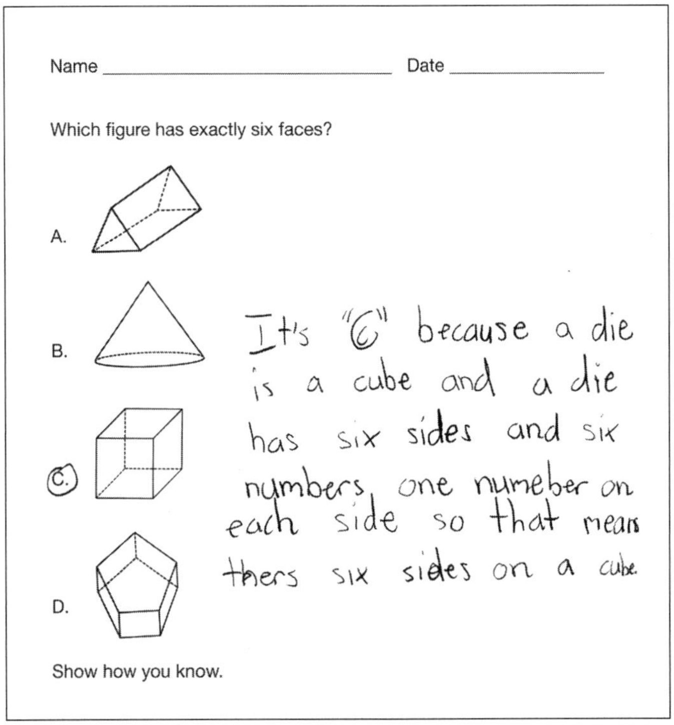

Name ____________________ Date __________

Which figure has exactly six faces?

A.

B.

(C.)

D.

It's "C" because a die is a cube and a die has six sides and six numbers, one numeber on each side so that means thers six sides on a cube.

Show how you know.

A Conversation with Pablo	Teacher Insights
T: Please tell me about your answer choice. **Pablo:** I know a die has six sides. They are numbered 1 to 6, one number on each side. Choice C looks like a die without the numbers or dots. Since there are six sides on a die, which is usually a cube, there must be six sides on the cube in the picture. **T:** What do you think the dotted lines mean in these pictures? **Pablo:** I think they put those there because you can't actually see through the shape, so the dotted line is telling you where the lines would be if you could see through the shape.	**T:** *Pablo's understanding is firm, and, like Ellie, he made a connection to his world by noticing a die is a cube. He used his knowledge and this connection to make the case that a cube has six faces. Pablo needs to learn that what he is calling a side should be referred to as a face.*

Informed Instructional Suggestions

Pablo would benefit from conversations about geometric figures that focus on and model correct vocabulary and require him to use this vocabulary to strengthen his knowledge and enhance his communication.

Student Work Sample: Alvin

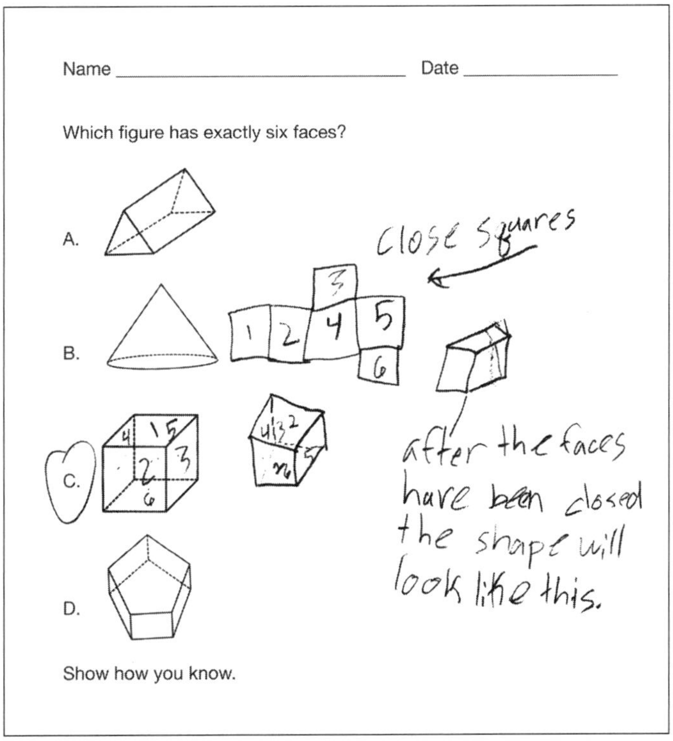

A Conversation with Alvin	Teacher Insights
T: What an interesting drawing you have on your paper. Please tell me more about it. **Alvin:** It's a picture of what a cube would look like if you cut it so it could lay flat. When I drew it that way, you could see all of the faces and there are six. When you fold it back up, it will be a cube again.	**T:** *Alvin was able to visualize a cube opened up and use this idea to verify that a cube has six faces.*

Informed Instructional Suggestions

Alvin would benefit from exploring to predict and verify what other 3-D shapes would look like when cut apart and laid flat.

Student Work Sample: Maya

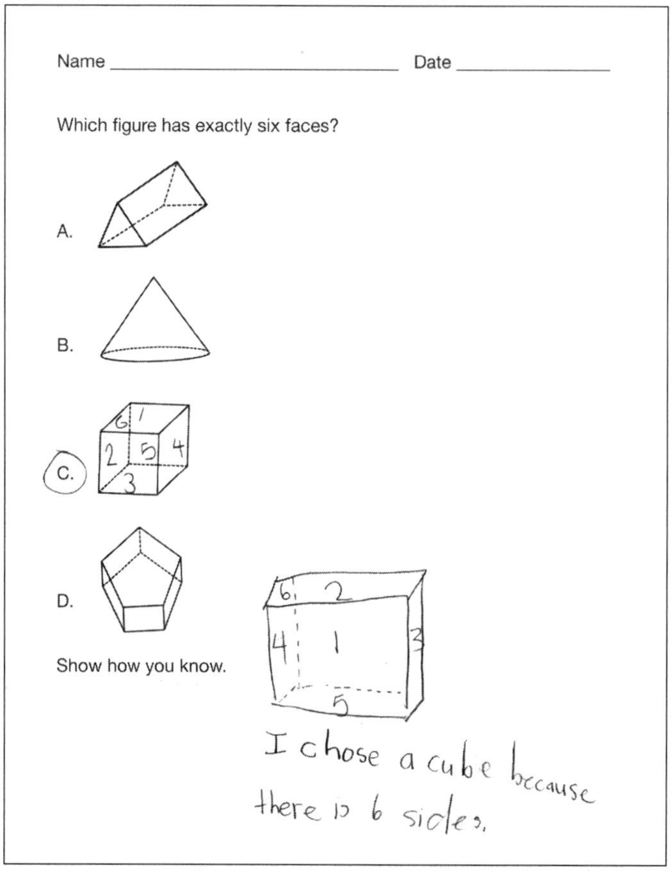

Name ________________________ Date ______________

Which figure has exactly six faces?

A.

B.

(C.)

D.

Show how you know.

A Conversation with Maya	Teacher Insights
T: How would you explain your thinking to a younger student? **Maya:** I would tell the student that a cube has square faces. Also, it has six faces. The face is the flat part. I already knew this so when I read the question I thought the right answer had to be a cube. I found the cube and I numbered the faces to show that there are six of them. [Maya points to her work.] **T:** Thank you for the clear explanation, Maya.	**T:** *Maya was able to use her knowledge to select a correct response and to clearly explain her decision.*

Informed Instructional Suggestions

Maya is ready to continue exploring the attributes—such as faces, edges, and vertices—of other polyhedra. Also, it would be helpful for Maya to investigate how polyhedra are made of other shapes or can be used to create other polyhedra. To encourage her to use the language of geometry in a meaningful context, we could provide her a list of appropriate vocabulary and ask her to work with a partner.

Student Work Sample: Josie

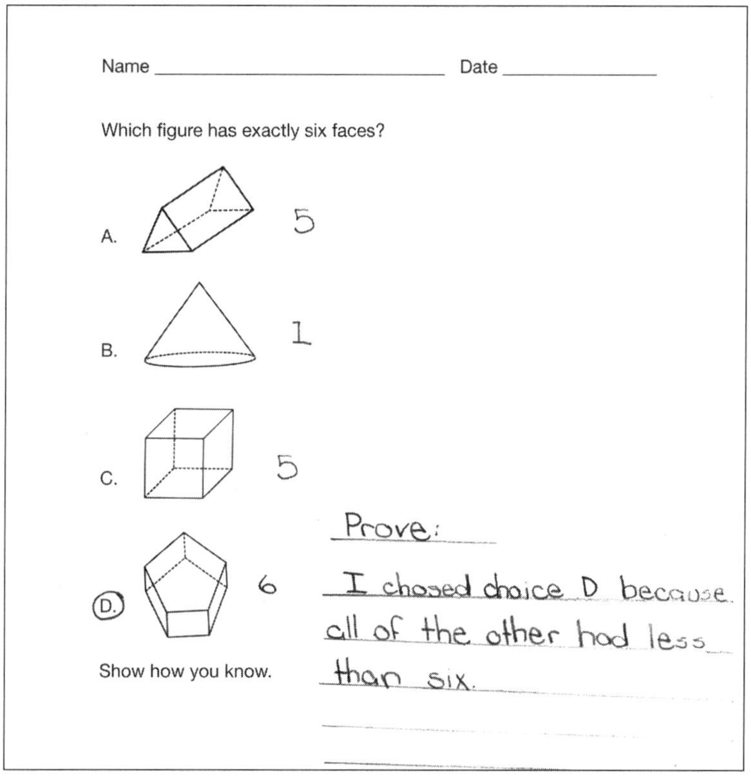
Name ______________________ Date ____________

Which figure has exactly six faces?

A. 5

B. 1

C. 5

(D.) 6

Show how you know.

Prove:

I chosed choice D because all of the other had less than six.

A Conversation with Josie	Teacher Insights
T: I noticed that you put a number by each of the polyhedra. What do the numbers mean? **Josie:** They tell the number of faces. Choice A has five, choice B has one, choice C has five, and choice D has six. The question wanted to know which one had six faces, so I chose choice D. **T:** Please show me how you counted the faces in choice D. **Josie:** There are five on the sides and one on the bottom. Five and one are six. **T:** Show me how you counted the faces in choice C. **Josie:** There are four on the sides and one on the bottom. Four and one are five, so it has five faces.	**T:** *Josie's error was consistent for both choices C and D—she did not count the top face of either polyhedron. I did not push her for an answer on choice B, as some sources say that a cone has two faces while others state it has one face. This was not the time to get into that discussion. She counted the faces of choice A correctly.*

Informed Instructional Suggestions

Providing Josie with geometric solids and asking her to count faces, edges, and vertices would help her correct her error and deepen her knowledge and understanding.

Student Work Sample: Mick

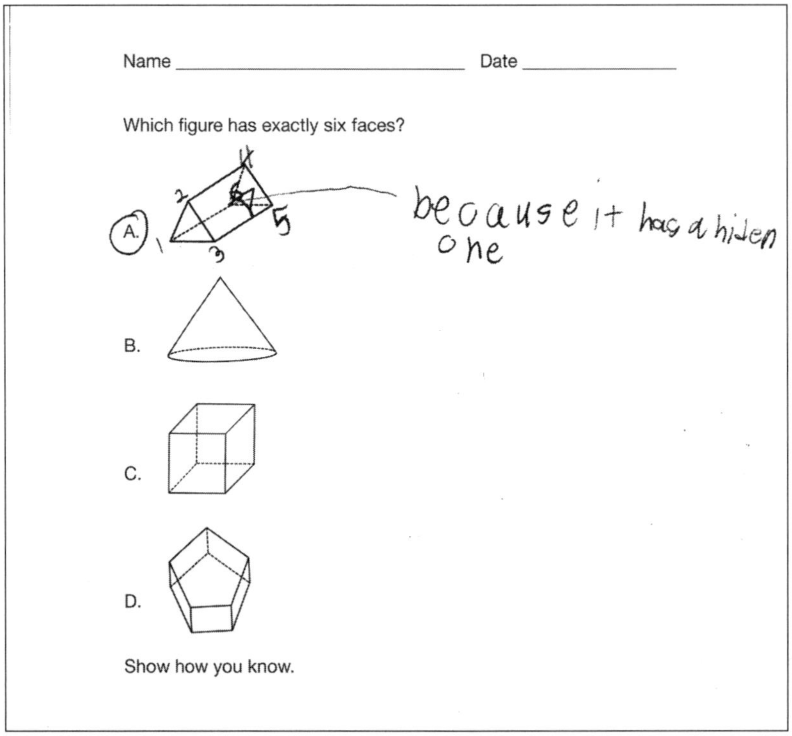
Name ______________________ Date ______________

Which figure has exactly six faces?

(A.) because it has a hiden one

B.

C.

D.

Show how you know.

A Conversation with Mick	Teacher Insights
T: How did you arrive at your choice of A? **Mick:** See where I put the numbers? I was counting the corners where the sides come together. There is a hidden one but I remembered to count it. Choice A has six.	**T:** *Mick believes that what is actually a vertex is a face. He counted the vertices of choice A correctly.*

Informed Instructional Suggestions

Mick needs concrete, hands-on experiences that will help him develop understanding of polyhedra and the geometric vocabulary related to them, for example, *face*, *vertex* (*vertices*), and *edge*. He needs to handle geometric solids, find them in everyday objects, draw them, label them, count their faces, edges, and vertices, and talk about them using the correct vocabulary.

Reassessment

1. Use a similar problem at the same level of difficulty.

   Which figure has exactly seven faces?

   A. 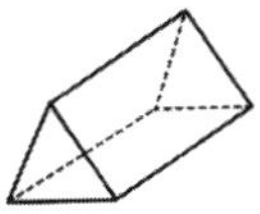

   B. 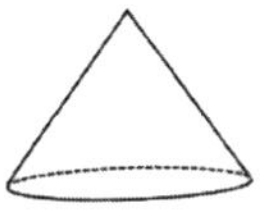

   C. 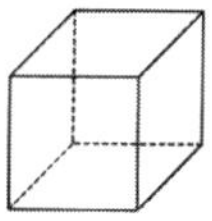

   D. 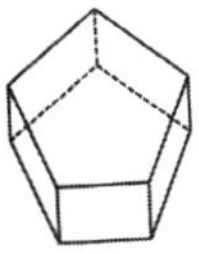

   Show how you know.

2. Choose a problem that is similar but slightly more challenging.

   Which figure has exactly six vertices?

   A. 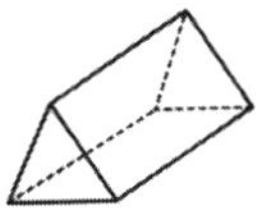

   B. 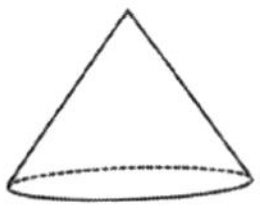

   C. 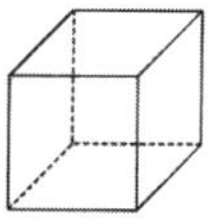

   D. 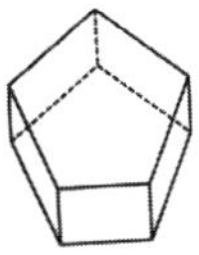

   Show how you know.

PROBLEM THREE

Overview

To answer this problem, students must use their knowledge of attributes of triangles, a key idea in geometry for second and third graders. Students need to apply their knowledge of sides and angles of triangles to identify a true statement.

Sample Problem

Which of these is a true statement about an equilateral triangle?

A. It has no equal sides and no equal angles.
B. It has 2 equal sides and 2 equal angles.
C. It has 4 equal sides and 4 equal angles.
D. It has 3 equal sides and 3 equal angles.

Show how you know.

Possible Student Solution Strategies

- Students apply their knowledge of triangles, recognizing that an equilateral triangle has three congruent sides and three congruent angles.
- Students select the correct answer based on partial knowledge: the word *equal* is a part of the larger word *equilateral* and a triangle has three sides and/or angles; therefore, an equilateral triangle can't have no equal sides or angles or four equal sides and angles.

Conversation Starters

- Please tell me all you know about triangles.
- What makes an equilateral triangle a special kind of triangle?
- Are all triangles equilateral?
- Which answer choice makes no sense to you? Explain.

Student Work Sample: Bart

Name ______________________ Date ____________

Which of these is a true statement about an equilateral triangle?

A. It has no equal sides and no equal angles.

B. It has 2 equal sides and 2 equal angles.

C. It has 4 equal sides and 4 equal angles.

D. It has 3 equal sides and 3 equal angles.

Show how you know.

Because a equalateral is a shape that has all equal sides And sence it's a triangle it has 3 sides and 3 angles that are equal.

A Conversation with Bart	Teacher Insights
T: What do you think makes an equilateral triangle a special type of triangle? **Bart:** The word *equilateral* sounds like *equal*, so it must be a triangle with all equal sides and angles. **T:** Are all triangles equilateral? **Bart:** No. Sometimes the sides are all different lengths. [Pauses.] Sometimes the angles are all different-looking, too. **T:** Which answer choice is the same as what you just described? **Bart:** I think A, no equal sides and no equal angles. **T:** Please draw me a picture of a triangle with no equal sides or angles. **Bart:** [Bart thinks a moment and then draws a triangle on his paper.] I can see the sides are different lengths and I think the angles are different too. I showed the top was big, the left angle was the middle, and the right was little.	**T:** *Bart had enough confidence in his understanding to select the correct answer choice and discuss his thinking in a manner that made sense. He made the connection between equal and equilateral and recognized that not all triangles are equilateral. He was able to state that there are triangles with no equal sides and angles, pick out a matching answer choice for this description, and draw an example of his thinking.*

Informed Instructional Suggestions

Bart has an understanding of triangles. As many children do, he needs to more fully develop the language of geometry via hands-on exploration with triangles and other polygons.

Student Work Sample: Greg

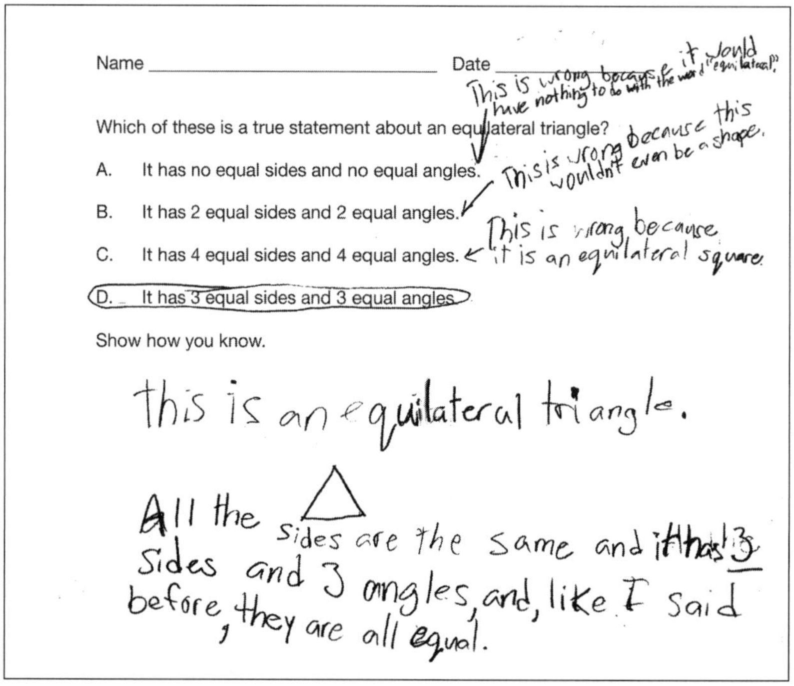
Name ______________________ Date ______

Which of these is a true statement about an equilateral triangle?

A. It has no equal sides and no equal angles.

B. It has 2 equal sides and 2 equal angles.

C. It has 4 equal sides and 4 equal angles.

D. It has 3 equal sides and 3 equal angles.

Show how you know.

This is wrong because it would have nothing to do with the word "equilateral."
This is wrong because this wouldn't even be a shape.
This is wrong because it is an equilateral square.
this is an equilateral triangle.
All the sides are the same and it has 3 sides and 3 angles, and, like I said before, they are all equal.

A Conversation with Greg	Teacher Insights
T: Greg, I appreciate the way you expressed your thinking for each of the answer choices. You did very complete work and it helps me to better understand what you know. I am interested in your comments about choices A and B. Please tell me more. **Greg:** I did the same thinking for choices A and B. They are silly and ridiculous choices. A shape with no sides or angles is no shape at all. It's nothing. So choice A would be nothing! Choice B says a shape with two sides and two angles. I think that's impossible too. You can't have a shape like a polygon, which is what an equilateral triangle is, with two sides and two angles. You can't have two angles with just two sides. The most angles you can get with just two sides is one angle. So choice B doesn't make any sense either. **T:** In choices A and B I see a word you haven't mentioned. Both choices say *equal* sides and *equal* angles. Could a polygon have only two sides or only two angles that are equal? **Greg:** You mean like there are three angles or sides and only two are equal? I didn't think of that. I am not sure about triangles, but rectangles have two opposite sides that equal, so maybe it's true for a four-sided figure but I don't know about triangles.	**T:** *Greg's written explanations about choices A and B indicated he might have misinterpreted the problem somewhat. This was verified by his verbal explanations. Greg showed some partial understanding and he was able to use the vocabulary of geometry effectively. However, there is room for growth, especially with respect to his understanding of triangles, which is still emerging.*

Informed Instructional Suggestions

Greg marked the correct answer but misunderstood to some extent what the question was actually asking. Greg will benefit greatly from hands-on experiences with creating, drawing, and classifying different types of triangles based on their attributes. He should explore equilateral, scalene, isosceles, acute, obtuse, right, and right isosceles triangles. Classifying triangles by both their sides and angles is important. Through these types of activities, Greg will come to recognize that triangles can have no equal sides or angles (scalene triangles), two equal sides and angles (isosceles triangles), all congruent sides and angles (equilateral triangles), right angles (right triangles), all acute angles (acute triangles), and an obtuse angle (obtuse triangles).

Student Work Sample: Blair

Name ______________________ Date ______________

Which of these is a true statement about an equilateral triangle?

A. It has no equal sides and no equal angles.

B. It has 2 equal sides and 2 equal angles.

C. It has 4 equal sides and 4 equal angles.

D. It has 3 equal sides and 3 equal angles.

Show how you know.

I think choice D is corect becaus c doesn't make sense to chaws c becaus it said a equilateral triangle has 4 sides and angles and I know that a equilateral triangle has 3 sides and 3 angles becaus Iv seen one before.

A Conversation with Blair	Teacher Insights
T: Are all triangles equilateral triangles? **Blair:** I don't know. I know that all triangles have three sides and three angles. The *tri-* in *triangle* means three, so they have to have three angles. I knew choice C was totally wrong because triangles don't have four sides or angles. Wouldn't something with four equal sides and four equal angles be a square? Well, a square is not a triangle! I knew choice C was wrong. **T:** Why didn't you pick choice A or B? **Blair:** I just skipped over them because in choice B I saw the number 2 and in choice A I saw the word no. I didn't even read them. **T:** Please read choice A for me now. [Blair reads aloud.] Is it possible for a triangle to have no equal sides and *no* equal angles? **Blair:** No, that's impossible. I know because I have seen triangles since kindergarten. They are the green pieces in the pattern blocks. That's what a triangle is. **T:** Have you seen triangles anywhere else? **Blair:** Nope, that's all.	**T:** *Blair marked the correct answer and knows that triangles have three sides and three angles. She also conjectured that a four-sided figure with equal sides and angles could be a square. She has some good beginning understanding upon which to build. Blair's understanding of a triangle is limited to the green triangles in pattern block sets.*

Informed Instructional Suggestions

Blair's correct response masked significant gaps in her understanding. Blair needs many concrete experiences to expand her idea of what a triangle is. She needs to build and draw triangles of all sorts. She needs to discover that triangles can have no congruent sides or angles, two congruent sides and angles, or three congruent sides and angles. Blair would also benefit from sorting and classifying many different kinds of triangles. She should begin by focusing on equilateral, scalene, and isosceles triangles, and then move on to experiences with right triangles, and later with acute and obtuse triangles. Blair also needs opportunities to find triangles in the world around her.

Student Work Sample: James

Name ______________________ Date ______________

Which of these is a true statement about an equilateral triangle?

A. It has no equal sides and no equal angles.

B. It has 2 equal sides and 2 equal angles.

C. It has 4 equal sides and 4 equal angles.

D. It has 3 equal sides and 3 equal angles.

Show how you know.

A Conversation with James	Teacher Insights
T: I see you marked choice D. What made you decide on that answer? **James:** Um, I guessed. **T:** What reasons were behind your guess? **James:** I was thinking about my dad and *dad* starts with a *d*. **T:** I see. What is this question asking you? **James:** Something about a triangle. **T:** What do you know about triangles? **James:** I know they have three sides. That's about all. **T:** That's important information to know. Can a triangle have four sides? **James:** No, that would be a square.	**T:** *James marked the correct answer, but, as revealed by the conversation, he has only basic knowledge about triangles. His response was just a lucky guess related to his thoughts about his dad.*

Informed Instructional Suggestions

James' verbal response revealed limited understanding of triangles. James, like several of the other students, needs to fully develop his knowledge and understanding of triangles through the concrete, hands-on activities described previously. James also needs to be encouraged to show his thinking on his paper using words, pictures, and numbers.

Student Work Sample: Alana

Name ______________________ Date ____________

Which of these is a true statement about an equilateral triangle?

A. It has no equal sides and no equal angles.

B. It has 2 equal sides and 2 equal angles.

C. It has 4 equal sides and 4 equal angles.

(D.) It has 3 equal sides and 3 equal angles.

Show how you know.

D because no triangle has a side because a side is (straight) like this
and every triangle has 3 angles.

A Conversation with Alana	Teacher Insights
T: I noticed that in your writing you said that triangles don't have sides because they don't have straight lines. I noticed also that you drew a picture to show what you meant. Please tell me more. **Alana:** A side has to go up and down like I drew in the picture. Triangles don't have that. **T:** Do you think I could turn the picture of the triangle that you drew so that the side goes straight up and down? **Alana:** I think so. [Alana rotates the paper until one side is vertical.] **T:** One of the lines on the triangle is now going vertically, or straight up and down. Is it a side now? **Alana:** I don't know. I'm confused and not sure. I do know for sure that a triangle does have three angles because *tri-* is a prefix that means three. That's why I chose choice D. It was closest to what I knew was right about triangles.	**T:** *Alana marked the correct answer but has fragile understanding of triangles. She also has a serious misunderstanding about the meaning of the word* side.

Informed Instructional Suggestions

Alana needs immediate intervention to correct her misunderstanding about sides. Through the use of concrete materials and perhaps drawings, she can develop her geometry vocabulary and understanding of triangles. She needs experiences similar to those recommended for the other students discussed thus far.

Student Work Sample: Kristin

Name ______________________ Date ______________

Which of these is a true statement about an equilateral triangle?

A. It has no equal sides and no equal angles.

(B) It has 2 equal sides and 2 equal angles.

C. It has 4 equal sides and 4 equal angles.

D. It has 3 equal sides and 3 equal angles.

Show how you know.

Because a triangle has One equal Side on the bottom and one side so they have 2 equal side but the top doesn't have an equal Side. so theres only 2 equal sides.

A Conversation with Kristin	Teacher Insights
T: Tell me what you know about triangles. **Kristin:** Triangles have three sides. **T:** I agree with you. Anything else? [Kristin shakes her head.] How many angles are in a triangle? **Kristin:** I don't know, maybe three or four? **T:** Tell me more about what you wrote on your paper. **Kristin:** A triangle has a side on the bottom and one on one side and they are both equal. There is still another side but there is no top, so there is no equal side for the top. **T:** It sounds a little to me like you are describing four sides rather than three. How many sides did you say were in a triangle? **Kristin:** Three? I'm not sure. Maybe I was confusing it for a rectangle. A rectangle has four sides and the side across from another side is the same length.	**T:** *Kristin may have confused a triangle for a rectangle when she tried to write and talk about sides. Kristin seemed unsure about the number of angles in a triangle as well.*

Informed Instructional Suggestions

Kristin's answer indicated a gap in her knowledge. Further probing through both written and verbal responses helped point to where to begin. She needs work in developing the meaning of such foundational ideas as *side* and *angle* and how many of each of these are in various polygons. Through the use of manipulatives, Kristin should recognize that polygons have the same number of angles as they do sides. For example, a polygon with three angles is a triangle just as a polygon with three sides is a triangle. Once Kristin has developed these concepts and the appropriate vocabulary, then she can move on with the activities that were recommended for the other students.

Reassessment

1. Use a similar problem at the same level of difficulty.

   Which of these is a true statement about an isosceles triangle?

   A. It has 3 equal sides and 3 equal angles.
   B. It has no equal sides and no equal angles.
   C. It has 2 equal sides and 2 equal angles.
   D. It has 4 equal sides and 4 equal angles.

   Show how you know.

2. Choose a problem that is similar but slightly more challenging.

   Which of these is a true statement about an acute triangle?

   A. It has no equal sides and no equal angles.
   B. It has a right angle and two equal sides.
   C. It has all angles less than 90 degrees.
   D. It has all angles greater than 90 degrees.

   Show how you know.

PROBLEM FOUR

Overview

This question tests students' ability to determine what 3-D shapes can be combined to make new 3-D shapes, requiring students to use spatial visualization skills. Students must also know some basic vocabulary, specifically the names of 3-D shapes. The notion of composing or decomposing shapes to make new shapes can be found in most mathematics curricula for the second and third grades.

Sample Problem

Stacy made this wooden shape. What two common figures make up this solid shape?

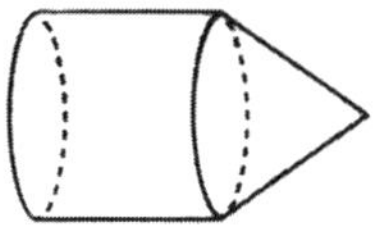

A. sphere and triangular prism
B. cylinder and cube
C. cone and cylinder
D. pyramid and cone

Show how you know.

Possible Student Solution Strategies

- Students recognize and correctly identify the appropriate polyhedra.
- Students attempt to draw the combinations of polyhedra.

Conversation Starters

- Where do you see these shapes in the world around you?
- What do you know about polyhedra that helped you make your choice?
- What do you think a cylinder or cone would look like if you cut it so you could lay it flat?
- What do all of the polyhedra listed have in common?
- What is the same about a cone and a cylinder? What is different?

Student Work Sample: Crystal

Name ______________________ Date ______________

Stacy made this wooden shape. What two common figures make up this solid shape?

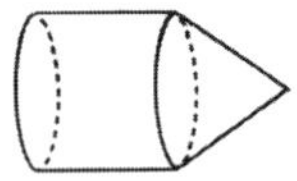

A. sphere and triangular prism

B. cylinder and cube

(C) cone and cylinder

D. pyramid and cone

Show how you know.

I know it is C because a cone looks like this: △ and a cylinder looks like this: ▭ and put them together and you get this ▭▷ and that is how I got my two shapes.

A Conversation with Crystal	Teacher Insights
T: I see that you marked choice C. What do you know about these shapes, called polyhedra, that helped you make your choice? **Crystal:** I know that a sphere is like a ball, a cylinder is a tube, a cone is like an ice-cream cone, and I am not too sure about a triangular prism or a pyramid. I drew a picture of a cylinder to show what it looks like and a picture of a cone and you put them together and you have the picture on the paper.	**T:** *Crystal made connections between some of the polyhedra listed and the real world. Her knowledge included understanding about cylinders and cones, enabling her to select the correct answer.*

Informed Instructional Suggestions

Crystal needs to continue to develop her understanding of polyhedra and the associated vocabulary. Her experiences should include the opportunity to count the edges, faces, and vertices of these 3-D shapes.

Student Work Sample: Justin

Name ______________________________ Date ______________

Stacy made this wooden shape. What two common figures make up this solid shape?

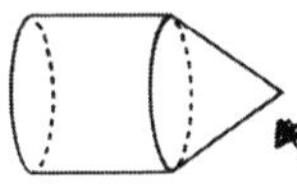

A. sphere and triangular prism

B. cylinder and cube

(C.) cone and cylinder

D. pyramid and cone

Show how you know. First, I had to look at: A, B, C, and D. Secondly, I had to disect the shape that Stacy made. I found a cone and a cylinder. Then, I had to find the matching choice. That's how I got C

A Conversation with Justin	Teacher Insights
T: Which of the shapes in the picture is a cone and which is a cylinder? **Justin:** The pointed shape is the cone and the other one is the cylinder. **T:** The way you wrote about the process you used is very clear and easy to understand. Where do you see cones and cylinders in the real world? **Justin:** Hmm, sometimes volcanoes look a little like a cone. Party hats and ice-cream cones are cones. We have orange cones at PE that mark the boundaries for soccer games. Paper towels come on cylinders, and there was this big machine fixing the street and it had a cylinder that was making the street flat. Some trash cans are cylinders, too, and sometimes cans and jars. **T:** What do you think a cylinder would look like if you cut it so it could lay flat? **Justin:** I think it would be a rectangle or a square. I think that because I can roll up a piece of paper into a cylinder, right? **T:** What about a cone? What would it look like if you cut it from its base to the point on top? **Justin:** Um, I am not too sure about that.	**T:** *Justin was able to clearly express how he solved this problem. He also has a clear understanding of what cones and cylinders are. He was able to give examples of each that could be found in the world around him.*

Informed Instructional Suggestions

Next, Justin should continue to explore polyhedra, their attributes, and the appropriate geometric vocabulary. Justin would also benefit from examining what polyhedra would look like as 2-D figures.

Student Work Sample: Casey

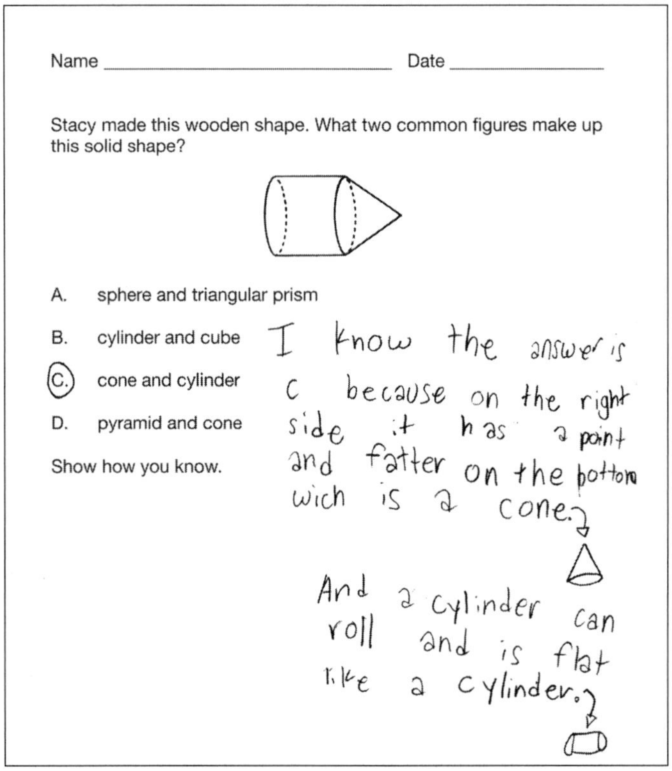
Name ______________ Date ________

Stacy made this wooden shape. What two common figures make up this solid shape?

A. sphere and triangular prism

B. cylinder and cube

(C.) cone and cylinder

D. pyramid and cone

Show how you know.

I know the answer is c because on the right side it has a point and fatter on the bottom wich is a cone. And a cylinder can roll and is flat like a cylinder.

A Conversation with Casey	Teacher Insights
T: Please explain a little more about your thinking. Where do you think the cone is in the picture? **Casey:** Right here by the point. [Casey points to the right side of the picture.] **T:** Where is the cylinder? **Casey:** Here. [Casey points to the left side of the picture.] **T:** You said a cylinder is flat. Please explain more about that. **Carla:** It's flat in two ways. You can stand it up on the end and it's flat. It won't fall over. Or you can think of it as flat because you can lay it on its side and it will roll in a straight line if you make it. If you do that to a cone, it will roll around in a circle. I wonder if that Stacy girl glued the cone to the cylinder because I don't see how it stayed together on its side like the picture shows!	**T:** *Casey has a basic foundational knowledge of cylinders and cones and is ready to continue to explore and to develop her understanding. As her knowledge and vocabulary increase, her communication about geometry will become more precise.*

Informed Instructional Suggestions

Casey would benefit from the same types of activities we suggested for Crystal and Justin.

Student Work Sample: Jackie

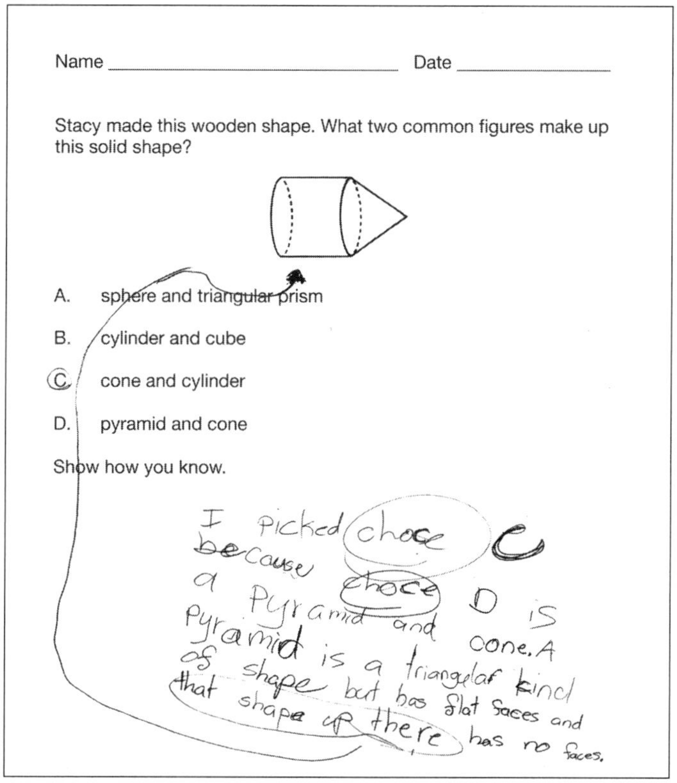
Name ______________________ Date ______________

Stacy made this wooden shape. What two common figures make up this solid shape?

A. sphere and triangular prism

B. cylinder and cube

(C.) cone and cylinder

D. pyramid and cone

Show how you know.

I picked choce C because choce D is a pyramid and cone. A pyramid is a triangular kind of shape but has flat faces and that shape up there has no faces.

A Conversation with Jackie	Teacher Insights
T: Do you know what all of the polyhedra, or shapes, on the list of choices look like? **Jackie:** I know all of them except for the triangular prism. It must have something to do with triangles because triangular sounds like triangle. **T:** What is a sphere? **Jackie:** It's a round thing like a ball or a globe. A cylinder is this. [Jackie points to the cylinder in the picture.] A cube looks like a box and a pyramid looks sort of like a cone because it has a point like a cone, but the faces of pyramids are flat and a cone's side is curved. If it was choice D, then there would be two points and I don't see two points, just one.	**T:** *Jackie provided a comparison of a pyramid and a cone, although a cone does have faces rather than sides. Jackie was able to explain what each of the polyhedra on the list would look like with the exception of the triangular prism. She inferred that a triangular prism has something to do with triangles based on the name, a useful connection for her to make.*

Informed Instructional Suggestions

Jackie would benefit from exploring polyhedra and sorting and classifying them according to their attributes, such as the number of faces, vertices, and edges.

Student Work Sample: Jason

Name ______________________ Date ______________

Stacy made this wooden shape. What two common figures make up this solid shape?

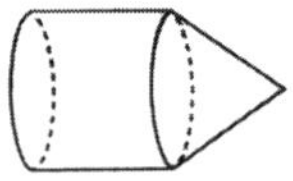

A. sphere and triangular prism

(B.) cylinder and cube

C. cone and cylinder

D. pyramid and cone

Show how you know.

I Khowe Becouse the CYlinder is a cube.

A Conversation with Jason	Teacher Insights
T: You wrote on your paper that a cylinder is a cube. Tell me more about that. **Jason:** I don't know. I guessed. A cube is a square so maybe a cylinder is a square too. Really, I just wrote it. **T:** Do you know what a sphere is? **Jason:** Not really. **T:** What do you think a cone is? **Jason:** I'm not sure. I really don't know this.	T: *Jason has very little knowledge of polyhedra. He believes a cube and a square are the same thing. A cube is made up of square faces, but a square is two-dimensional while a cube is three-dimensional.*

Informed Instructional Suggestions

Jason needs many foundational, concrete experiences to begin to build and develop his understanding of polyhedra. Before beginning work with 3-D figures, it will be important to find out what Jason knows about polygons and other 2-D shapes and develop that knowledge, if necessary, so he can build on it and connect to polyhedra.

Student Work Sample: Philip

Name ______________________ Date ______________

Stacy made this wooden shape. What two common figures make up this solid shape?

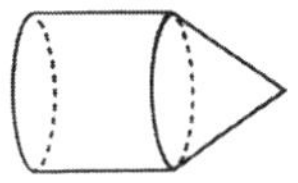

● sphere and triangular prism

B. cylinder and cube

C. cone and cylinder

D. pyramid and cone

Show how you know.

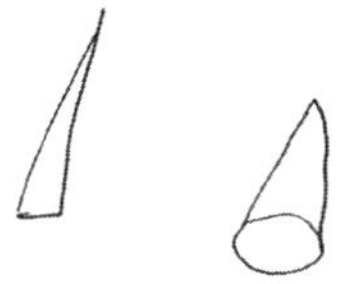

I Know that it is A because the shape that this Girl or Boy made it is just like a triangle.

A Conversation with Philip	Teacher Insights
T: Tell me about your thinking. **Philip:** It has to be choice A because there is a triangle in the shape and there is a word in choice A that also has the word *triangle*. It's the only choice like that.	**T:** *Philip interpreted the drawing of the cone as a triangle, disregarding the rest of the polyhedron.*

Informed Instructional Suggestions

Philip needs work with developing concepts of 2-D geometry. Once he has acquired understanding of that information, then he needs to make connections between 2-D and 3-D geometry as he begins to explore and learn about polyhedra.

Reassessment

1. Use a similar problem at the same level of difficulty.

   Bobby made a make-believe ice-cream cone with these wooden solids. What two common figures make up this solid shape?

   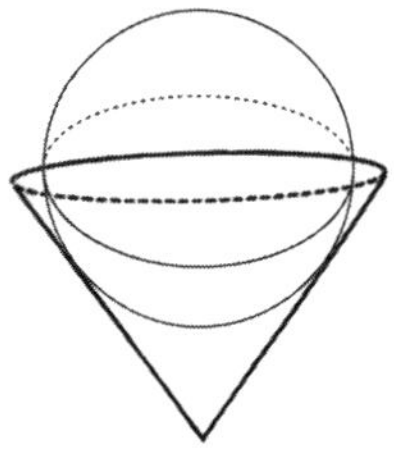

   A. cylinder and pyramid
   B. pyramid and cone
   C. sphere and cone
   D. triangular prism and cube

   Show how you know.

2. Choose a problem that is similar but slightly more challenging. (Note: Students often confuse pyramids and prisms, which makes the following problem difficult for some.)

   Camille made this solid shape. What two common figures make up this solid shape?

   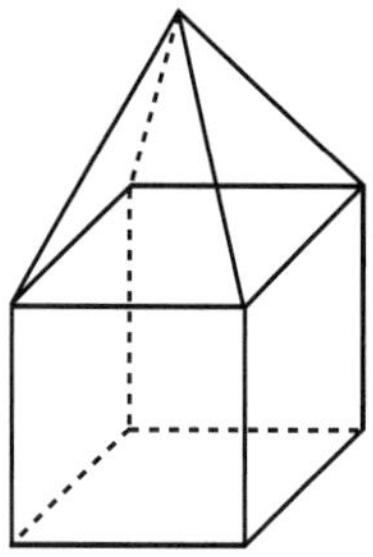

   A. pyramid and cube
   B. cube and cylinder
   C. rectangular prism and cube
   D. sphere and cube

   Show how you know.

PROBLEM FIVE

Overview

This question tests students' knowledge of angles. Typically, the right angle is used as a reference, or benchmark angle, to determine if another angle is right, acute, or obtuse. Students often have a poor understanding of angles. They have difficulty interpreting the spread of the rays and instead sometimes focus on the length of the illustrated rays.

Sample Problem

Look at the four angles marked on the picture below. Which numbered angle measures *less* than a right angle?

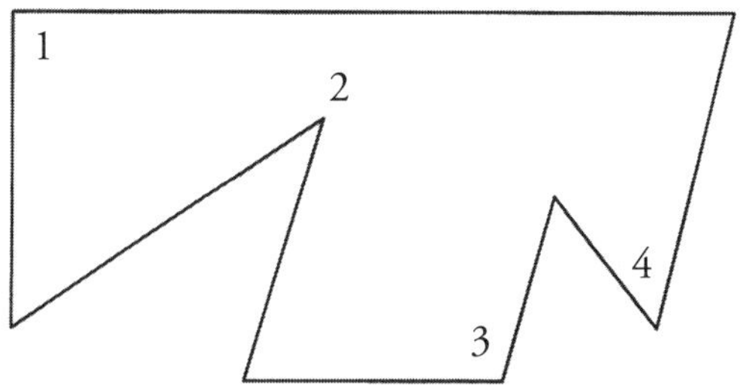

A. 1
B. 2
C. 3
D. 4

Show how you know.

Possible Student Solution Strategies

- o Students use their knowledge of a right angle to identify angles less than 90 degrees.
- o Students used partial knowledge in an attempt to make sense of this problem.

Conversation Starters

- o What do you know about a right, or 90-degree, angle?
- o Are all angles right angles?
- o How could you identify a right angle?

Student Work Sample: Ben

Name ____________________ Date ____________

Look at the four angles marked on the picture below. Which numbered angle measures *less* than a right angle?

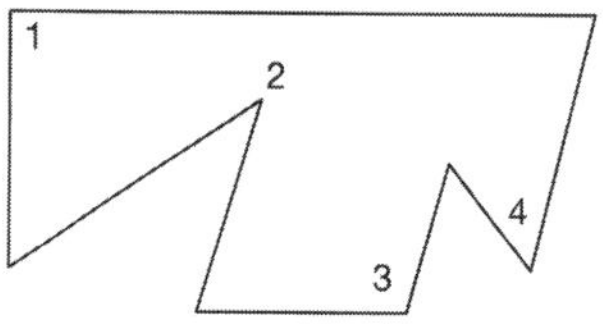

A. angle 1

B. angle 2

C. angle 3

D. angle 4 (circled)

Show how you know. Because the 4 number angle is smaller than a right angle.

A Conversation with Ben	Teacher Insights
T: Ben, where do you see a right angle on this page? **Ben:** On the corner. **T:** Tell me more. **Ben:** It's right here, the corner of the paper. **T:** I agree the corner of the paper is a right angle. Now, look at the polygon. Is there a right angle in the polygon? **Ben:** Yes, right here where number 1 is. **T:** You wrote that number 4 is smaller than a right angle. What do you mean by that exactly? **Ben:** The sides are closer together than a right angle. **T:** Do you know the name of an angle less than 90 degrees, or a right angle? **Ben:** No. I forget. I think I learned it before but I forgot.	**T:** *Ben's written explanation indicated some understanding, and when questioned, he revealed that he knew more about angles. He correctly identified a right angle in the polygon as well as recognizing that the page had at least one right angle.*

Informed Instructional Suggestions

Ben has a nice foundational understanding. He needs to continue using concrete, hands-on experiences to further develop his knowledge and vocabulary. It will be important to continue to provide Ben and his classmates with geometry experiences over time to help them retain the concepts and vocabulary of geometry.

Student Work Sample: Cori

Name ______________________ Date ____________

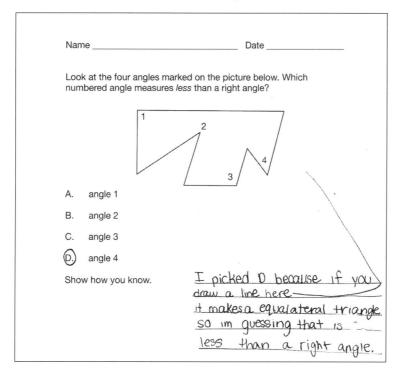

Look at the four angles marked on the picture below. Which numbered angle measures *less* than a right angle?

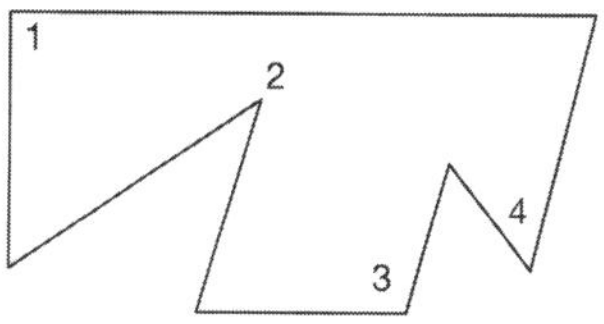

A. angle 1

B. angle 2

C. angle 3

(D.) angle 4

Show how you know. I picked D because if you draw a line here it makes a equalateral triangle so im guessing that is less than a right angle.

A Conversation with Cori	Teacher Insights
T: You have an interesting explanation. Tell me more about it. **Cori:** I learned that an equilateral triangle has equal sides and angles and all the angles are less than a right angle. So I drew a line to make that part of the shape into an equilateral triangle and guessed that angle 4 is less than a right angle. **T:** Do you see any right angles on this paper? **Cori:** Yes, angle 1 looks like a right angle. **T:** How can you prove that the sides and angles of the triangle you made are equal, or congruent? **Cori:** Um . . . I don't know. It just looks like it is.	**T:** *Cori tried to make sense of this problem by using her prior knowledge of equilateral triangles and her understanding of right angles. She was able to correctly identify angle 1 as a right angle. The triangle she drew is not an equilateral triangle, although it appears to be close. Using her picture and the knowledge that equilateral triangles have angles less than 90 degrees, she selected the correct answer.*

Informed Instructional Suggestions

Cori's correct answer alone would have hidden her fragmented knowledge. Further hands-on exploration, along with opportunities to discuss what she is learning, will strengthen her conceptual knowledge of geometry.

Student Work Sample: Chris

Name ______________________ Date ______________

Look at the four angles marked on the picture below. Which numbered angle measures *less* than a right angle?

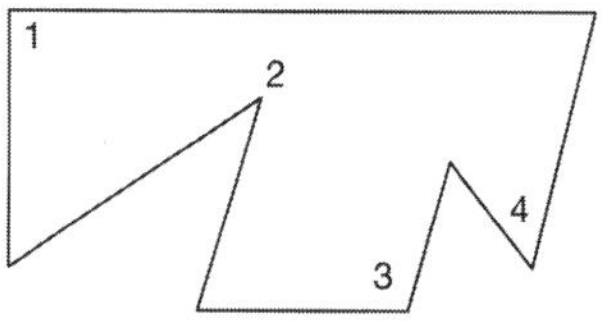

A. angle 1

B. angle 2

C. angle 3

(D) angle 4

Show how you know.

becqase that is the only right sid in The questoin,

A Conversation with Chris	Teacher Insights
T: I see you selected choice D. Tell me what you mean by "the only right side." **Chris:** That's easy. There is a right side, a left side, a top, and a bottom. [Chris points to each as he explains.] Four is on the right side, 1 is on the left, 3 is on the bottom, and 2 is above 3.	**T:** *Chris knows directions (right, left, etc.) and used this knowledge to make sense of this problem.*

Informed Instructional Strategies

Chris' correct guess was coincidental and masked his true level of knowledge. He needs foundational experiences that will help him understand what a right angle is and how to use that information to identify angles less than or greater than 90 degrees.

Student Work Sample: Max

Name ______________________________ Date _______________

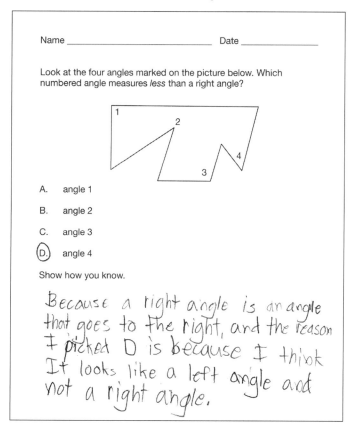

Look at the four angles marked on the picture below. Which numbered angle measures *less* than a right angle?

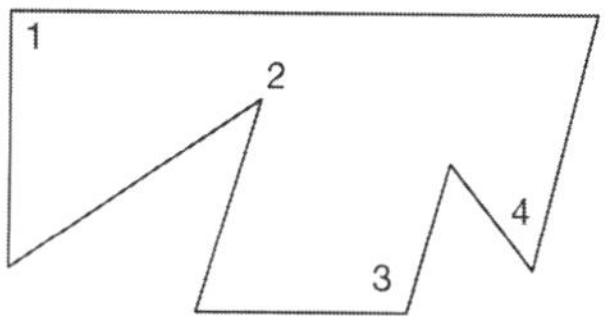

A. angle 1

B. angle 2

C. angle 3

(D.) angle 4

Show how you know.

Because a right angle is an angle that goes to the right, and the reason I picked D is because I think It looks like a left angle and not a right angle.

A Conversation with Max	Teacher Insights
T: Tell me what you know about angles. **Max:** A right angle goes right and a left angle goes left. That's why I chose D. It's going left, not right, right? **T:** According to your thinking, do you see any right angles in the polygon? **Max:** I think angle 3 is maybe a right angle.	**T:** *Max showed no understanding of right angles. He thinks that an angle's name is directional, that is, it is based on the direction in which it opens rather than its measurement in degrees. When asked to identify a right angle, he was unable to do so correctly.*

Informed Instructional Suggestions

Max needs foundational experiences to build his knowledge of right angles and angles in general. Learning and using the appropriate vocabulary are critical to developing understanding of geometric concepts.

Student Work Sample: Gavin

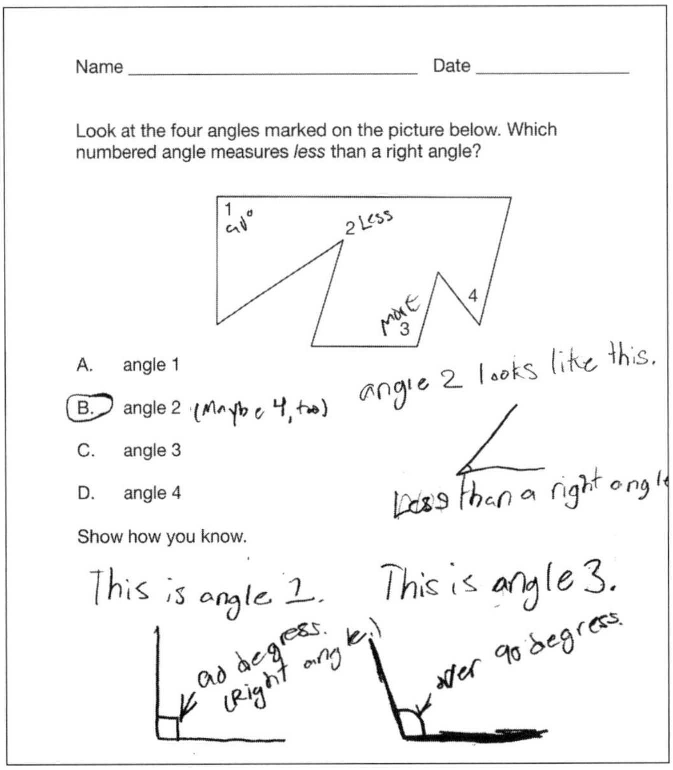
Name ______________________ Date ______________

Look at the four angles marked on the picture below. Which numbered angle measures *less* than a right angle?

A. angle 1

(B.) angle 2 (Maybe 4, too)   angle 2 looks like this.

C. angle 3

D. angle 4   less than a right angle

Show how you know.

This is angle 2.   This is angle 3.

90 degress. (Right angle)   over 90 degress.

A Conversation with Gavin	Teacher Insights
T: Gavin, I appreciate your written explanation. I notice that you drew a picture of angle 2. Show me where you see angle 2 in the picture above. **Gavin:** I see it right here. [Gavin points to the exterior angle rather than the interior angle indicated by the location of the 2.] **T:** The angle you are pointing to is outside the polygon. The number 2 is inside the polygon and shows you what angle to consider. **Gavin:** I thought that might be true, which is why I wrote on my paper that it might be angle 4. I wasn't sure and I didn't think about if it was important for the angle to be inside or outside the shape. Now that I know that, I can see it should be angle 4, which is choice D. I made a mistake.	**T:** *Gavin has solid understanding of what a right angle is and how to determine if an angle is greater or less than a right angle. His error was the result of not understanding that the placement of the 2 indicated which angle to consider.*

Informed Instructional Suggestions

Gavin's incorrect answer alone would have indicated the need for remediation of this skill, when none is really needed. Reteaching would be a poor use of resources and of his time. Through the brief conversation, Gavin learned about his error. He needs to continue to practice to reinforce his knowledge.

Student Work Sample: Larry

Name ______________________________ Date _______________

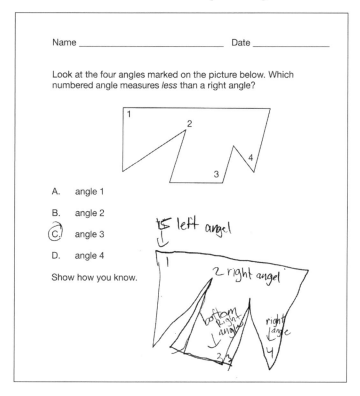

Look at the four angles marked on the picture below. Which numbered angle measures *less* than a right angle?

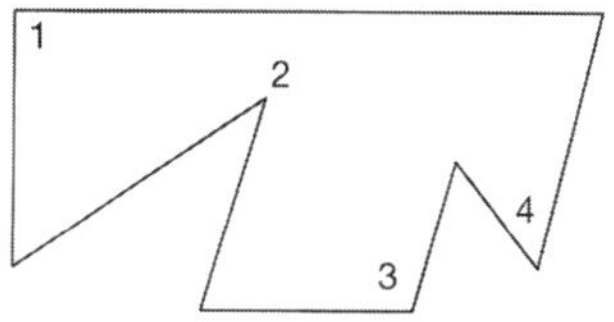

A. angle 1

B. angle 2

(C.) angle 3

D. angle 4

Show how you know.

A Conversation with Larry

T: Your drawing tells me a lot about your thinking and understanding, which is very helpful. Each of the corners of the paper is a right angle: the one on the left top, the right top, the left bottom, and the right bottom. All four are called right angles or 90-degree angles. Do you see an angle in the polygon that looks like the corner of the paper?

Larry: All of the corners of the paper are right angles? Ohh! Is angle 1 a right angle then?

T: Yes. Do you see any other right angles in the polygon?

Larry: No, I don't think so.

T: Do you see one that is less than, or smaller than, a right angle?

Larry: The sides by number 4 are closer, so I guess that is smaller, so angle 4?

T: That's it. You got it.

Teacher Insights

T: *Larry's drawing was very telling and allowed for instruction in the moment. Once he understood more clearly what a right angle is, he was able to select an angle that was less than 90 degrees.*

Informed Instructional Suggestions

Larry's initial understanding was lacking. As the result of a few carefully chosen questions that provided a quick introduction to right angles, he was able to build on that understanding. However, this new learning is fragile and needs to be supported through many different concrete experiences. Some children do not understand how the distance between the sides of an angle relates to the measure of the angle, but Larry was able to make sense of this idea and use it when discussing this problem.

Student Work Sample: Stephan

Name ______________________ Date ____________

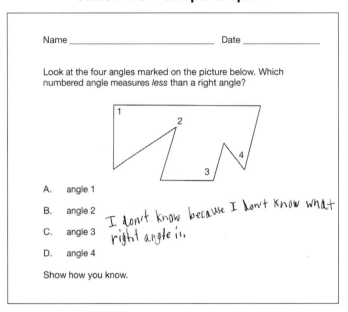

Look at the four angles marked on the picture below. Which numbered angle measures *less* than a right angle?

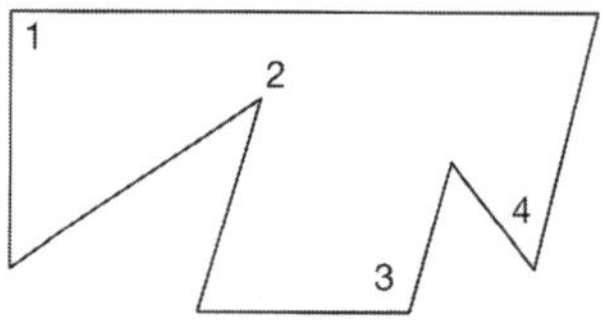

A. angle 1

B. angle 2

C. angle 3

D. angle 4

I don't know because I don't know what right angle is.

Show how you know.

A Conversation with Stephan	Teacher Insights
T: Stephan, I appreciate how you could identify what caused you to be unable to do this problem. However, when confronted with a multiple-choice test, it is usually a good idea to make your best guess. So, which of these answers would you choose as your best guess? **Stephan:** I don't think it would be choice B, which is angle 2, because it doesn't look like an angle, see? [Stephan uses his index finger to indicate the wide space created by angle 2.] Angle 1 looks like a square corner, so I don't think that would be less than anything. Angle 3 is sort of like that, too, so I think maybe it's angle 4, which is choice D, but I don't really know. **T:** A square corner is a right angle. Knowing that, can you answer the question now? **Stephan:** Oh, then it is angle 4, which is choice D.	**T:** *Stephan's truthful response provided accurate information about his level of knowledge. After I gave him the definition of a right angle, he was able to identify the correct answer.*

Informed Instructional Suggestions

Stephan's self-professed lack of knowledge provided the perfect opportunity for immediate intervention. After linking his prior knowledge of a square corner to the term *right angle*, he was able to easily solve the problem. He also learned that on most multiple-choice tests, it is better to reason through all answer choices and make a best guess. In this case, he was able to reason enough to make the correct choice. Stephan would benefit from further study of angles.

Reassessment

1. Use a similar problem at the same level of difficulty.

   Look at the four angles marked on the picture below.

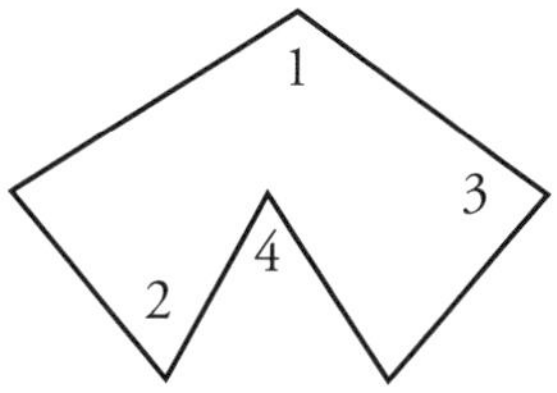

   Which numbered angle measures *more* than a right angle?

   A. angle 1
   B. angle 2
   C. angle 3
   D. angle 4

   Show how you know.

2. Choose a problem that is similar but slightly more challenging.

   Look at the four angles marked on the picture below.

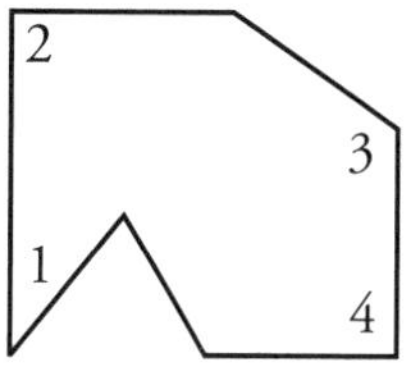

   Which two angles are right angles (that is, measure exactly 90 degrees each)?

   A. 1 and 2
   B. 3 and 4
   C. 2 and 4
   D. 2 and 3

   Show how you know.

PROBLEM SIX

Overview

Studying the number of faces, edges, and vertices of three-dimensional shapes is commonly a part of mathematics curricula for the second and third grades. Students need to be familiar with both the vocabulary and how to count faces, vertices, and edges on 3-D (solid) figures when not all faces, edges, and vertices are visible simultaneously.

Sample Problem

How many faces does a cube have?

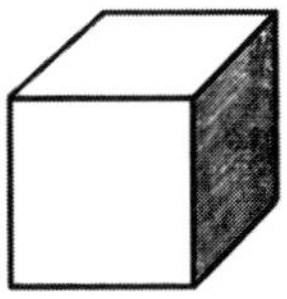

A. 4
B. 6
C. 12
D. 8

Show how you know.

Possible Student Solution Strategies

- Students use drawings to count the faces of the cube.
- Students draw a cube unfolded to show the six faces.
- Students relate the cube to familiar everyday objects.

Conversation Starters

- What do you know about a cube?
- What shape are the faces of all cubes?
- Where do you see cubes or how do you use cubes in your life?
- What things can you think of that are made from cubes?
- How are cubes and squares different? Alike?

Student Work Sample: Germaine

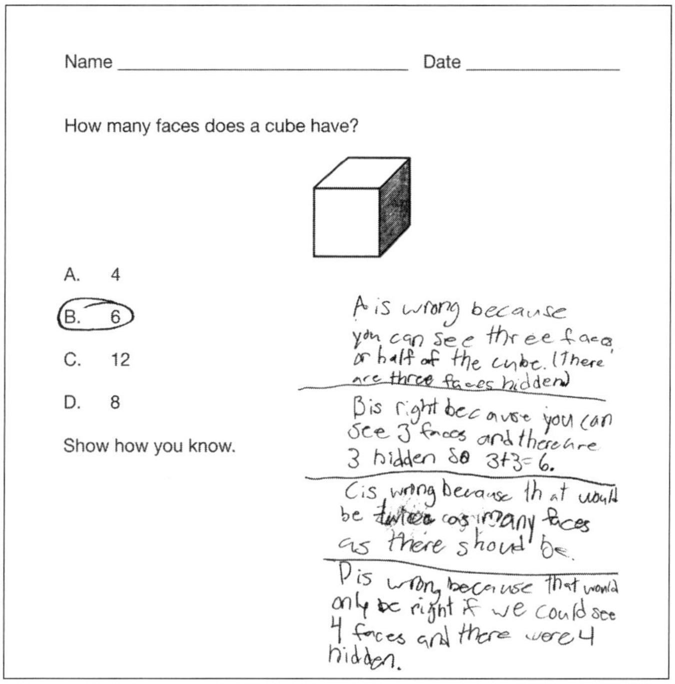
Name ______________________ Date ____________

How many faces does a cube have?

A. 4

B. 6 (circled)

C. 12

D. 8

Show how you know.

A is wrong because you can see three faces or half of the cube. (There are three faces hidden)

B is right because you can see 3 faces and there are 3 hidden so 3+3=6.

C is wrong because that would be ~~twice~~ as many faces as there should be.

D is wrong because that would only be right if we could see 4 faces and there were 4 hidden.

A Conversation with Germaine	Teacher Insights
T: You wrote a very complete explanation of your thinking. You said in your explanation about choice B that there are three hidden faces. Where are they? **Germaine:** They're hidden in the picture, but if you had a real cube, you could just turn it around and see the other faces. In the picture, there is a hidden face on the left of the cube, one behind it, and one under it. **T:** What shape are all of the faces? **Germaine:** Squares. All cubes have square faces. **T:** What is different about a cube and a square? **Germaine:** A square is flat. A cube stands up. A cube is made out of square faces. Squares have right angles and the square faces on a cube have right angles. **T:** Where do you see or use cubes? **Germaine:** Boxes are cubes. **T:** Are all boxes cubes? **Germaine:** I'm not too sure about that.	**T:** *Although Germaine's knowledge of cubes is strong, it is not complete. Through careful questioning, I uncovered a direction for new learning: Germaine is unsure if all boxes are cubes, so he needs to explore that idea further.*

Informed Instructional Suggestions

Rather than work on foundational activities with cubes, Germaine needs to explore cubes and other rectangular prisms together to come to his own understanding that a cube is a special kind of rectangular prism, just as a square is a special kind of rectangle. This understanding will help Germaine answer the question about whether or not all boxes are cubes.

Student Work Sample: Brittany

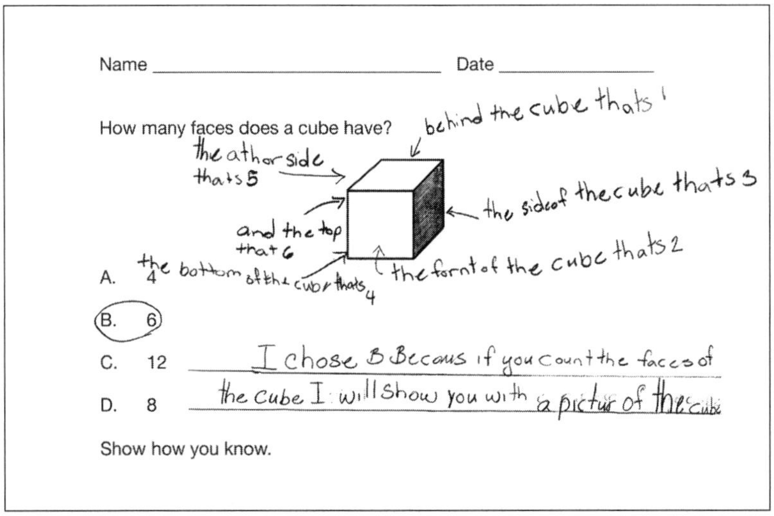
Name ______ Date ______

How many faces does a cube have?

A. 4

B. 6

C. 12

D. 8

I chose B Becaus if you count the faces of the cube I will show you with a pictur of the cube

Show how you know.

A Conversation with Brittany	Teacher Insights
T: Very nice explanation, Brittany. What would you like to say about it? **Brittany:** Well, I know the answer is choice B because you can actually see three of the faces. The faces are the flat part on the cube. I know that there is a face I can't see behind the cube, and the cube has to be sitting on something, so I know there is a face under the cube, and there is a face hidden on the left side of the cube. So that's three faces I can see and three that are hidden. Three plus three is six, so there are six faces. **T:** What makes a cube a cube and not a square? **Brittany:** A cube is like a square except that it is tall and a square is flat. A cube is made out of squares, six squares to be exact! Even the gray square in the picture is a square, but it doesn't look like it. If there was a real cube, the gray one would be a square. **T:** Can a cube have a face that is rectangular? **Brittany:** No, I don't think so . . . maybe . . . no, that would make it something else.	**T:** *Brittany is able to visualize a cube's hidden faces. She knows that the faces of a cube are square, although she expressed some uncertainty when asked if a cube could have a rectangular face.*

Informed Instructional Suggestions

Brittany has a good foundational understanding of cubes. Like Germaine, she needs hands-on experiences with rectangular prisms, including opportunities to explore differences and similarities of cubes and other rectangular prisms.

Student Work Sample: Jose

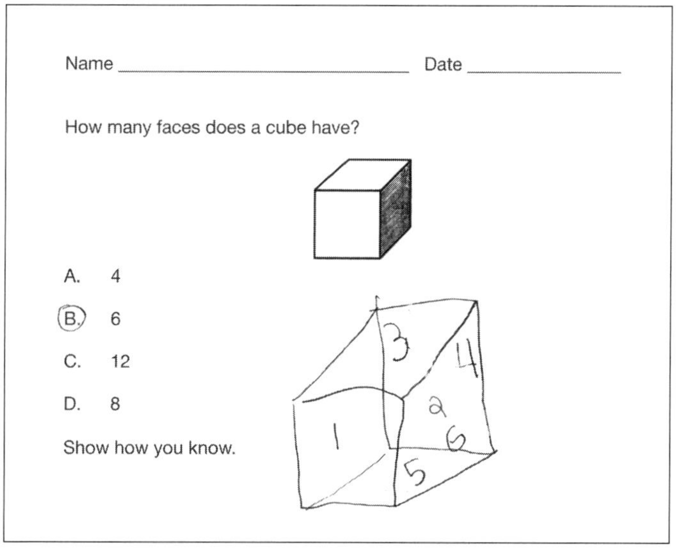
Name ______________________ Date ______________

How many faces does a cube have?

A. 4

(B.) 6

C. 12

D. 8

Show how you know.

A Conversation with Jose	Teacher Insights
T: I see you drew a picture. **Jose:** Yep, I drew a cube so you could see the hidden faces and then I numbered them to show that there are six faces. [Jose points to each of the faces he drew as he counts them aloud to emphasize.] **T:** What do you call this? [I point to a face.] **Jose:** It's the flat part, so it's a face. **T:** What do you call this? [I point to an edge of the cube.] **Jose:** A side? **T:** How about this? [I point to a vertex.] **Jose:** A corner. **T:** What makes a cube a cube? **Jose:** It looks like a square. **T:** Are a square and a cube the same thing? **Jose:** Yes, one is just taller is all.	**T:** *Jose can count the faces of a cube. He correctly used the vocabulary word* face *but did not use the terms* edge *and* vertex *when I asked what those parts were called. Jose also needs further opportunities to explore cubes and squares to develop his conceptual understanding of the differences between the two.*

Informed Instructional Suggestions

Jose needs to develop the basic vocabulary associated with polyhedra. To do so, he could participate in some hands-on experiences with polyhedra, focusing on their different parts by discussing them, labeling them, and writing about them. To further support all students' acquisition and use of vocabulary, we should post in a clearly visible spot a vocabulary chart with words and pictures. Jose and others can then easily check the list when needed to support their oral and written explanations.

Student Work Sample: Preston

Name ______________________ Date ____________

How many faces does a cube have?

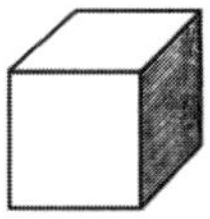

A. 4

(B) 6

C. 12

D. 8

Show how you know.

It's "B" because I know that a die is a cube and a die has a number on each side and there's 6 numbers on a die so that means that there's six faces on a cube.

A Conversation with Preston	Teacher Insights
T: What do you know about a cube? **Preston:** It has six square faces just like in the picture. I chose B because really, a die is a cube with dots on it to show numbers. The numbers start with one, and then two, and then three, and then four, and then five, and then six, and then there are no more faces so there are no more numbers. Six faces on a die and six faces on a cube. That's how I know!	**T:** *Preston made a useful connection between something in real life and the mathematical idea of a cube. He was articulate in his explanation and confident in his reasoning.*

Informed Instructional Suggestions

Preston's next steps should be the same as those for Brittany and Germaine.

Student Work Sample: Jerry

Name ______________________ Date ____________

How many faces does a cube have?

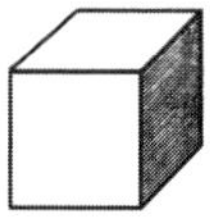

A. 4

(B) 6

C. 12

D. 8

Show how you know.

I know there are 6 cubes because 3 sides can be seen but the others cannot. All you have to do is multiply what you see.

A Conversation with Jerry	Teacher Insights
T: You wrote that there are six cubes because three sides can be seen. The question asked you how many faces are on a cube. Please tell me more about your thinking. **Jerry:** I'm not too sure actually. **T:** Do you know what a face on a cube is? **Jerry:** The front? Like our face is the front of our head. **T:** How many faces can you see in the picture? **Jerry:** I see one face and three sides.	**T:** *Jerry marked the correct answer but does not understand what a face is. He used an everyday meaning of* face *rather than the mathematical meaning. When he referred to the faces of the cube, he used the term* side. *Jerry also seemed to confuse the word* cube *for* square *in his written explanation, so he needs to work on vocabulary. Also, Jerry wrote about multiplication, which I needed to investigate next.*
T: Jerry, you said you multiply what you see. Please help me understand what you mean by that. **Jerry:** I don't really know. We were just studying multiplication, so I thought maybe multiplication was part of the problem. **T:** What did you multiply? **Jerry:** I didn't really. I just thought maybe I should because I can see three sides but the smallest answer is 4, not 3, so I thought maybe if I multiplied 3 times 2 I could get 6, and that was one of the answers. **T:** Are a square and a cube the same thing? **Jerry:** Yes.	**T:** *The last question shed some light on Jerry's first written sentence,* I know there are 6 cubes . . . . *He considers cubes and squares to be the same thing, and if you substitute the word* squares *for* cubes, *his writing makes sense. Jerry did what many students do: he overgeneralized, assuming that the last operation he learned—in this case, multiplication—was the strategy to solve all problems.*

Informed Instructional Suggestions

From Jerry's confused explanation, it is clear he needs help. Jerry needs opportunities such as verbal discussions to develop his vocabulary and conceptual understanding. He needs to learn the attributes of both squares and cubes so that he recognizes that they are not the same. Many of the activities suggested for the previous students would also benefit Jerry. Additionally, Jerry needs reinforcement in multiplication to help him understand when multiplication is appropriate and when it is not.

Student Work Sample: MG

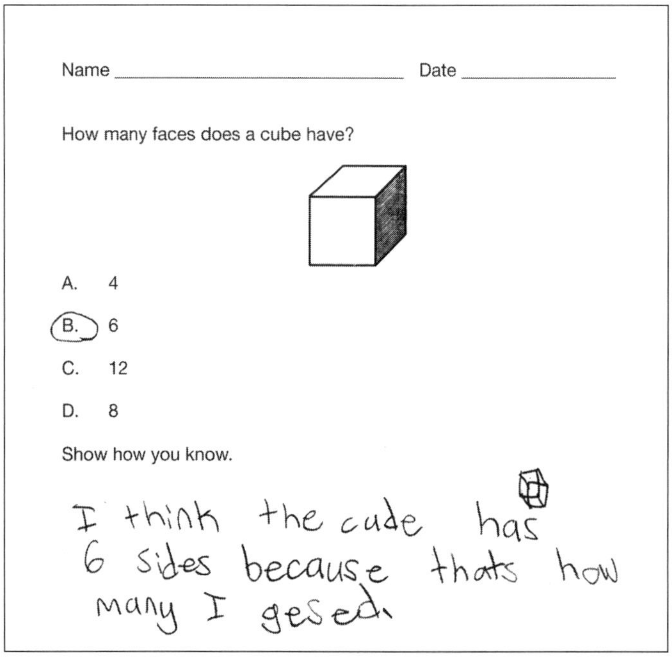
Name ______________________ Date ____________

How many faces does a cube have?

A. 4

(B.) 6

C. 12

D. 8

Show how you know.

I think the cude has 6 sides because thats how many I gesed.

A Conversation with MG	Teacher Insights
T: The question asked you about faces, but you wrote about sides. What is a face? **MG:** It's a side, like this. [MG points to the front face of the pictured cube.] **T:** Mathematicians call that a face. So in your writing you are using the word *side* to mean face? **MG:** Yes. **T:** How do you know that a cube has six faces? **MG:** I guessed, but I drew a picture and pretended I could see through it and it looked like maybe there were six sides, I mean faces. But they are sort of on top of each other and that makes it hard to count, but I think there are six.	**T:** *MG has an emerging understanding. He intuitively knew to draw a transparent cube to determine the number of faces. He came up with the correct number of faces but wasn't confident in his answer.*

Informed Instructional Suggestions

As with Jerry, the multiple-choice answer alone would not have indicated MG's instructional needs. His understanding is fragile and he needs work to develop accurate vocabulary. MG needs the same type of experiences as Jerry and the previous students.

Student Work Sample: Frank

Name ______________________ Date ____________

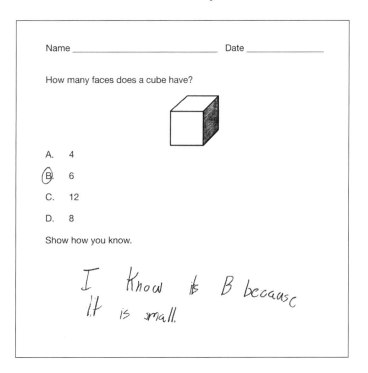

How many faces does a cube have?

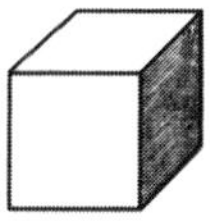

A. 4

(B.) 6

C. 12

D. 8

Show how you know.

I Know its B becausc it is small.

A Conversation with Frank	Teacher Insights
T: What does being small have to do with being a cube? **Frank:** I don't know. I guessed. I don't even know what a face is, so I don't know how many faces on the cube.	**T:** *Frank marked the correct answer, but he knows very little about faces or perhaps even cubes.*

Informed Instructional Strategies

Frank's lucky guess covered up his lack of understanding. He needs to start with foundational geometry activities. He must develop the concepts and vocabulary associated with cubes and other basic geometric shapes before he can move forward in this strand.

Student Work Sample: Stuart

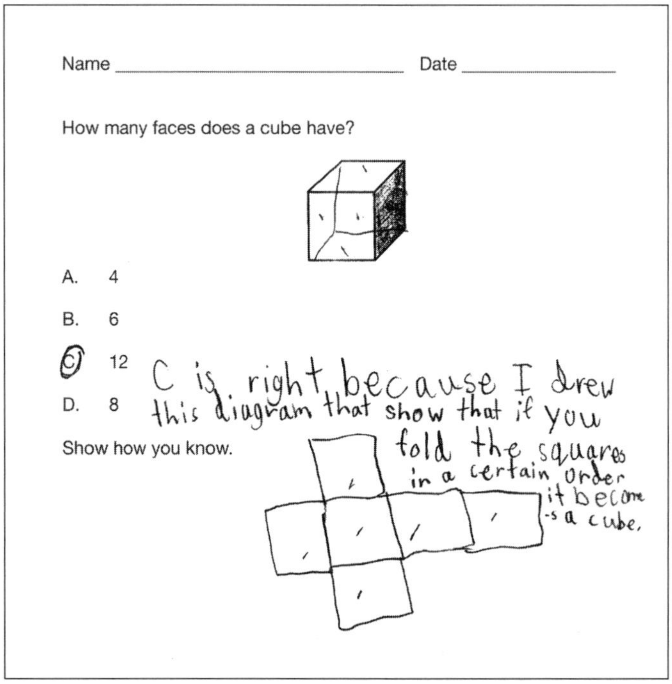
Name ____________ Date ________

How many faces does a cube have?

A. 4

B. 6

C. 12

D. 8

Show how you know.

C is right because I drew this diagram that show that if you fold the squares in a certain order it becomes a cube.

A Conversation with Stuart	Teacher Insights
T: Tell me more about your drawing. **Stuart:** Well, I drew what a cube would look like when it is opened up. It would be six squares. And then you could fold it back up in a certain order and it would go back to being a cube. The top and bottom square would fold up and the other four squares would fold around, sort of like a belt. **T:** You marked choice C for your answer. **Stuart:** Uh-oh! Choice C says twelve. There are really six faces. Oops! I guess I should check my work. It should be choice B.	**T:** *Stuart marked the wrong answer. He even restated that choice C was correct in his written explanation, but his thinking supported choice B.*

Informed Instructional Suggestions

Although he mistakenly selected an incorrect multiple-choice answer, Stuart has a good understanding of cubes. The written and verbal explanations are helpful for choosing the appropriate next steps for Stuart. He is ready to move on to exploring the edges and vertices of cubes and the attributes of other polyhedra. Stuart needs to be encouraged to read questions carefully and double-check his answers.

Student Work Sample: Damon

Name ______________________ Date ____________

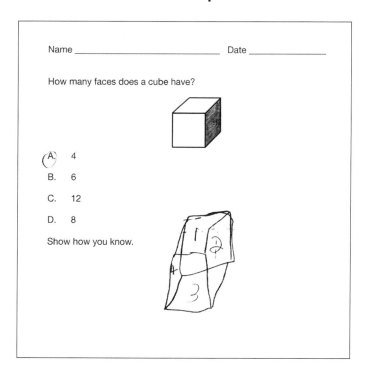

How many faces does a cube have?

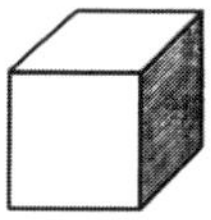

(A.) 4

B. 6

C. 12

D. 8

Show how you know.

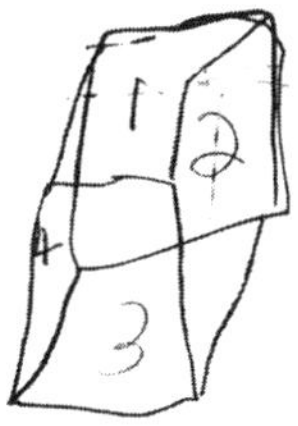

A Conversation with Damon	Teacher Insights
T: I see that you marked choice A, four, as your answer. Show me how you counted the faces of the cube. **Damon:** I drew it and then I counted like this. [Damon numbers the faces of the cube as he counts aloud.] See, there are four faces. **T:** Can you think of an example of a cube in real life? **Damon:** Not really. **T:** Do you think there are really cubes? **Damon:** Well, the cube looks like a square to me, so maybe a cube is a square.	**T:** *Damon has little understanding of cubes and probably squares since he is wondering if the two are the same thing. He used a good strategy, drawing a picture, but still had difficulty counting the faces accurately.*

Informed Instructional Suggestions

Damon needs hands-on, concrete experiences to develop his understanding of cubes and squares. As he develops this understanding, he needs many opportunities to learn the appropriate vocabulary as well.

Reassessment

1. Use a similar problem at the same level of difficulty.

   How many faces does a rectangular prism have?

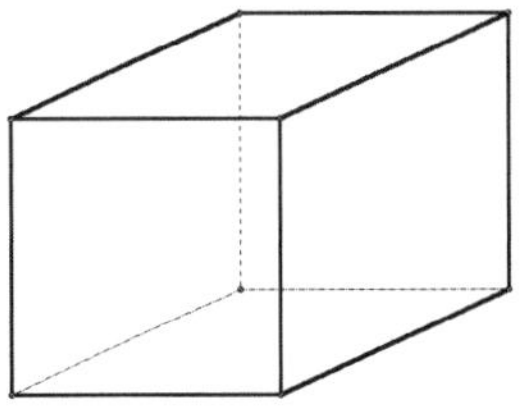

   A. 8
   B. 6
   C. 12
   D. 10

   Show how you know.

2. Choose a problem that is similar but slightly more challenging.

   How many edges does a triangular pyramid have?

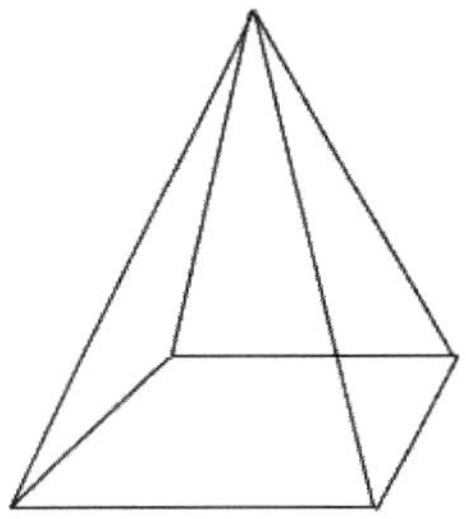

   A. 3
   B. 4
   C. 5
   D. 6

   Show how you know.

Probability

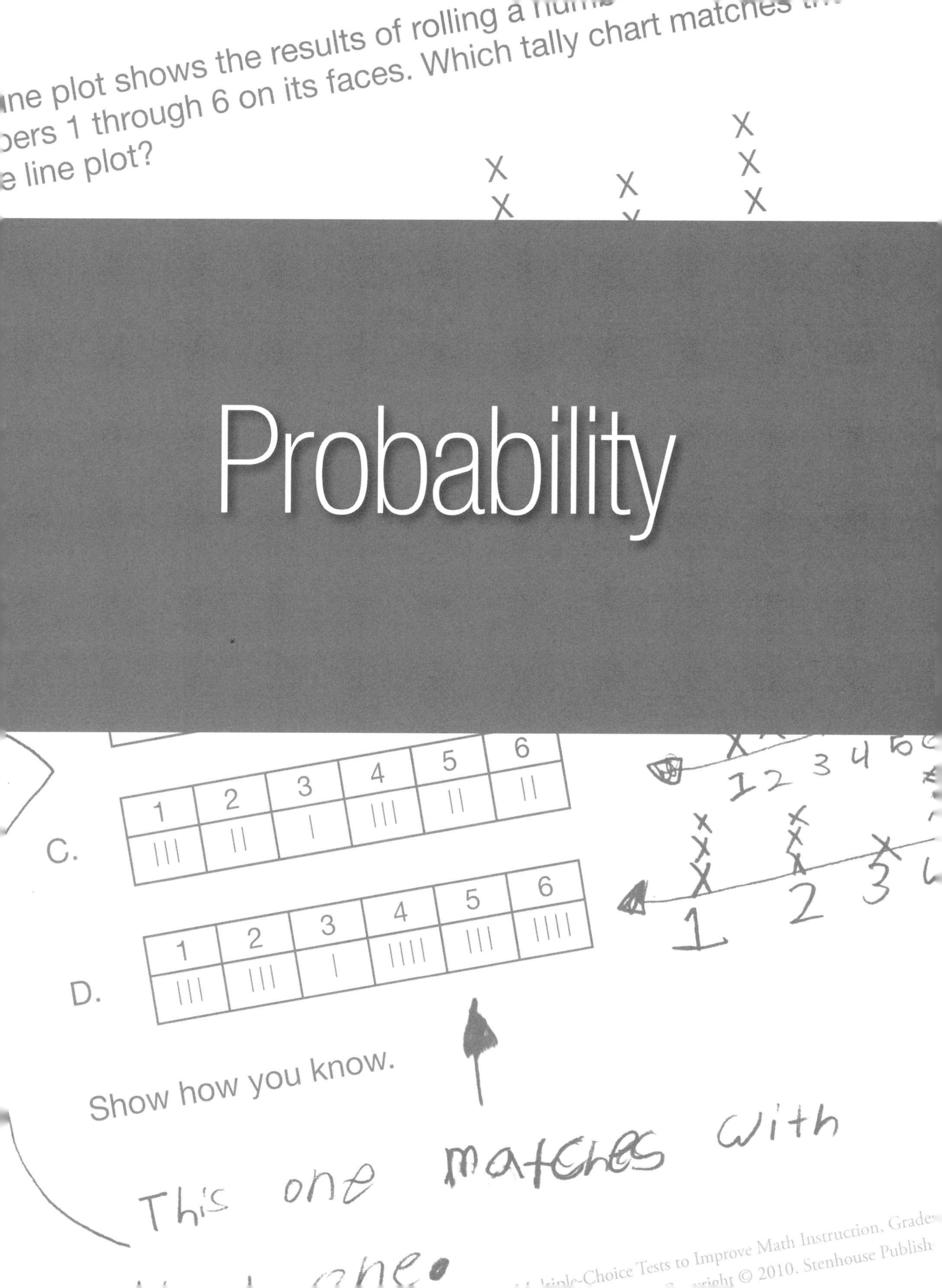

PROBLEM ONE

Overview

This problem asks students to consider concepts in probability such as *certain*, *possible*, *likely*, *unlikely*, and *impossible*. The idea is that the more there is of a certain color of marble, the more likely that color is to be chosen at random. Children who do not understand this may choose an answer based on color preference or some other characteristic.

Sample Problem

A jar had 5 red marbles, 2 blue marbles, 6 yellow marbles, and 8 green marbles. Without looking, Juan reached into the jar and picked 1 marble. What color did he *most* likely pick?

A. blue
B. green
C. yellow
D. red

Show how you know.

Possible Student Solution Strategies

- Students represent the data by drawing pictures.
- Students represent the data using a tally chart.
- Students represent the data using a bar graph.

Conversation Starters

- How did your picture [or tally chart or graph] help you solve the problem?
- What did you do to prove that your answer choice was correct?
- Would you choose the same answer if the number of green and yellow marbles were reversed? If the number of blue and red marbles were reversed, would you choose a different answer?
- How did you think about this problem?
- How would you explain your thinking to another student?

Student Work Sample: Rocky

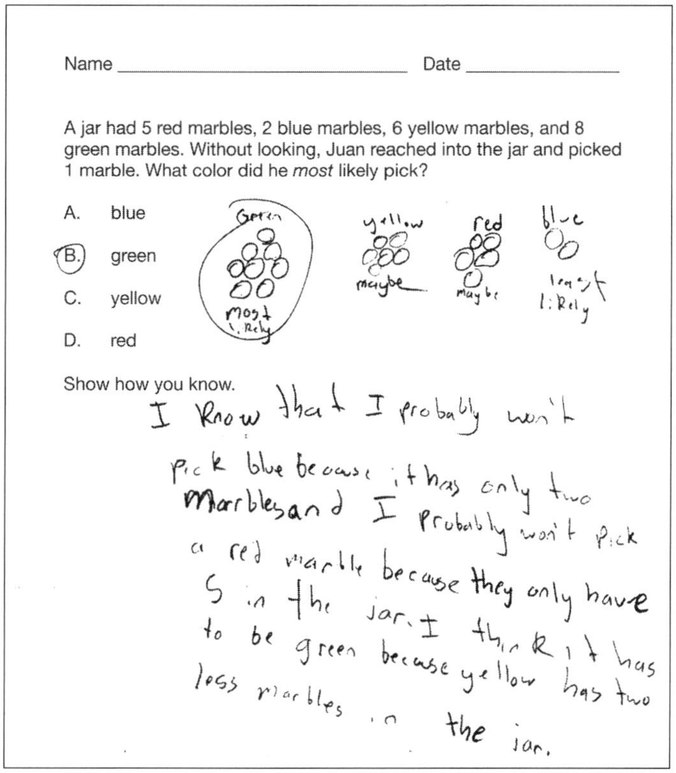

Name ______________________ Date ____________

A jar had 5 red marbles, 2 blue marbles, 6 yellow marbles, and 8 green marbles. Without looking, Juan reached into the jar and picked 1 marble. What color did he *most* likely pick?

A. blue

(B.) green

C. yellow

D. red

Show how you know.

I know that I probably won't pick blue because it has only two marbles and I probably won't pick a red marble because they only have 5 in the jar. I think it has to be green because yellow has two less marbles in the jar.

A Conversation with Rocky	Teacher Insights
T: I noticed that you drew pictures and labeled them. How did that help you think about the problem? **Rocky:** The pictures helped me to see the number of each of the colors of marbles. I wouldn't pick blue because there are only two blue in my picture. I can see in my picture that there are the most green. The picture made it easy. **T:** Would your answer choice be the same if the number of green marbles and yellow marbles were reversed? **Rocky:** No. I would have to switch the labels and then I would see that there were more yellow than green. So my answer would change.	**T:** *Rocky has a strong understanding of the concepts of likely and unlikely and he effectively used the language in his written work. His response to the last question indicated he has a solid conceptual understanding of probability for this situation.*

Informed Instructional Strategies

Rocky is ready to explore increasingly complex situations involving probability. This might include experiments involving more colors of marbles or a greater number of marbles.

Student Work Sample: Catalina

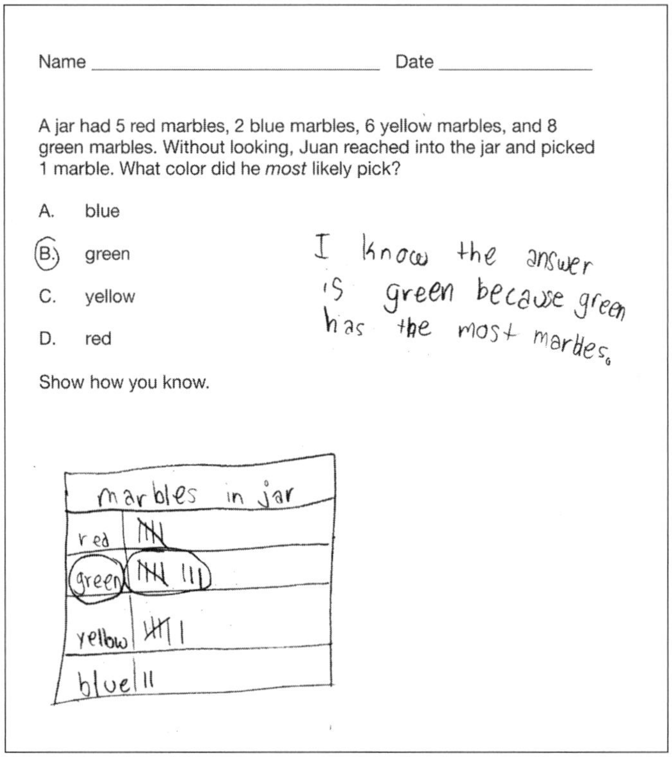
Name ______________________ Date ____________

A jar had 5 red marbles, 2 blue marbles, 6 yellow marbles, and 8 green marbles. Without looking, Juan reached into the jar and picked 1 marble. What color did he *most* likely pick?

A. blue

(B.) green

C. yellow

D. red

Show how you know.

I know the answer is green because green has the most marbles.
marbles in jar
red
green
yellow
blue

A Conversation with Catalina	Teacher Insights
T: Catalina, I see you used tally marks. What do the tally marks represent? **Catalina:** Each tally stands for a marble. So for red there are five tallies because there are five red marbles. Green has eight tallies because there were eight green marbles. I did the same for the yellow and blue. The word *most* is italic, so I looked for the one that was the most because it could happen the most. That's green, so I circled it. With tallies it made it easy to see which was the most. You can just look and see it!	**T:** *One of Catalina's strengths was her ability represent the data in a way that was meaningful to her and communicate her understanding clearly to others.*

Informed Instructional Strategies

Like Rocky, Catalina is ready to move on to more sophisticated problems.

Student Work Sample: Brielle

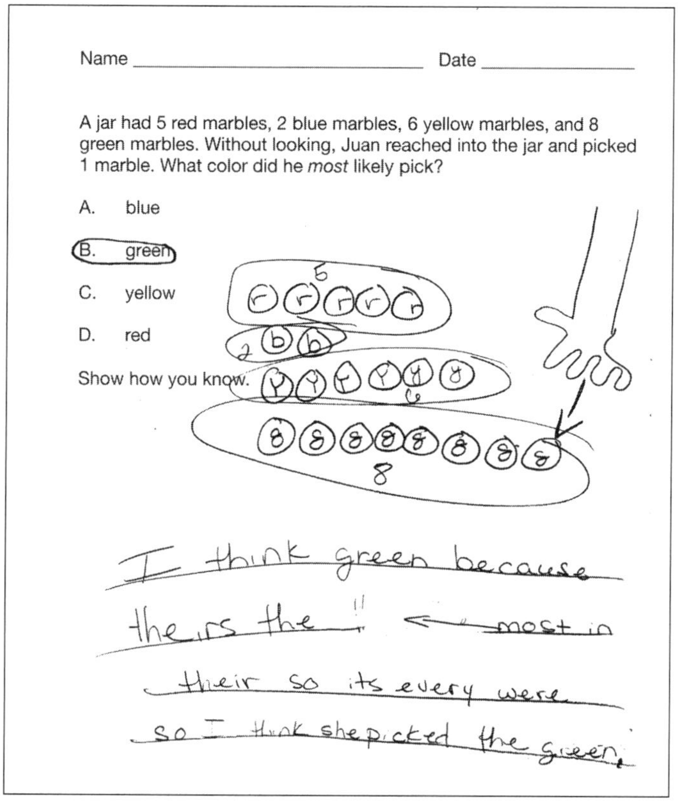
Name ______________________ Date ____________

A jar had 5 red marbles, 2 blue marbles, 6 yellow marbles, and 8 green marbles. Without looking, Juan reached into the jar and picked 1 marble. What color did he *most* likely pick?

A. blue

B. green

C. yellow

D. red

Show how you know.

I think green because the.rs the !! ← most in their so its every were so I think shepicked the green.

A Conversation with Brielle	Teacher Insights
T: How does your picture show that your answer choice is correct? **Brielle:** Easy. I just drew a picture of what the words told me to do. I put five circles for the reds, two for the blue ones, six for the yellow, and eight for the green. Then I drew my hand to show me picking the green one. **T:** Why is your hand picking the green one and not a blue one? **Brielle:** Because there are mostly green ones and hardly any blue marbles. That's why!	**T:** Brielle used a picture to show her clear thinking about this problem. Her verbal explanation also supported her written explanation.

Informed Instructional Suggestions

Brielle is also ready to move on to more complex problems.

Student Work Sample: Marci

Name ______________________ Date ____________

A jar had 5 red marbles, 2 blue marbles, 6 yellow marbles, and 8 green marbles. Without looking, Juan reached into the jar and picked 1 marble. What color did he *most* likely pick?

A. blue

(B.) green

C. yellow

D. red

Show how you know. because maybe it had the most marbles. And maybe those ones are less and maybe he likes green.

A Conversation with Marci	Teacher Insights
T: Tell me about your thinking. **Marci:** I think Juan likes green because he has the most of them. So when he puts them all together in a jar, I think he likes to see green best so he puts the most in. He can see in the jar so he can pick his favorite color, which is green. **T:** What if the marbles were in a can and Juan couldn't see them? **Marci:** Well, because he likes green and has the most of them, I think he would still get green. **T:** Do you think he would still get green if he had only two green and eight blues but still liked green best? **Marci:** Yep, it's his favorite color.	**T:** *Although Marci marked the correct answer, her written and verbal explanations revealed she thought Juan would most likely draw a green marble because it was his favorite color rather than the most abundant one. Marci has not yet developed an understanding of the role of chance. She saw this problem in very literal terms.*

Informed Instructional Suggestions

In this situation, Marci's correct answer masked gaps in her knowledge and understanding. While it is possible that Juan's favorite color is green and that is the reason he has mostly green marbles, that is not a known factor in this problem. Marci needs to physically conduct this probability experiment by placing the marbles in a paper bag so she cannot see them and then drawing and replacing the marbles, recording the results of each draw. By doing this type of sampling experiment and examining the results, Marci will begin to develop an understanding of chance and sample size. In addition to this probability experience, Marci needs to do several other similar experiments to further develop and solidify her understanding.

Student Work Sample: Joey

Name ______________________ Date ____________

A jar had 5 red marbles, 2 blue marbles, 6 yellow marbles, and 8 green marbles. Without looking, Juan reached into the jar and picked 1 marble. What color did he *most* likely pick?

A. blue

(B.) green

C. yellow

D. red

Show how you know.

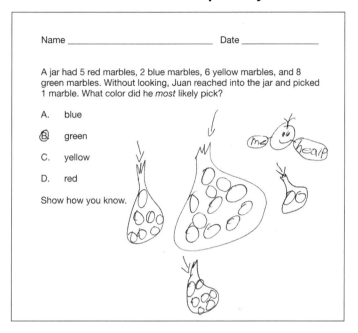

A Conversation with Joey	Teacher Insights
T: I see you drew some pictures. How were they helpful to your thinking about this problem? **Joey:** The problem was about marbles. So I drew some bags with marbles in them on my paper. I also put me. I need some help solving this problem. That's why I wrote "help." **T:** How did you know how many marbles to put in the bags? **Joey:** I just made bags and marbles. The biggest bag has the most marbles. See? [Joey points to the largest bag.] It has eleven marbles. **T:** Why did you put eleven marbles in the largest bag? **Joey:** I needed to have a bag with the most. [Joey points to the word *most* in the problem.] **T:** Why did you pick green for your answer? **Joey:** It's my favorite color.	**T:** *Joey, like Marci, saw color preference as an influencing factor in the outcome of this problem. He understood that* most *was involved somehow in the problem but did not connect this idea to any of the data provided.*

Informed Instructional Suggestions

Joey's answer selection revealed his favorite color rather than an understanding of ideas of probability. Like Marci, he needs foundational experiences to develop basic knowledge of chance.

Student Work Sample: Fritz

Name ______________________ Date ____________

A jar had 5 red marbles, 2 blue marbles, 6 yellow marbles, and 8 green marbles. Without looking, Juan reached into the jar and picked 1 marble. What color did he *most* likely pick?

A. blue

(B) green

C. yellow

D. red

I Know that he likes the green marbles because it has the most marbles.

Show how you know.

I Know that he doesn't like the other marbles because he has a little bit of marbles

A Conversation with Fritz	Teacher Insights
T: Fritz, how do you know Juan liked green the best? **Fritz:** I don't know that he does like it the best. The problem says he has the *most* green because he has eight and all the rest have a little bit. **T:** Pretend Juan likes all the colors the same. What color do you think he would pick if he reached in the jar and picked one without looking? **Fritz:** The green! There are the most, so that's what he'd pick the most.	**T:** *Fritz is a second-language learner. His imprecise language can be misleading, as it was in this case. When Fritz orally clarified his thinking for me, it became clear that he didn't actually think the outcome was based on a color preference; he understood that Juan would most likely pick a green because there was a higher number of green marbles than of the other colors.*

Informed Instructional Suggestions

Fritz's needs are similar to those of Rocky. However, he would benefit from a focus on language, perhaps through the use of sentence frames, vocabulary lists, and other tools to support more precise language use.

Student Work Sample: Jamie

Name ______________________ Date ____________

A jar had 5 red marbles, 2 blue marbles, 6 yellow marbles, and 8 green marbles. Without looking, Juan reached into the jar and picked 1 marble. What color did he *most* likely pick?

(A.) blue

B. green

C. yellow

D. red

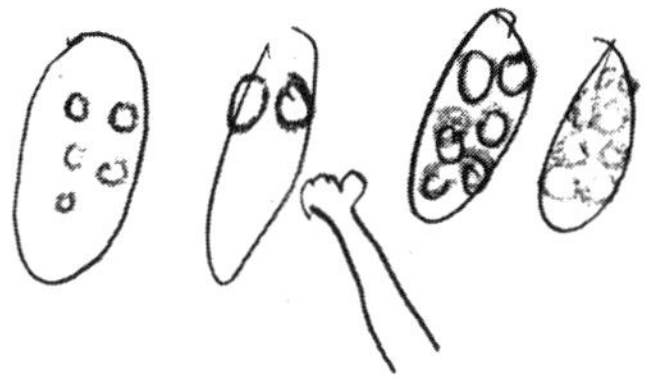

Show how you know.

I think blue becanse
it has the less
marbals so she
proply picked
that one you see
that chart I
made it has the
less marbels.

A Conversation with Jamie	Teacher Insights
T: Jamie, please reread the problem aloud and then tell me what it is that you think you need to do. **Jamie:** It wants me to tell the one with the littlest. **T:** What does most mean? **Jamie:** The littlest bit. **T:** *Most* means the one that has the greatest or many. Which one of your pictures has many? **Jamie:** [Pointing to the drawing on the right] It's this one.	**T:** *Jamie is a second-language learner and frequently confuses words such as* most *and* least, *as she did in this case.*

Informed Instructional Suggestions

Like Fritz, Jamie needs many hands-on, concrete experiences, with a focus on language development.

Reassessment

1. Use a similar problem at the same level of difficulty.

   Maria had a bag of jelly beans. The bag had 3 red jelly beans, 9 blue jelly beans, 5 green jelly beans, and 7 yellow jelly beans. Without looking, Maria reached into the bag and picked one jelly bean. What color did Maria *most* likely pick?

   A. yellow
   B. blue
   C. red
   D. green

   Show how you know.

2. Choose a problem that is similar but slightly more challenging.

   Josh is doing a probability experiment using colored tiles in a bag. He draws out a tile, records the color, and replaces the tile. In the bag, there are 2 red tiles, 9 green tiles, 5 yellow tiles, and 7 blue tiles. Which color of tile is Josh *least* likely to draw out of the bag?

   A. yellow
   B. blue
   C. red
   D. green

   Show how you know.

PROBLEM TWO

Overview

The important concept of chance appears on most standardized multiple-choice tests, as well as on most district and other local multiple-choice tests. Children often view the ideas behind chance through the lenses of their daily lives. Some children see all things as possible, while others are overwhelmed and consider everything impossible. Their answers may reflect these outlooks rather than the mathematics that underlies questions such as this one. Therefore, it is important to provide many hands-on experiences to help students grasp the mathematical ideas of chance.

Sample Problem

Yasmine is tossing a cube with the numbers 2, 4, 6, 8, 10, and 12 on the faces. When the cube lands, is it certain, likely, unlikely, or impossible that the face on the top of the cube will show the number 1?

A. certain
B. likely
C. unlikely
D. impossible

Show how you know.

Possible Student Solution Strategies

- Students use a picture.
- Students recognize the pattern of even numbers and eliminate 1 because it is odd.
- Students recognize that six numbers are listed and the number 1 is a seventh number and there are no more faces on the die for a seventh number.

Conversation Starters

- What patterns do you see?
- What does *impossible* mean? *Certain*? *Likely*? *Unlikely*?
- How could a picture help you solve this problem?
- What other numbers would be impossible to roll with this die? Why?
- How could you renumber the die so that 2 was the most likely number to roll but not certain?

Student Work Sample: Melei

Name ______________________ Date ______________

Yasmine is tossing a cube with the numbers 2, 4, 6, 8, 10, and 12 on the faces. When the cube lands, is it certain, likely, unlikely, or impossible that the face on the top of the cube will show the number 1?

A. certain

B. likely

C. unlikely

D. impossible (circled)

Show how you know.

It is impossible because it is a even pattern and 1 is a odd number.

A Conversation with Melei	Teacher Insights
T: What patterns did you notice, Melei? **Melei:** The numbers on the die are all even. They also count up by twos. **T:** How did that help you answer the question? **Melei:** One is an odd number, so it would be impossible for it to be on a die with all even numbers. **T:** What does *impossible* mean? **Melei:** It can't happen. **T:** What other numbers would be impossible on this die? **Melei:** Any odd number can't be on this die if all numbers have to be even.	**T:** *Melei saw a pattern in the numbers on the die. Her explanations indicated a good grasp of odd and even numbers. She applied this understanding to determine that it would be impossible to roll a 1 in this situation.*

Informed Instructional Suggestions

While Melei found a pattern to the numbers on the die and applied this to justify her answer selection, she needs to explore to find out if there are other possible reasons that a 1 wouldn't be on this particular die, for example, because all numbers on the die are multiples of two. Melei needs activities that will push her to become a more flexible thinker.

Student Work Sample: Jaycee

Name ______________________ Date ____________

Yasmine is tossing a cube with the numbers 2, 4, 6, 8, 10, and 12 on the faces. When the cube lands, is it certain, likely, unlikely, or impossible that the face on the top of the cube will show the number 1?

no 1

A. certain

B. likely

C. unlikely

(D) impossible

Show how you know.

I picked choice D because Yasmine is thowing a dice that has only numbers 2, 4, 6, 8, 10, and 12. So do you see a 1 in the numbers.

A Conversation with Jaycee	Teacher Insights
T: Your answer is clear, Jaycee. You have convinced me. Why couldn't I just add a 1 to the list? **Jaycee:** Well, there are six faces on a cube and that would make seven numbers. There isn't enough room! **T:** How could you renumber the die so that 2 was the most likely but not certain? **Jaycee:** You could put on two 2s and take one of the other numbers off.	**T:** *Jaycee's understanding is strong and she was able to consider a more difficult question and articulate a solid, appropriate response.*

Informed Instructional Suggestions

Jaycee needs experiences in which she can apply and stretch her understanding. For example, she could make up a game involving probability that included such concepts as *likely*, *equally likely*, *fair*, and *unfair*. For the game, she could create spinners or dice that players would use to generate random outcomes.

Student Work Sample: Brandon

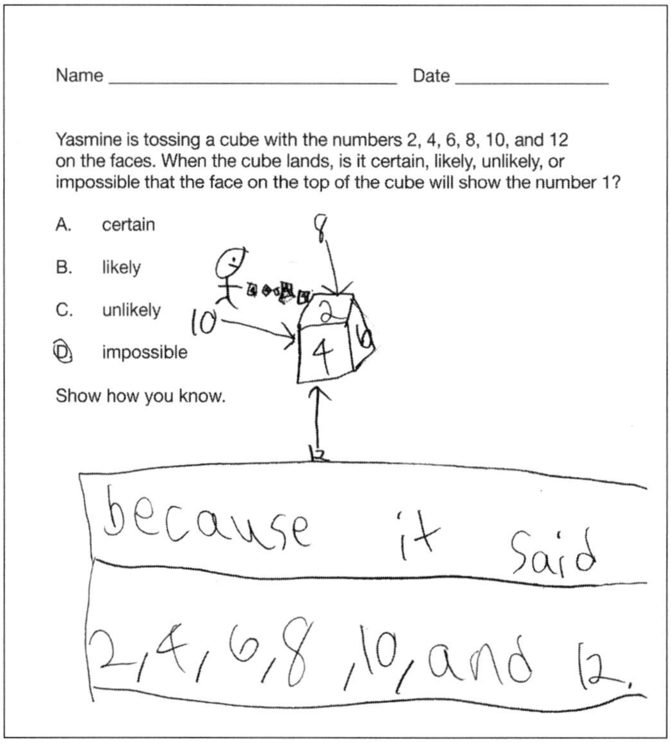
Name ______________________ Date ____________

Yasmine is tossing a cube with the numbers 2, 4, 6, 8, 10, and 12 on the faces. When the cube lands, is it certain, likely, unlikely, or impossible that the face on the top of the cube will show the number 1?

A. certain

B. likely

C. unlikely

(D) impossible

Show how you know.

A Conversation with Brandon	Teacher Insights
T: Why did you decide to draw a picture? **Brandon:** Because I wanted to show all sides of the cube. See the guy in the picture? He's tossing the cubes and it shows the numbers he could get. When I looked at the list and put the numbers on the cubes in the picture, 1 was not one of them. The list says 2, 4, 6, 8, 10, and 12. The only place there is a 1 is in the 10 and the 12, and that's not 1, that's really one ten. **T:** What is the difference between *impossible* and *unlikely*? **Brandon:** Oh, unlikely means it could maybe in a million trillion years happen, but probably not. Like I could go to Disneyland on a field trip tomorrow. It could happen, but I don't think so. Impossible means it will never ever, ever never happen. Like it's impossible I'll eat broccoli. It will never ever, ever never happen. It's gross!	**T:** *Brandon's drawing and verbal responses provided entertaining and enlightening insight into his strong understanding.*

Informed Instructional Suggestions

Brandon's understanding and instructional needs are similar to Jaycee's. They could work together on the types of activities we suggested for Jaycee, such as creating and playing games.

Student Work Sample: Alisa

Name ______________________ Date ____________

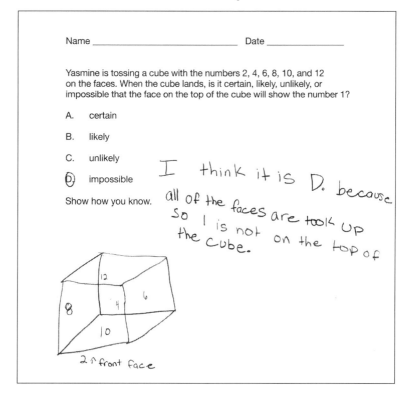

Yasmine is tossing a cube with the numbers 2, 4, 6, 8, 10, and 12 on the faces. When the cube lands, is it certain, likely, unlikely, or impossible that the face on the top of the cube will show the number 1?

A. certain

B. likely

C. unlikely

(D.) impossible

Show how you know. I think it is D. because all of the faces are took up so 1 is not on the top of the cube.

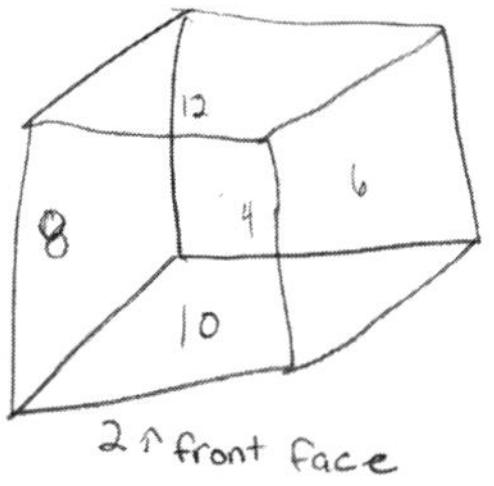

A Conversation with Alisa	Teacher Insights
T: I see you have explained your thinking. Please tell me more about what "took up" means. **Alisa:** There are no more faces on the cube for 1 because the other numbers took up the spaces for numbers. I drew a picture to show you. No more spaces! **T:** Do you see any patterns in the numbers that are on the cube? **Alisa:** No . . . wait, yes! They're all even numbers. That's cool. I didn't notice that before. One wouldn't be there anyway because it's odd and the others are even!	**T:** *Alisa initially looked at the problem spatially. She stated there was no more room on the cube for the number 1. Of course, this makes sense. However, there was another way to look at the problem. Through questioning, Alisa came to see that there was a pattern to the numbers on the cube and she could also justify her answer in this way.*

Informed Instructional Suggestions

While Alisa correctly answered this question and was able to justify her thinking, giving her opportunities to discover more than one strategy would strengthen her understanding and help her think with greater flexibility. When appropriate, we should encourage Alisa to show a second solution strategy.

Student Work Sample: Sandy

Name ______________________ Date ____________

Yasmine is tossing a cube with the numbers 2, 4, 6, 8, 10, and 12 on the faces. When the cube lands, is it certain, likely, unlikely, or impossible that the face on the top of the cube will show the number 1?

A. certain

B. likely

C. unlikely

● impossible

Show how you know.

because there is no why to get a 1 on a fraction di. You can only get 2, 4, 6, 8, 10, and 12

A Conversation with Sandy	Teacher Insights
T: We have been using fraction dice lately and I see you mentioned that in your explanation. Please tell me how that relates to this situation. **Sandy:** Well, they're both dice and, well, I just thought maybe since we had been using them, this problem would have something to do with them. **T:** Are the numbers 2, 4, 6, 8, 10, and 12 numbers you could roll on a fraction die? **Sandy:** If you put a 1 above the 2, it would be 1/2, and that's on a fraction die. You can put a 1 over the 4 and that's 1/4. **T:** The problem says there is a 2 on one face of the cube. Is one-half the same as two? **Sandy:** No. **T:** So according to the problem, is 1/2 on any of the faces of the cube? **Sandy:** Well, no . . . oh, now I see. It's not fractions. It's the other kind of numbers. So the numbers at the top are the only numbers on the cube and so just a 1 would not work.	**T:** *Sandy's understanding has lots of room for growth and development.*

Informed Instructional Suggestions

While Sandy marked the correct answer, she had only beginning understanding of the problem. Sandy needs basic conceptual, hands-on experiences with number cubes to develop her understanding. In addition, she needs clarification of fractions and whole numbers.

Student Work Sample: Sadie

Name ______________________ Date ____________

Yasmine is tossing a cube with the numbers 2, 4, 6, 8, 10, and 12 on the faces. When the cube lands, is it certain, likely, unlikely, or impossible that the face on the top of the cube will show the number 1?

A. certain

B. likely

(C.) unlikely

D. impossible

Show how you know.

It is unlikely because the dice only has the numbers 2, 4, 6, 8, 10, and 12. But yeah sure there are dices with 1 on it.

A Conversation with Sadie	Teacher Insights
T: Tell me what *unlikely* means. **Sadie:** It could happen, you never know. It probably won't happen. **T:** Is there a 1 on the cube? **Sadie:** Not on this one, but there are 1s on some cubes. **T:** How would you get a 1 on this cube? **Sadie:** You wouldn't. You'd have to get a different cube with a 1 on it. **T:** This problem says the cube has a 2, 4, 6, 8, 10, and 12. There is no other cube to get. **Sadie:** Oh, OK. I thought I could get another cube. It's impossible then.	**T:** *Sadie's prior knowledge and creative problem solving led her to come up with an unexpected response. Her reasoning made sense, and she used her experience with dice to think of a way to get a 1, but her thinking was outside the parameters of this problem. If I hadn't had this conversation with Sadie, I wouldn't have been aware of her true understanding and creativity.*

Informed Instructional Suggestions

Sadie marked an incorrect response because of her creativity and prior knowledge. Sadie needs to learn when to think within the parameters of a problem and when to think outside the box. The opportunity to solve a variety of problems and discuss her thinking with others can support her in this endeavor.

Reassessment

1. Use a similar problem at the same level of difficulty.

   Raylin is tossing a cube with the numbers 1, 3, 5, 7, 9, and 11 on the faces. When the cube lands, is it certain, likely, unlikely, or impossible that the face on the top of the cube will show the number 6?

   A. certain
   B. likely
   C. unlikely
   D. impossible

   Show how you know.

2. Choose a problem that is similar but slightly more challenging.

   Marylou is designing a number cube for a new game. She wants the number 7 to be the *most likely* outcome when rolling the cube. Which set of numbers should she use to label the number cube?

   A. 1, 3, 5, 7, 9, 11
   B. 1, 1, 5, 5, 7, 7
   C. 1, 3, 7, 7, 7, 9
   D. 1, 3, 3, 3, 9, 11

   Show how you know.

PROBLEM THREE

Overview

Gathering, recording, and interpreting data are big ideas of statistics. It takes hands-on experience and practice with doing all three to develop conceptual understanding. Hopefully, by the time students see a question such as the following, they will have had hands-on experiences similar to the one described in the problem.

Sample Problem

Sasha tossed a dime 20 times. It landed on heads 9 times and on tails 11 times. Which tally chart shows these results?

A.

heads	tails
𝍸 𝍸	𝍸 𝍸 𝍷

B.

heads	tails
𝍸 𝍷𝍷𝍷𝍷	𝍸 𝍸

C.

heads	tails
𝍸 𝍷𝍷𝍷𝍷	𝍸 𝍸 𝍷

D.

heads	tails
𝍸 𝍷𝍷𝍷	𝍸 𝍸 𝍷

Show how you know.

Possible Student Solution Strategies

- Students add the tally marks to find the totals in each chart.
- Students count the tally marks.
- Students change the tally marks to “fix” an incorrect solution.

Conversation Starters

- What kind of mathematics did you use to solve this problem?
- Explain how your answer makes sense.
- What did you do to check your answer?

Student Work Sample: Turner

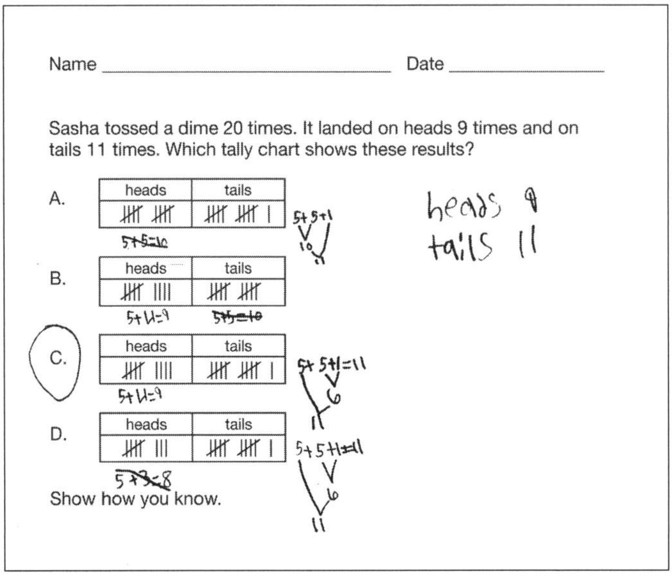

Name ______________________ Date ____________

Sasha tossed a dime 20 times. It landed on heads 9 times and on tails 11 times. Which tally chart shows these results?

A.

heads	tails
卌 卌	卌 卌 |

5+5=10   5+5+1 = 11

B.

heads	tails
卌 ||||	卌 卌

5+4=9   5+5=10

C. (circled)

heads	tails
卌 ||||	卌 卌 |

5+4=9   5+5+1=11

D.

heads	tails
卌 |||	卌 卌 |

5+3=8   5+5+1=11

Show how you know.

heads 9
tails 11

A Conversation with Turner	Teacher Insights
T: What kind of mathematics did you use to solve the problem? **Turner:** It shows collecting data like we did in our heads-and-tails experiment. **T:** [Pointing to a tally mark under "heads" in choice A] What does this tally mark represent? **Turner:** It means the dime landed with the head up one time. **T:** I agree. What other mathematics did you use? **Turner:** I used addition to add up the tally marks and I showed it with numbers. I crossed out answers that weren't either 9 or 11 because I knew that the right answer had to have both of those numbers. I crossed out a 10 in choices A and B and an 8 in choice D, so I knew it couldn't be any of those. That left choice C, and sure enough choice C has a 9 and an 11. It was easy, actually.	**T:** *Turner understands what he's doing. One of Turner's strengths is that he looked at all possibilities and recorded the results of his calculations to show evidence of his work. This thoroughness—looking at all components of the problem—and care further ensure clear thinking and accuracy.*

Informed Instructional Suggestions

Turner understood all aspects of this problem and is ready to do other similar experiments. We should encourage him to develop his own experiments and to collect and analyze data from them.

Student Work Sample: Michael

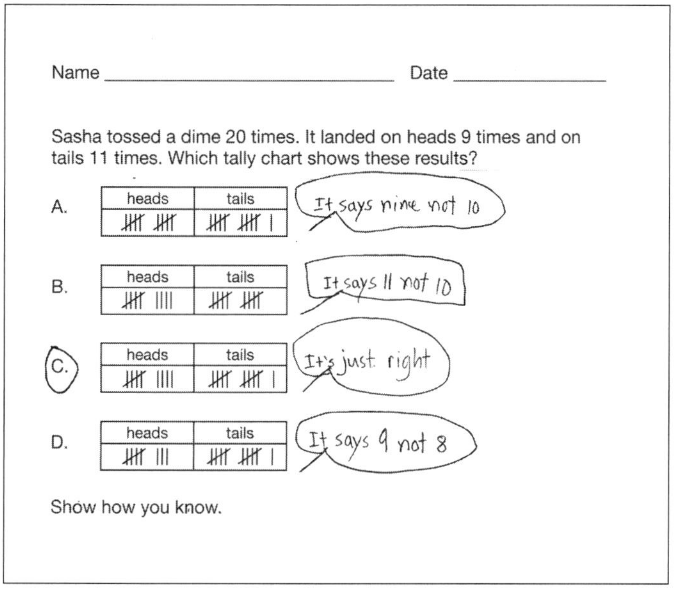
Name ______________________ Date ____________

Sasha tossed a dime 20 times. It landed on heads 9 times and on tails 11 times. Which tally chart shows these results?

A.

heads	tails
𝍸 𝍸	𝍸 𝍸 |

B.

heads	tails
𝍸 ||||	𝍸 𝍸

(C.)

heads	tails
𝍸 ||||	𝍸 𝍸 |

D.

heads	tails
𝍸 |||	𝍸 𝍸 |

Show how you know.

A Conversation with Michael	Teacher Insights
T: Explain how your answer makes sense. **Michael:** Well, it's sort of like the fairy tales we have been reading where things are sometimes too big, too small, or just right. Choice C is just right! In the problem it says there are nine heads, and choice A has ten heads. Too big! Choice B was a little different. The problem says eleven tails, and choice B says ten tails. Too small! Choice C was just right. It has nine heads and eleven tails. But, I checked choice D just to be sure. It had eight heads, not nine. Too small again!	**T:** *Michael had a clear understanding of the problem and was able to easily solve it. Because Michael and Turner both had strong understanding of the mathematics involved, this was a good opportunity for them to share and discuss their work to find similarities and differences in their written solutions.*
T: Michael and Turner, please look at each other's papers. In a few moments I am going to ask you to share what is the same about your solutions and what is different. **Turner:** We both got the same answer! I used addition. Michael didn't. **Michael:** I did too! I did it in my head. **Turner:** I didn't know that because you didn't write it. We're supposed to show what's in our heads. **Michael:** Well I got ten for the heads in choice A, like you. See, I wrote it here. [Michael points to his writing next to choice A.] I got ten for tails in choice B like you. I wrote it here. [Again, Michael points.] We really did do the same thing. You just wrote more.	**T:** *Although both boys answered the question correctly, Turner's thinking was more evident. After some supervised discussion, both boys were able to come to value the other's work.*

Informed Instructional Suggestions

Michael's needs are similar to Turner's. The boys could work together to solve similar problems and develop and investigate their own experiments. This will help them gain insight and strengths from each other's thinking. Michael would also benefit from encouragement to practice writing more complete explanations.

Student Work Sample: Katie

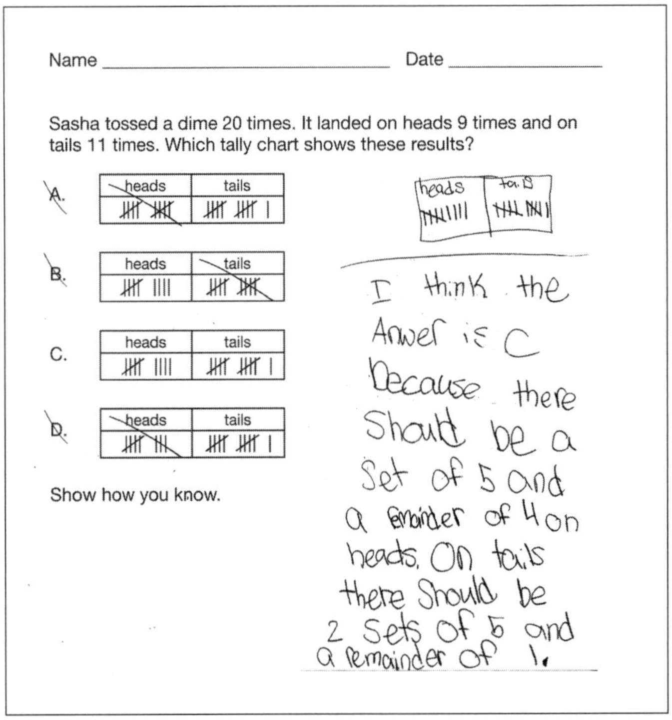
Name ______________________ Date ______________

Sasha tossed a dime 20 times. It landed on heads 9 times and on tails 11 times. Which tally chart shows these results?

A.

heads	tails
𝍸 𝍸	𝍸 𝍸 I

B.

heads	tails
𝍸 IIII	𝍸 𝍸

C.

heads	tails
𝍸 IIII	𝍸 𝍸 I

D.

heads	tails
𝍸 𝍸	𝍸 𝍸 I

Show how you know.

heads
tails
I think the Anwer is C because there Shoud be a Set of 5 and a emainder of 4 on heads. On tails there Should be 2 Sets of 5 and a remainder of 1.

A Conversation with Katie	Teacher Insights
T: What did you do to check your answer? **Katie:** I counted the tally marks by fives because they are mostly in sets of fives. But sometimes there were remainders. **T:** What do you mean by "remainders"? **Katie:** Oh, they're the ones that aren't in groups of five. It's sort of like the ones. So in choice A under "heads," there are two groups of five and no remainders. Two times five equals ten. Under "tails," there are two groups of five and one remainder. So two times five equals ten plus one leftover equals eleven.	**T:** *Katie has a strong understanding of the concepts involved in this problem. Her use of the word* remainder, *which is often associated with division, clearly explained her thinking about groupings of five and the ones that were left over.*

Informed Instructional Suggestions

Katie's needs are similar to those of the previous students.

Student Work Sample: Noey

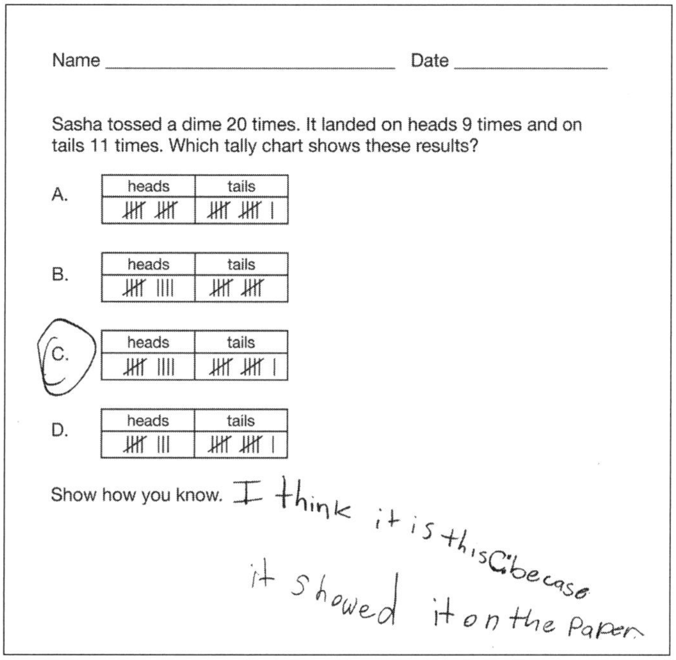
Name ______________________ Date ____________

Sasha tossed a dime 20 times. It landed on heads 9 times and on tails 11 times. Which tally chart shows these results?

A.

heads	tails
卌 卌	卌 卌 |

B.

heads	tails
卌 ||||	卌 卌

C.

heads	tails
卌 ||||	卌 卌 |

D.

heads	tails
卌 |||	卌 卌 |

Show how you know. I think it is this C. becase it showed it on the Paper

A Conversation with Noey

T: What do you mean by "it showed it on the paper"? Can you explain that?

Noey: Well, at the top of the paper the problem has a 9. And right here on choice C there are nine tally marks. So it has to be choice C. That's what I wrote and that's what I mean by "it showed it."

T: [Pointing to the "heads" column in choice B] What about right here in choice B? How many tally marks are there?

Noey: Uh-oh! There are nine. Hmm. Does that mean my answer is wrong?

T: What other information in the problem could you use to help you figure that out?

Noey: I'm not sure.

T: Let's read the problem together to find out.

Noey: [After rereading the problem] Does the 11 have something to do with this? Maybe it does or it wouldn't be in the problem. Hmm! [Noey quickly counts the tallies for tails in choice C.] There are eleven tails in choice C, so I think my answer is probably right because it has both a nine and an eleven.

Teacher Insights

T: *Noey's answer was correct, but her written and verbal explanations indicated only partial understanding. Also, Noey did not seem to recognize the important connection between the information in the problem and the tally charts. Noey considered only one piece of information from the problem when selecting her answer.*

Informed Instructional Suggestions

Noey's partial understanding indicates a need to solve similar problems and discuss the important connection between the information in a problem and its representation in charts or other forms in the answers. It is also crucial for Noey to learn to consider all information provided in a problem. As Noey moves in this direction, she will experience increased success and gain strategies to check the reasonableness of her work, ultimately raising her confidence level.

Student Work Sample: Tiffie

A Conversation with Tiffie	Teacher Insights
T: Tell me about your thinking. **Tiffie:** I put a flower around the 20 to remind me that was the answer. I know that ten plus ten is twenty. I saw the ten in choice B right here. [Tiffie points to the tally marks under "tails" in choice B.] Then I looked at the "heads" part and there were only nine. I think they made a mistake, so I fixed it. I just made one more tally mark. Now it's ten plus ten makes twenty. **T:** Do any of the tally marks in the other choices make twenty? **Tiffie:** I don't think so because then there would be two right answers. None of the other choices say ten plus ten, and that's how you make twenty. That's why I had to fix choice B to make twenty. Ten plus ten is the only way.	**T:** *Tiffie believes that the only way to make twenty is ten plus ten. This is an important misconception that needs immediate attention. Additionally, she focused only on the 20 and seemed unaware of the rest of the information included in the problem.*

Informed Instructional Suggestions

We must address Tiffie's notion that the only way to make 20 is 10 plus 10. But before investigating what Tiffie knows about ways to make 20, we should assess whether she can make smaller numbers with a variety of combinations. For example, can she make 10 using 10 objects arranged into groups of 6 and 4, 7 and 3, or even 8, 1, and 1, and so on? Once she understands that smaller numbers can be made using a variety of combinations, then she can build on that knowledge to strengthen her understanding about 20 and similar numbers.

Reassessment

1. Use a similar problem at the same level of difficulty.

   Paul tossed a nickel 19 times. It landed on heads 8 times and on tails 11 times. Which tally chart shows these results?

A.

<table><tr><th>heads</th><th>tails</th></tr><tr><td>卌 卌</td><td>卌 卌 |</td></tr></table>

B.

<table><tr><th>heads</th><th>tails</th></tr><tr><td>卌 ||||</td><td>卌 卌</td></tr></table>

C.

<table><tr><th>heads</th><th>tails</th></tr><tr><td>卌 ||||</td><td>卌 卌 |</td></tr></table>

D.

<table><tr><th>heads</th><th>tails</th></tr><tr><td>卌 |||</td><td>卌 卌 |</td></tr></table>

Show how you know.

2. Choose a problem that is similar but slightly more challenging.

   Barney was flipping a two-color counter. It landed on red 27 times and yellow 23 times. Which tally chart shows these results?

A.

red	yellow
𝍸 𝍸 𝍸 𝍸 𝍸	𝍸 𝍸 𝍸 𝍸 𝍸

B.

red	yellow
𝍸 𝍸 𝍸 𝍸 𝍸 𝍷𝍷	𝍸 𝍸 𝍸 𝍸 𝍷𝍷𝍷

C.

red	yellow
𝍸 𝍸 𝍸 𝍸 𝍸 𝍷𝍷	𝍸 𝍸 𝍸 𝍸 𝍷𝍷𝍷𝍷

D.

red	yellow
𝍸 𝍸 𝍸 𝍸 𝍷𝍷𝍷	𝍸 𝍸 𝍸 𝍸 𝍸 𝍷𝍷

Show how you know.

PROBLEM FOUR

Overview

After students have had hands-on experiences with collecting, recording, and interpreting data, it is important for them to discover that there are multiple ways in which to record data. For example, the same information can be represented on both a chart and a bar graph. Providing students with opportunities to represent the same data in multiple forms is an effective way to deepen their understanding of statistical ideas. The following question is designed to test children's skill in matching two different representations of the same data.

Sample Problem

This line plot shows the results of rolling a number cube with the numbers 1 through 6 on its faces. Which tally chart matches the data in the line plot?

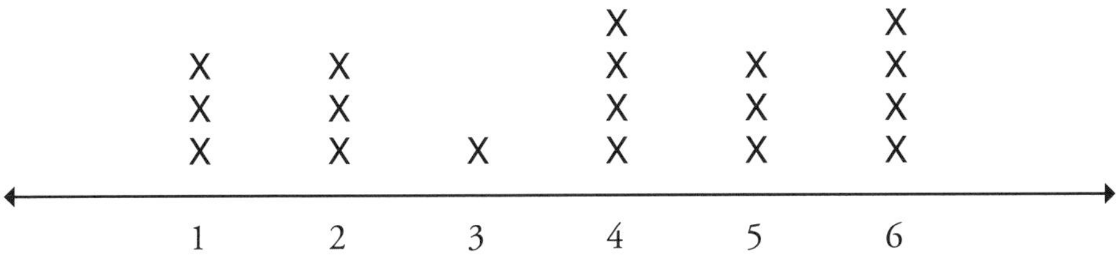

A.

<table><tr><td>1</td><td>2</td><td>3</td><td>4</td><td>5</td><td>6</td></tr><tr><td>||</td><td>||</td><td></td><td>||||</td><td>||</td><td>|||</td></tr></table>

B.

<table><tr><td>1</td><td>2</td><td>3</td><td>4</td><td>5</td><td>6</td></tr><tr><td>||</td><td>||</td><td></td><td>|||</td><td>||</td><td>|||</td></tr></table>

C.

<table><tr><td>1</td><td>2</td><td>3</td><td>4</td><td>5</td><td>6</td></tr><tr><td>|||</td><td>||</td><td>|</td><td>|||</td><td>||</td><td>||</td></tr></table>

D.

<table><tr><td>1</td><td>2</td><td>3</td><td>4</td><td>5</td><td>6</td></tr><tr><td>|||</td><td>|||</td><td>|</td><td>||||</td><td>|||</td><td>||||</td></tr></table>

Show how you know.

Possible Student Solution Strategies

- Students represent each answer choice using numbers or a line plot.
- Students count the *X*s in the line plot and the tallies in the answer choices.
- Students look for the answer choice with the highest number of tally marks.
- Students use only part of the information from the line plot to find an answer.

Conversation Starters

- What did you do to help you select your answer?
- How did you think about the problem?
- What ideas have you learned before that helped you solve this problem?
- [To encourage conversation between students] You have the same answer, but your work looks different. What is alike and what is different about your work?

Student Work Samples: Colin and Terrence

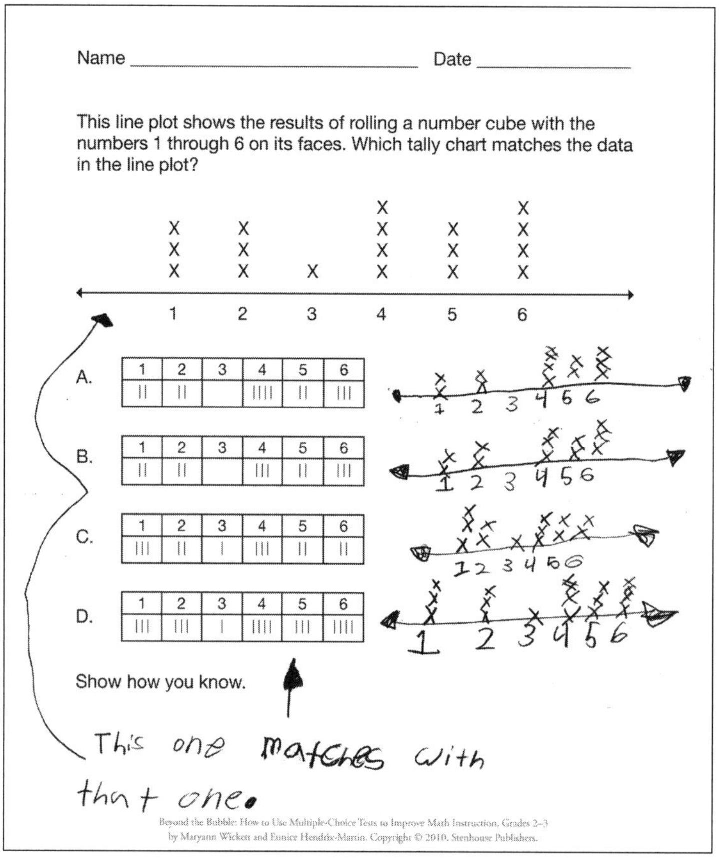

Name ______________________ Date ____________

This line plot shows the results of rolling a number cube with the numbers 1 through 6 on its faces. Which tally chart matches the data in the line plot?

A.

1	2	3	4	5	6
||	||		||||	||	|||

B.

1	2	3	4	5	6
||	||		|||	||	|||

C.

1	2	3	4	5	6
|||	||	|	|||	||	||

D.

1	2	3	4	5	6
|||	|||	|	||||	|||	||||

Show how you know.

This one matches with that one.

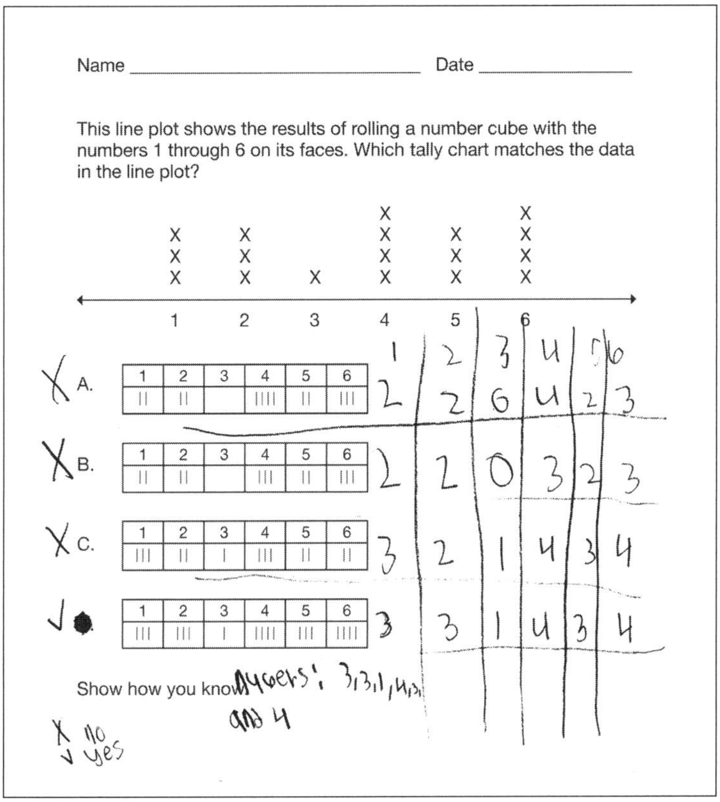
Name ______________________ Date ____________

This line plot shows the results of rolling a number cube with the numbers 1 through 6 on its faces. Which tally chart matches the data in the line plot?

A.

1	2	3	4	5	6
||	||		||||	||	|||

B.

1	2	3	4	5	6
||	||		|||	||	|||

C.

1	2	3	4	5	6
|||	||	|	|||	||	||

D.

1	2	3	4	5	6
|||	|||	|	||||	|||	||||

Show how you know Answers: 3,3,1,4,3, and 4

X no
✓ yes

A Conversation with Colin and Terrence	Teacher Insights
T: I notice that you both have the same answer, but your work certainly looks different. Talk with each other and decide what is alike about your work and what is different. **Terrence:** I drew a chart and put numbers for the tally marks. **Colin:** I drew a line plot to show the numbers. **Terrence:** Hey, my numbers match your *X*s! That's cool! **Colin:** It's the same because we got the same right answer, but it's different because you used numbers and I used a line plot, but really that's the same because your numbers and my *X*s match. Wow!	**T:** *By sharing their solutions, both boys came to see the problem from another perspective, realizing that there is more than one way to represent similar thinking.*

Informed Instructional Suggestions

Colin and Terrence have a solid understanding of how to approach this type of problem. One suggestion would be for them to conduct their own probability experiment and create a line plot and matching chart. Each boy could also be challenged to use the other boy's strategy to solve a problem.

Student Work Samples: Miguel and Joana

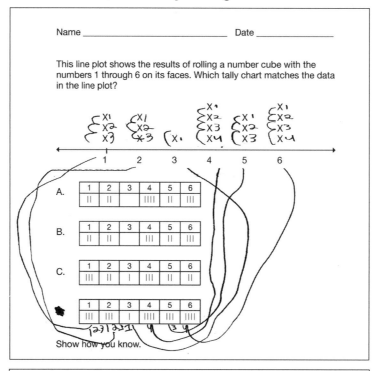

Name ______________________________ Date ______________

This line plot shows the results of rolling a number cube with the numbers 1 through 6 on its faces. Which tally chart matches the data in the line plot?

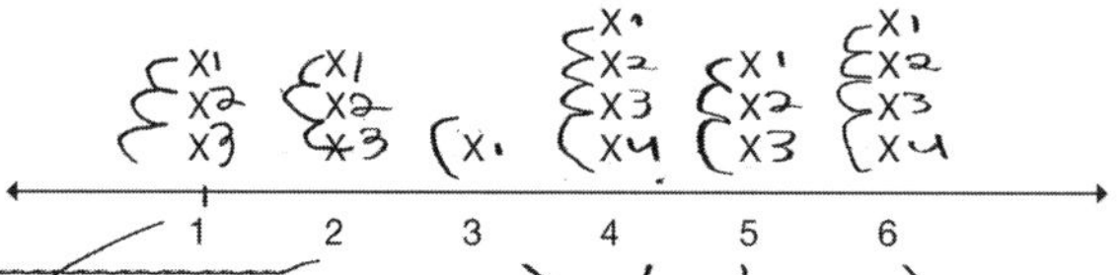

A.

1	2	3	4	5	6
II	II		IIII	II	III

B.

1	2	3	4	5	6
II	II		III	II	III

C.

1	2	3	4	5	6
III	II	I	III	II	II

●

1	2	3	4	5	6
III	III	I	IIII	III	IIII

Show how you know.

Name ______________________________ Date ______________

This line plot shows the results of rolling a number cube with the numbers 1 through 6 on its faces. Which tally chart matches the data in the line plot?

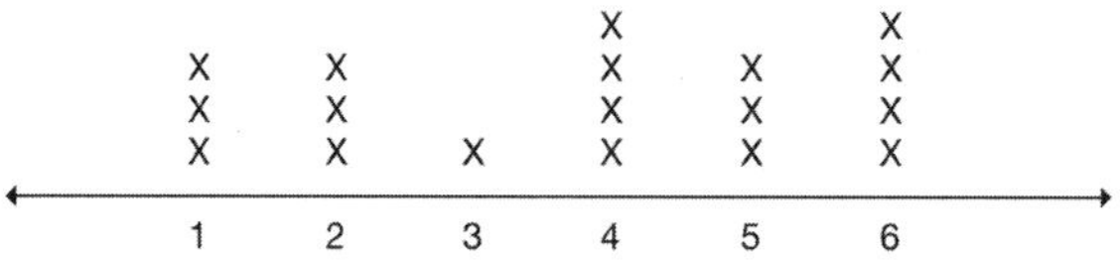

A.

1	2	3	4	5	6
II	II		IIII	II	III

B.

1	2	3	4	5	6
II	II		III	II	III

C.

1	2	3	4	5	6
III	II	I	III	II	II

●.

1	2	3	4	5	6
III	III	I	IIII	III	IIII

Show how you know.

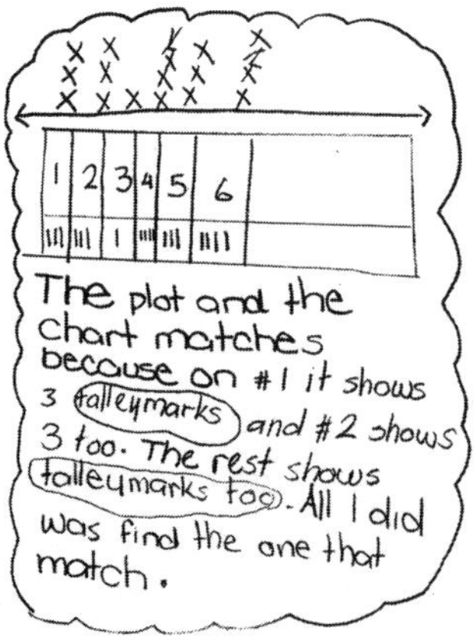
The plot and the chart matches because on #1 it shows 3 talleymarks and #2 shows 3 too. The rest shows talleymarks too. All I did was find the one that match.

A Conversation with Miguel and Joana	Teacher Insights
T: Joana and Miguel, please share with each other how you thought about this problem. As you share, listen closely and look at each other's work to find out what is the same and what is different. **Miguel:** I counted each of the *X*s on the line plot. When I was finished counting them all, I looked at the tally charts and found the one that matched. I drew lines to show that they matched. **Joana:** That's cool! I didn't think of that. First I redrew the line plot. Then I drew my own tally chart underneath it to show how my chart matches the line plot. Then I looked for the answer choice that matched it. It was D. **Miguel:** Our papers look different but in a way we were thinking the same thing. Oh, I know another way they are the same: we both showed our thinking! **Joana:** We both got the right answer, too!	**T:** Like Colin and Terrence, Miguel and Joana were able to discuss their ideas and understand each other's thinking even though their representations looked different.

Informed Instructional Suggestions

An important reason to ask students to explain their thinking about a multiple-choice question is to uncover the variety of strategies they used to solve the problem. Sharing their work with one another gives students additional insights, strengthening their understanding and flexibility. This particular problem lent itself to several ways of representing thinking. Explaining and sharing their thinking was a valuable opportunity for growth. As a next step, these students could select another student's strategy and solve a similar problem using that strategy.

Student Work Sample: Tyler

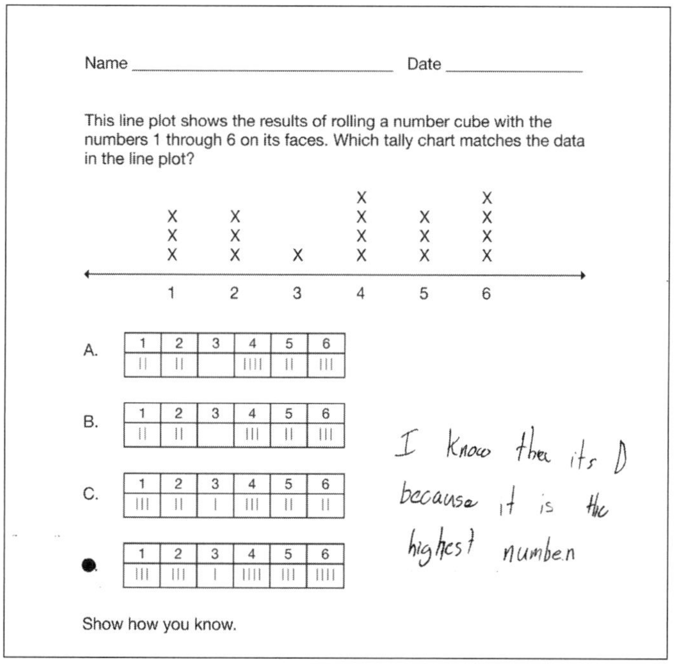

Name ______________________ Date ____________

This line plot shows the results of rolling a number cube with the numbers 1 through 6 on its faces. Which tally chart matches the data in the line plot?

A.

1	2	3	4	5	6
II	II		IIII	II	III

B.

1	2	3	4	5	6
II	II		III	II	III

C.

1	2	3	4	5	6
III	II	I	III	II	II

D.

1	2	3	4	5	6
III	III	I	IIII	III	IIII

I know thea its D because it is the highest numben

Show how you know.

A Conversation with Tyler	Teacher Insights
T: What did you do to help you select your answer? **Tyler:** I looked for the one with the highest numbers. **T:** Why did that make sense to you to do? **Tyler:** It looks like there are a lot of *X*s. I see one *X* on the 3 in the line plot, and choices A and B don't have any tally marks for 3. So I thought the right chart should have the most *X*s. **T:** Please tell me a more about how the line plot and the tally charts are related. **Tyler:** I'm not too sure. Maybe the *X*s and the tallies should be the same?	**T:** *Tyler's understanding is just beginning to emerge. He was uncertain about the connection between the line plot and the tally charts but seemed to realize that some connection existed, as indicated by his comparison of the X marked for 3 on the line plot and the tallies marked for 3 in the charts below. His written explanation that choice D must be correct because it had the highest number of tallies revealed misconceptions.*

Informed Instructional Suggestions

Tyler marked the correct answer for misguided reasons. To strengthen his understanding, Tyler needs opportunities to represent the same data in multiple ways and explain how they are connected.

Student Work Sample: Darren

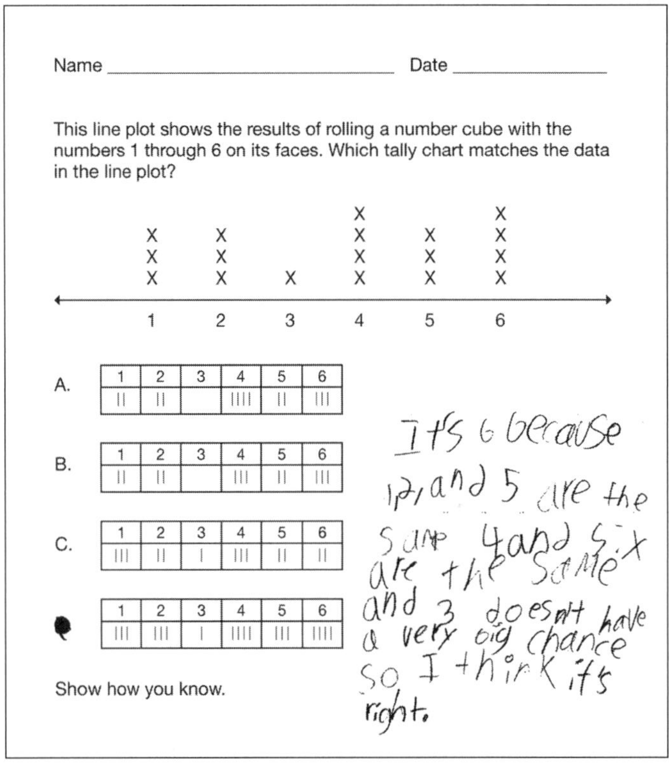
Name ______________________ Date ____________

This line plot shows the results of rolling a number cube with the numbers 1 through 6 on its faces. Which tally chart matches the data in the line plot?

1	2	3	4	5	6
X X X	X X X	X	X X X X	X X X	X X X X

A.

1	2	3	4	5	6
II	II		IIII	II	III

B.

1	2	3	4	5	6
II	II		III	II	III

C.

1	2	3	4	5	6
III	II	I	III	II	II

D. (filled in)

1	2	3	4	5	6
III	III	I	IIII	III	IIII

Show how you know.

A Conversation with Darren	Teacher Insights
T: How did you think about this problem? **Darren:** I remember when we were doing dice experiments that all the faces should have an equally likely chance. So I looked for the tally chart where they were sort of equal. In choice B, most of the numbers happened either two or three times. That's pretty equal. And when we did our dice experiment, 3 didn't happen very much even though it was supposed to. **T:** What do you think is the purpose of the line plot? **Darren:** Oh . . . I just looked at the tally charts and thought it was like the dice experiment. I guess I should have looked at the line plot. **T:** Look at the line plot now and decide if you want to keep or change your answer. **Darren:** Well it's easy now. The answer should be choice D because the *X*s on the line plot match the tally marks. I get it now!	**T:** It's a good thing that Darren tries to connect real-life experiences to problems. However, in this case, he misunderstood the task and overlooked important information, causing him to select an incorrect response. After his verbal explanation, it was evident that Darren understands the concepts being tested.

Informed Instructional Suggestions

Darren's incorrect multiple-choice response was misleading. His use of the word *chance* in his written explanation provided a clue that he had misinterpreted the problem. Through further conversation, it became clear that Darren has a good understanding of the concepts and does not need remediation. This experience reinforced for Darren the value of reading everything carefully. He would benefit from the same instructional suggestions as Colin and Terrence.

Reassessment

1. Use a similar problem at the same level of difficulty.

   This line plot shows the results of rolling a number cube with the numbers 1 through 6 on its faces. Which tally chart matches the data in the line plot?

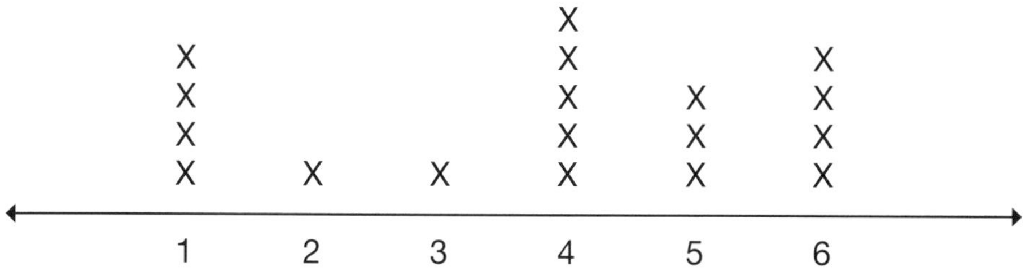

A.

1	2	3	4	5	6
IIII	I	I	𝍸	IIII	III

B.

1	2	3	4	5	6
𝍸	IIII	IIII	III	I	I

C.

1	2	3	4	5	6
IIII	I	I	𝍸	III	IIII

D.

1	2	3	4	5	6
III	II	III	III	II	III

Show how you know.

2. Choose a problem that is similar but slightly more challenging.

This tally chart shows the results of rolling a number cube with the numbers 1 through 6 on its faces. Which line plot matches the data in the tally chart?

1	2	3	4	5	6
IIII	III	𝍸	IIII	II	𝍸 I

A.

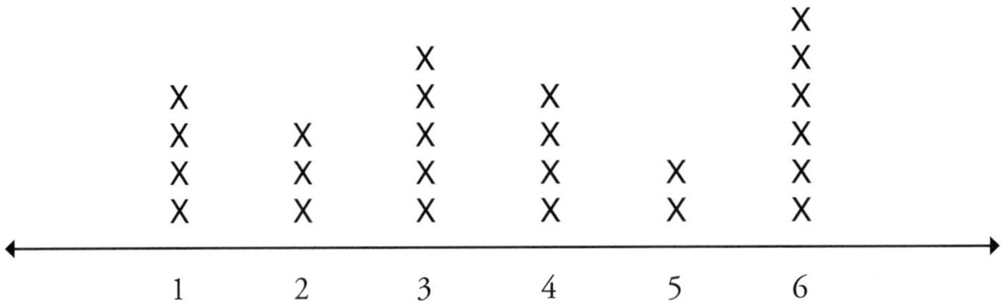

B.

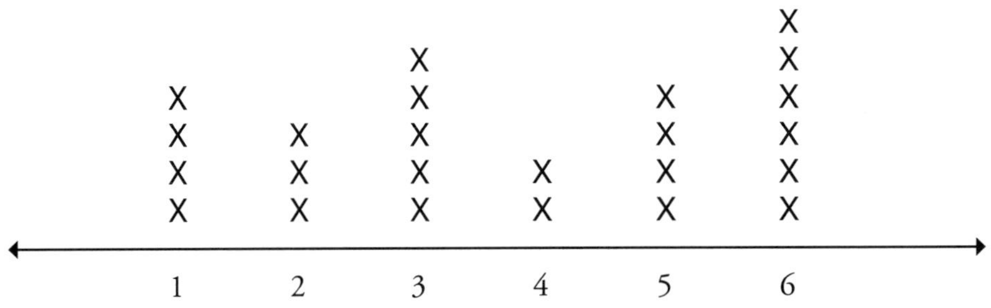

C.

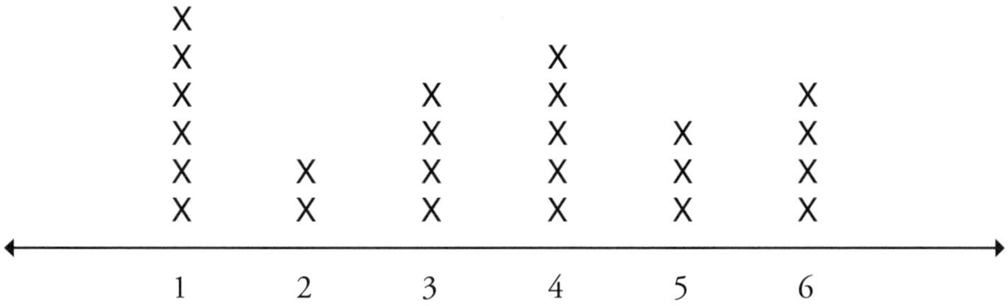

D.

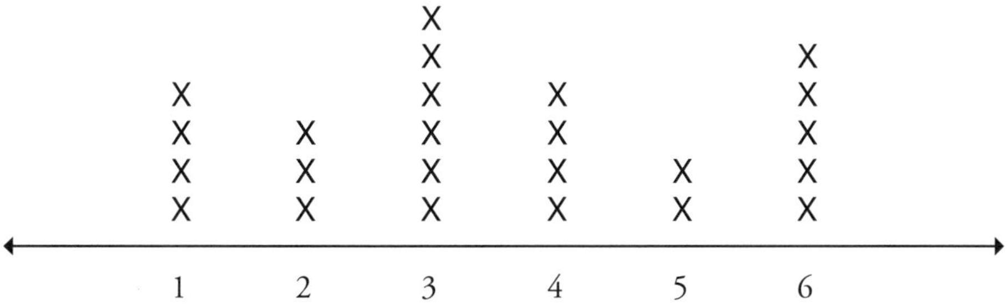

Show how you know.

PROBLEM FIVE

Overview

This question is similar to those found on many multiple-choice tests. The intent is to test the student's knowledge of chance. The big idea is that the more items of a particular type there are in a collection of items, the greater chance that type has of being selected in a blind draw. The inverse is also true: the fewer items of a certain type there are in the collection, the less likely an item of that type is to be randomly selected. Students who misunderstand this problem often do not relate to concepts of chance and instead answer the problem according to personal color preference or location of the gumball within the machine.

Sample Problem

There are 14 gumballs in a gumball machine. There are 1 red, 7 yellow, 2 green, and 4 blue gumballs. Is it certain, likely, unlikely, or impossible that the red gumball will come out of the machine next?

A. certain
B. likely
C. unlikely
D. impossible

Show how you know.

Possible Student Solution Strategies

- Students correctly apply ideas related to chance.
- Students determine the likelihood of an event based on location rather than the number of certain objects in a collection.

Conversation Starters

- Why do you think your answer is reasonable?
- What would happen if there were five reds instead of only one?
- How could you change this problem to make the likelihood of getting a red gumball impossible?
- Could you get a purple gumball? Explain.
- What would be in the gumball machine if it were certain you would get a blue gumball? Explain.

Student Work Sample: Juanita

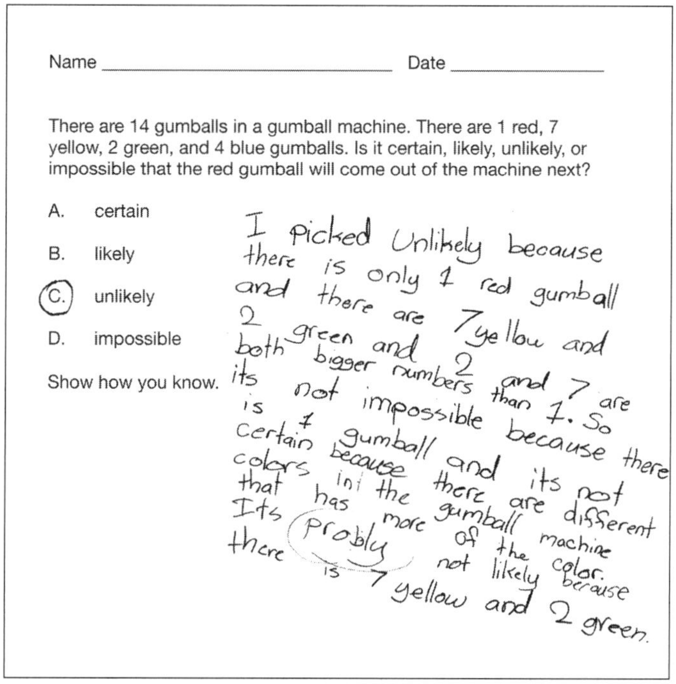
Name ______________________ Date ____________

There are 14 gumballs in a gumball machine. There are 1 red, 7 yellow, 2 green, and 4 blue gumballs. Is it certain, likely, unlikely, or impossible that the red gumball will come out of the machine next?

A. certain

B. likely

(C.) unlikely

D. impossible

Show how you know.

I picked Unlikely because there is only 1 red gumball and there are 7 yellow and 2 green and 2 and 7 are both bigger numbers then 1. So its not impossible because there is 1 gumball and its not certain because there are different colors in the gumball machine. Its Probly not likely because there is 7 yellow and 2 green.

A Conversation with Juanita	Teacher Insights
T: Your explanation is very complete and clear. It helps me to know that you understand this problem and how to solve it. How could you change this problem so that it would be impossible to get a red gumball? **Juanita:** That's easy. All you would have to do is take out the red gumball. If there is no red gumball, how can you possibly get a red? It's impossible. No red, no possibility! **T:** What would have to be in the gumball machine to make it certain to get a blue gumball? **Juanita:** There would have to be all blue gumballs, nothing else. Then it would be certain.	**T:** *Juanita has a clear understanding of the skills being assessed by this question. She was also able to extend her understanding to solve different but related problems during our conversation.*

Informed Instructional Suggestions

Since Juanita was able to clearly articulate her understanding, she is ready for a new challenge that would provide her the opportunity to apply her understanding. An appropriate task for Juanita would be to create a game that involves the ideas of chance. Outcomes should include some that are certain, likely, unlikely, and impossible. Juanita should be able to identify and explain the outcomes according to these ideas.

Student Work Sample: Marlee

Name ______________________ Date ____________

There are 14 gumballs in a gumball machine. There are 1 red, 7 yellow, 2 green, and 4 blue gumballs. Is it certain, likely, unlikely, or impossible that the red gumball will come out of the machine next?

A. certain

B. likely

(C.) unlikely

D. impossible

Show how you know.

because you can't pick from a machine so it is unlikely.

A Conversation with Marlee	Teacher Insights
T: Tell me more about why you think your answer is reasonable. **Marlee:** Everyone knows that when a machine chooses for you, you have no choice. My favorite color is red and I know the machine probably won't give me my favorite color, so it's unlikely that I'll get a red gumball. Machines never give you what you want.	**T:** *The reality is that a red gumball is unlikely to come out of the machine because there is only one red gumball out of the fourteen gumballs. Marlee seemed to think that machines and her favorite color of gumballs would determine the likelihood of getting a red gumball rather than the principles of chance.*

Informed Instructional Suggestions

Marlee needs many opportunities to explore ideas of chance using a variety of materials—such as spinners, dice, and two-color counters—to help her begin to make sense of outcomes that are certain, likely, unlikely, and impossible.

Student Work Sample: Derek

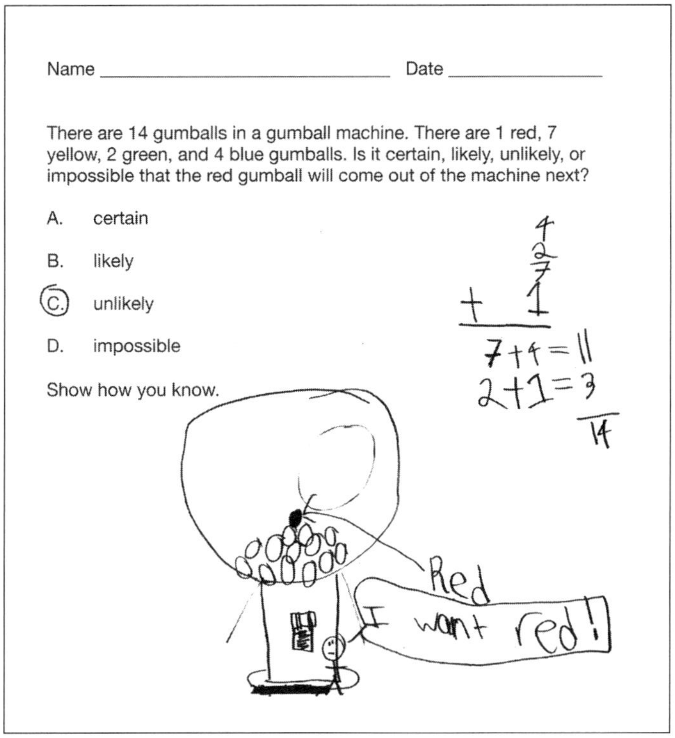

Name ______________________ Date ____________

There are 14 gumballs in a gumball machine. There are 1 red, 7 yellow, 2 green, and 4 blue gumballs. Is it certain, likely, unlikely, or impossible that the red gumball will come out of the machine next?

A. certain

B. likely

(C.) unlikely

D. impossible

Show how you know.

A Conversation with Derek	Teacher Insights
T: I see you did some computation. Tell me how this helped you solve this problem. **Derek:** I saw all the numbers and I added them to be sure they added up to fourteen. They did. After I added the numbers, I drew a picture. Red is on top. I want red. That's me in the picture saying, "I want red!" But there is only one red and it's on top. Oh no! I probably won't get it because it is on top, so I marked choice C, unlikely. Too bad for me, huh? **T:** If we took all the gumballs out of the machine and put them in a paper bag and you took one out without looking, would it still be unlikely that you would get red? **Derek:** I'm not too sure. Maybe it would still be unlikely because there aren't too many reds, maybe not.	**T:** *Derek chose the correct answer, but his thinking, while it did make sense, did not reflect the thinking the test makers had intended to assess. The red gumball at the top of the machine is less likely to come out than one at the bottom; however, this idea is based on location rather than probability. His final verbal response indicated a glimmer of emerging understanding.*

Informed Instructional Suggestions

Derek and Marlee have similar needs, so the suggestions we made for Marlee would also be appropriate for Derek. It would benefit both students if they worked together.

Student Work Sample: Amy

Name ______________________ Date ____________

There are 14 gumballs in a gumball machine. There are 1 red, 7 yellow, 2 green, and 4 blue gumballs. Is it certain, likely, unlikely, or impossible that the red gumball will come out of the machine next?

A. certain

(B) likely — Likely because there are more yellows than any other coler.

C. unlikely

D. impossible

Show how you know.

R= Red
Y= yellow
G= Green
B= blue

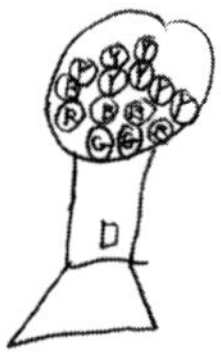

A Conversation with Amy	Teacher Insights
T: Amy, please reread this problem and then tell me what you think it is asking you to do. **Amy:** [After reading the problem] Oh no! I did it again. I didn't read carefully. I thought they wanted to know which would be most likely. Yellow would be because there are the most. It's not certain because there are other colors, but mostly there are yellow. The right answer is really choice C. There is only one red out of fourteen. That's not very likely, but it is possible!	**T:** *Amy understands the concept being tested but misread the problem. After rereading the problem, Amy was able to show clear understanding through a verbal explanation.*

Informed Instructional Suggestions

Although Amy marked an incorrect answer, she has strong understanding, as indicated by her verbal explanation. Her multiple-choice answer by itself would have implied she needed reteaching, which would not have benefited Amy or been a good use of valuable instructional time. Instead, Amy would benefit from the same types of activities we suggested for Juanita. She would also benefit from practice with reading questions carefully and determining what they are asking her to do.

Student Work Sample: Conrad

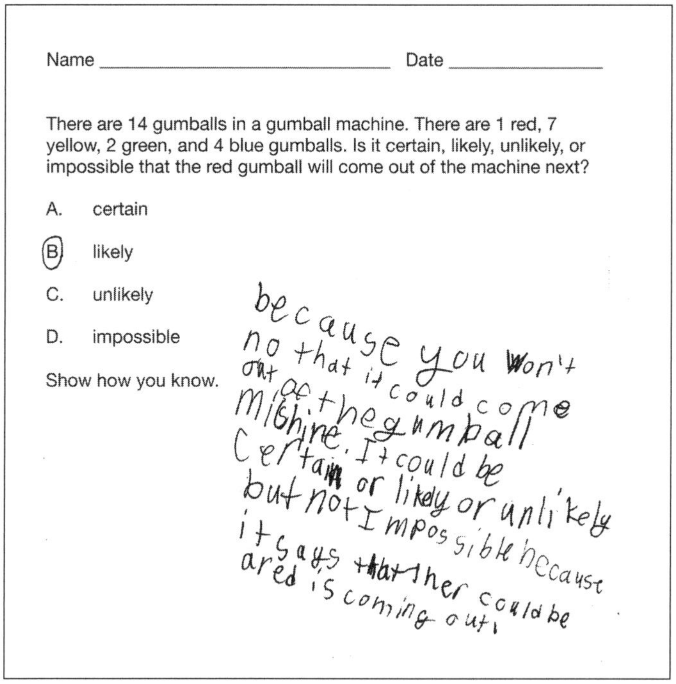
Name ______________________ Date ____________

There are 14 gumballs in a gumball machine. There are 1 red, 7 yellow, 2 green, and 4 blue gumballs. Is it certain, likely, unlikely, or impossible that the red gumball will come out of the machine next?

A. certain

(B.) likely

C. unlikely

D. impossible

Show how you know.

because you won't no that it could come out of the gumball mishine. It could be certain or likely or unlikely but not Impossible because it says that ther could be a red is coming out.

A Conversation with Conrad	Teacher Insights
T: Why do you think it is likely for the red gumball to come out of the machine? **Conrad:** Because there is one in the machine, so it could happen. **T:** Would it be possible for a purple gumball to come out of the machine? **Conrad:** Nope; there isn't one in there, so one can't come out. Won't happen! **T:** Which color gumball do you think would be most likely? **Conrad:** It could be yellow, green, red, or blue. You can't tell until it happens.	**T:** Conrad has little understanding of likelihood. He understands when something is impossible but doesn't seem to differentiate between certain, likely, and unlikely.

Informed Instructional Suggestions

Like Marlee, Conrad needs opportunities to develop his understanding of likelihood. The same activities that will help Marlee will also help Conrad.

Student Work Sample: Carter

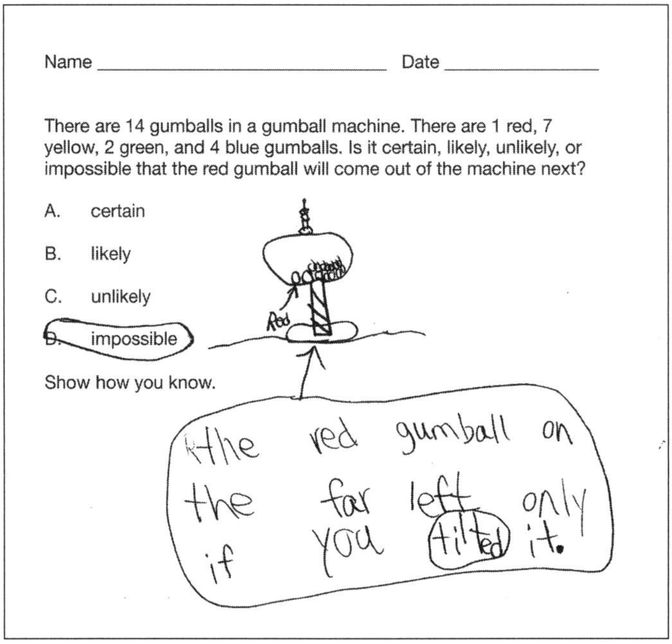
Name ____________________ Date ____________

There are 14 gumballs in a gumball machine. There are 1 red, 7 yellow, 2 green, and 4 blue gumballs. Is it certain, likely, unlikely, or impossible that the red gumball will come out of the machine next?

A. certain

B. likely

C. unlikely

D. impossible

Show how you know.

Red
the red gumball on the far left only if you tilted it.

A Conversation with Carter	Teacher Insights
T: Why do you think red is impossible? **Carter:** Because you will have to tilt the machine to get the red and everybody knows you can't tilt a real gumball machine so how could you get the red? It's impossible.	**T:** *Carter did not apply ideas of likelihood to this situation. His thinking was similar to Derek's, and while it made a degree of sense, there was no indication of understanding of probability.*

Informed Instructional Suggestions

Carter needs experiences with sampling and recording outcomes and conversations with other students that focus on the ideas of likelihood such as certain, likely, unlikely, and impossible.

Reassessment

1. Use a similar problem at the same level of difficulty.

   There are 17 teddy bear counters in a brown paper bag. There are 3 red teddy bears, 5 yellow teddy bears, 1 green teddy bear, and 8 blue teddy bears. If Jason picked a teddy bear counter out of the bag without looking, is it certain, likely, unlikely, or impossible that it would be a green teddy bear?

A. certain
B. likely
C. unlikely
D. impossible

Show how you know.

2. Choose a problem that is similar but slightly more challenging.

There are 16 jelly beans in a box. Which combination would give you the least likely chance of drawing a black jelly bean if you picked one without looking?

A. 3 red, 8 black, 1 green, 4 yellow
B. 2 red, 2 black, 6 green, 6 yellow,
C. 7 red, 1 black, 4 green, 4 yellow
D. 4 red, 4 black, 4 green, 4 yellow

Show how you know.

PROBLEM SIX

Overview

Mean, median, mode, and range are all ideas used to explain and summarize statistical data. They permeate our daily lives and it is important for students to be wise about how such statistics are reported and how to interpret them. The following question asks students to determine the range of some real-world information.

Sample Problem

Mrs. Parker's class recorded the temperature each day for one week. What was the range in temperature between the highest and lowest temperatures?

Sunday: 60
Monday: 65
Tuesday: 73
Wednesday: 62
Thursday: 75
Friday: 64
Saturday: 70

A. 20
B. 15
C. 62
D. 70

Show how you know.

Possible Student Solution Strategies

- Students find the highest and the lowest temperatures and find the difference between the two to determine the range of temperatures.
- Students select a temperature that is somewhere in the middle of the range of temperatures.

Conversation Starters

- What did you do first?
- What do you think *range* means?
- What did you do to figure the range?
- Why does your answer make sense?

Student Work Sample: JoLissa

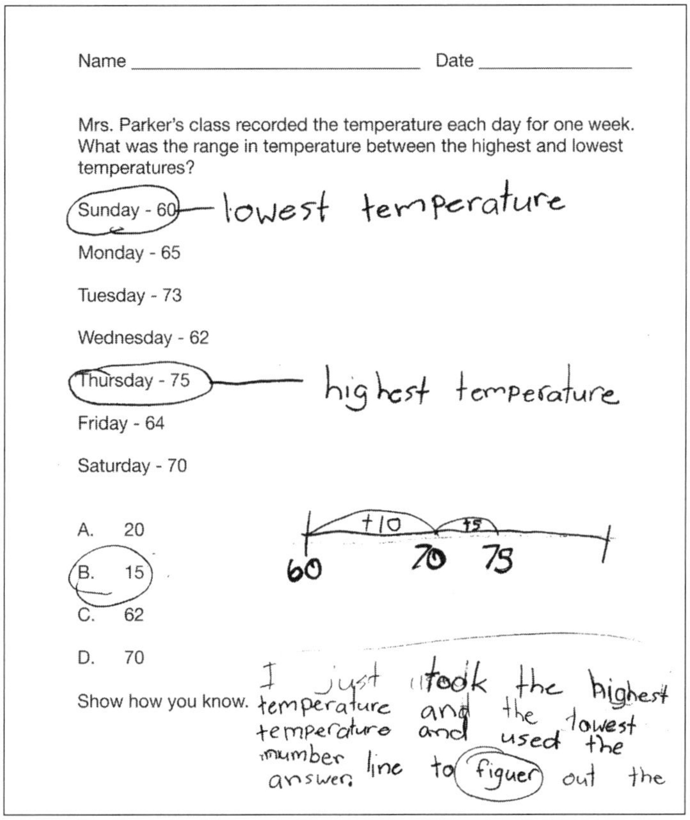

Name ______________________ Date ______________

Mrs. Parker's class recorded the temperature each day for one week. What was the range in temperature between the highest and lowest temperatures?

Sunday - 60 — lowest temperature

Monday - 65

Tuesday - 73

Wednesday - 62

Thursday - 75 — highest temperature

Friday - 64

Saturday - 70

A. 20

B. 15

C. 62

D. 70

Show how you know. I just took the highest temperature and the lowest temperature and used the number line to figuer out the answer.

A Conversation with JoLissa	Teacher Insights
T: What did you do first? **JoLissa:** Well, I looked at all the temperatures. I found the lowest one and circled it; then I found the highest one and circled that one. **T:** Why did you do that? **JoLissa:** Because the range is how much is between the lowest and highest. Then I figured out the difference by counting up from sixty to seventy-five. I showed it on the number line. The difference is fifteen.	**T:** *JoLissa indicated a clear understanding of the meaning of* range *and had an effective strategy for how to find it.*

Informed Instructional Suggestions

JoLissa showed an understanding of range and applied it appropriately to this problem. She is ready for a challenge, such as a similar problem with larger numbers.

Student Work Sample: Madeline

Name ______________________ Date ____________

Mrs. Parker's class recorded the temperature each day for one week. What was the range in temperature between the highest and lowest temperatures?

Sunday - 60

Monday - 65

Tuesday - 73

Wednesday - 62

Thursday - 75

Friday - 64

Saturday - 70

A. 20

(B) 15

C. 62

D. 70

I couted up to 15

Show how you know.

A Conversation with Madeline	Teacher Insights
T: What do you think *range* means? **Madeline:** I am not really sure. I just counted fifteen. **T:** How did you count fifteen? **Madeline:** Um, I don't know, I just did.	**T:** *Madeline did mark the correct answer, but neither her written nor her verbal explanation indicated knowledge of what range is or how to find it. Madeline needs additional experiences to build this understanding.*

Informed Instructional Suggestions

Madeline was not able to explain why she chose the answer she did. Madeline needs many hands-on experiences to develop her understanding of range, such as gathering data for a group of students of the number of tally marks each can draw in a minute. She also needs opportunities to explain her thinking whenever possible.

Student Work Sample: Joselle

Name ______________________ Date ____________

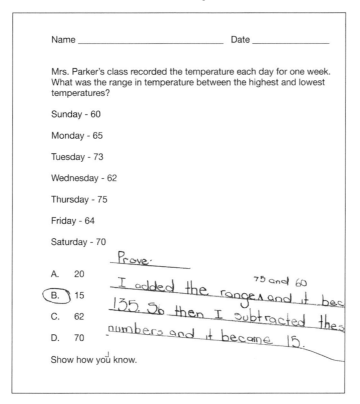

Mrs. Parker's class recorded the temperature each day for one week. What was the range in temperature between the highest and lowest temperatures?

Sunday - 60

Monday - 65

Tuesday - 73

Wednesday - 62

Thursday - 75

Friday - 64

Saturday - 70

A. 20

(B.) 15

C. 62

D. 70

Show how you know.

Prove:

I added the range (75 and 60) and it bec 135. So then I subtracted thes numbers and it became 15.

A Conversation with Joselle

T: What do you think *range* means?

Joselle: Well, it has something to do with the highest and the lowest. The highest number was 75 and the lowest was 60. I added them together to get 135, but that wasn't a choice. So I decided to subtract 60 from 75. The answer is 15 and that was a choice, so it must be the right answer.

T: Why don't you think 62 is the right answer?

Joselle: Well, um . . . it isn't the highest and it isn't the lowest; it's in the middle.

T: If 15 is the correct answer, what does that tell you about the range?

Joselle: Maybe that it's the difference between the highest and lowest?

Teacher Insights

T: *Joselle marked the correct answer, but she had only partial understanding about the meaning of* range. *She knew it had something to do with highest and lowest, but didn't know if it was the sum or the difference of the two. She figured the answer based on the answer choices and her partial understanding. Even after I talked with Joselle and presented her with leading questions, she was still not entirely certain.*

Informed Instructional Suggestions

Joselle has memorized many procedures and facts out of context. Often she is not sure how to apply them or when to apply them. In this case, she tried both addition and subtraction and selected the answer choice that matched one of the answers she figured. Joselle needs additional experiences to help her clarify what *range* means and how to find it.

Student Work Sample: Suki

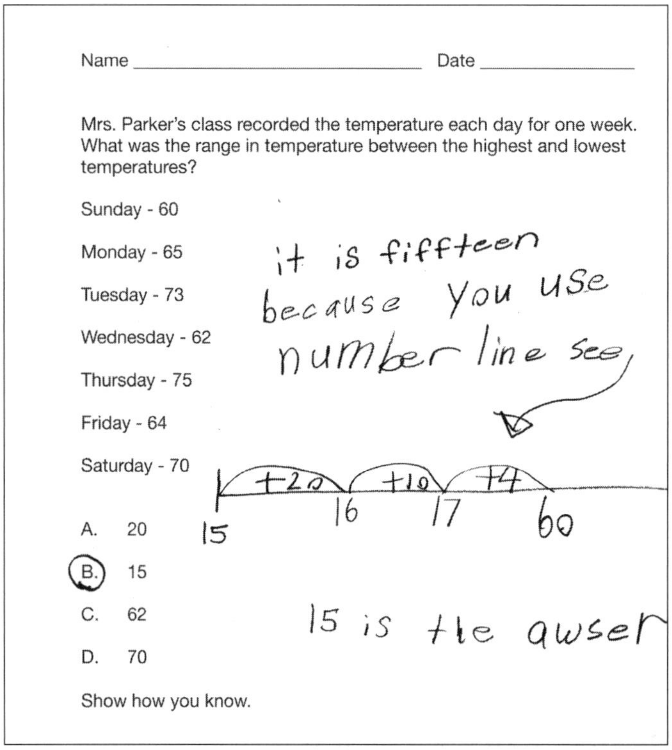

Name ______________________ Date ____________

Mrs. Parker's class recorded the temperature each day for one week. What was the range in temperature between the highest and lowest temperatures?

Sunday - 60

Monday - 65

Tuesday - 73

Wednesday - 62

Thursday - 75

Friday - 64

Saturday - 70

A. 20

(B.) 15

C. 62

D. 70

Show how you know.

A Conversation with Suki	Teacher Insights
T: I see you marked choice B. What do think *range* is? **Suki:** I don't really know. **T:** How did you figure the answer of 15? **Suki:** I used a number line. **T:** How did a number line help you? **Suki:** Um . . . I started with 15 and did some jumps and stopped at 60. Oh, I don't really know.	**T:** *Suki marked the correct answer but did not understand what range is or how to figure it. Her number line made no sense, nor was it clear why she started with 15 or made the jumps she did on the number line.*

Informed Instructional Suggestions

Suki needs many more experiences and opportunities to think about and discuss what range is and how to figure it. She also needs opportunities to make sense of number lines.

Student Work Sample: Janae

Name ______________________ Date ____________

Mrs. Parker's class recorded the temperature each day for one week. What was the range in temperature between the highest and lowest temperatures?

Sunday - 60

Monday - 65

Tuesday - 73

Wednesday - 62

Thursday - 75

Friday - 64

Saturday - 70

A. 20

B. 15

(C.) 62

D. 70

Show how you know.

I think it is ancer C. becaus in reall life it's warm like 80 degreece is hot.

A Conversation with Janae	Teacher Insights
T: Why does your answer of 62 make sense? **Janae:** Because like I said, mostly in real life, the temperature is like 62. It's not usually 15 or 20. I think maybe it could be 70, but I'm not sure. **T:** What do you think *range* means? **Janae:** Range is probably what usually happens, I think.	**T:** *Janae marked the incorrect answer and clearly has no understanding of range. To Janae's credit, she did try to make sense of the question by relating it to her real-life experiences.*

Informed Instructional Suggestions

Like Suki, Joselle, and Madeline, Janae needs opportunities to make sense of what range is and how to find it.

Reassessment

1. Use a similar problem at the same level of difficulty.

   Seven friends were jumping rope. Following is the number of jumps each made. What is the range of the number of jumps they made?

   Jesus: 48
   Dominique: 68
   Frances: 13
   Tommy: 25
   Jessie: 37
   Betty: 42
   Miranda: 65

   A. 20 jumps
   B. 5 jumps
   C. 52 jumps
   D. 55 jumps

   Show how you know.

2. Choose a problem that is similar but slightly more challenging. (Note: In the following problem, the magnitude of the numbers increases the complexity.)

   Students in Mr. Gomez's class each took a handful of beans and counted them. What is the range of the number of beans in their handfuls?

   Tenisha: 86
   Simon: 113
   Jazmin: 101
   Bobby: 56
   Tami: 74
   Maria: 120
   Randolf: 66

   A. 64
   B. 76
   C. 54
   D. 57

   Show how you know.

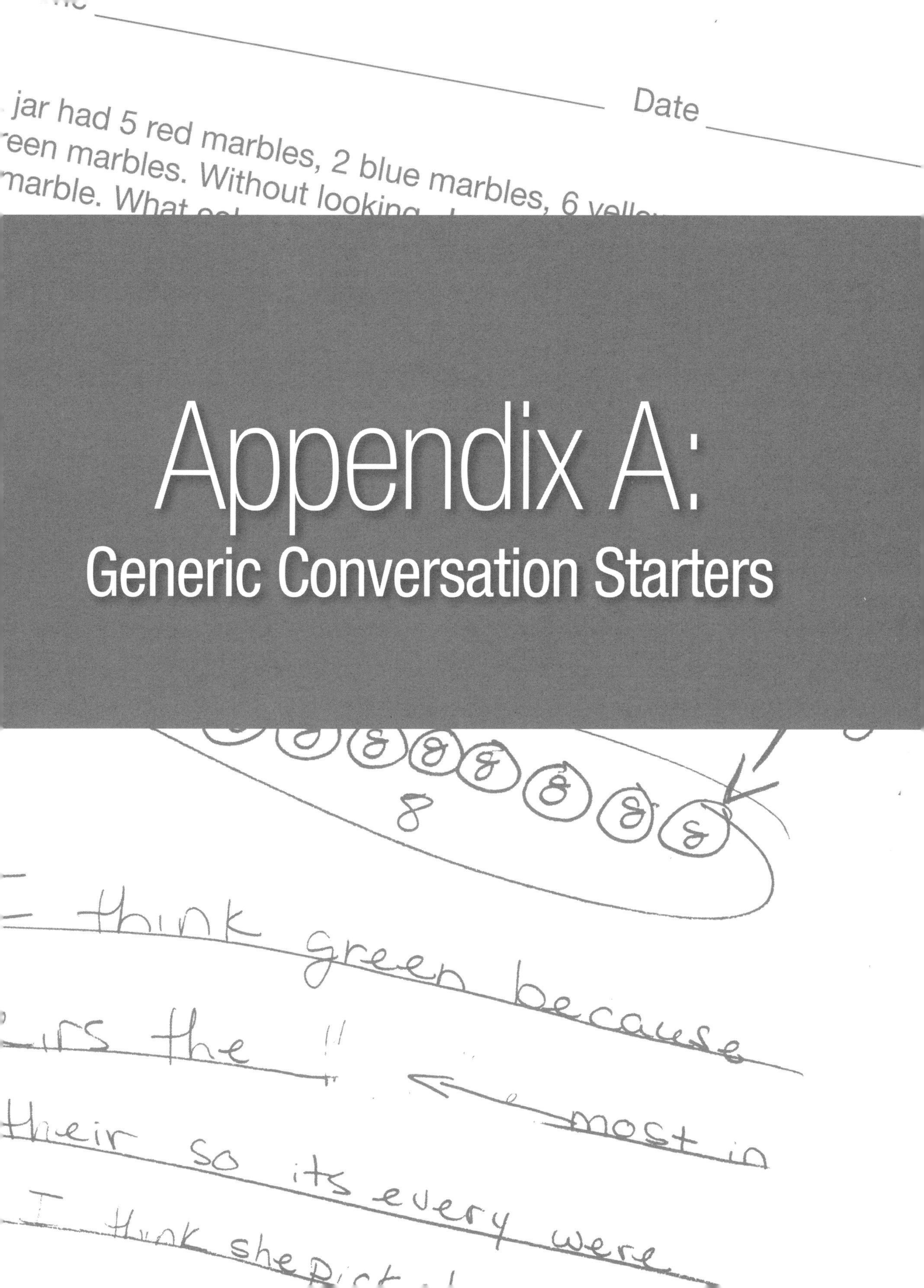

Appendix A:
Generic Conversation Starters

Generic Conversation Starters

- Restate the problem in your own words.
- How is this problem like others you've done before?
- What do you know about this problem? What do you need to find out?
- How would you use manipulatives or pictures to help you solve this problem?
- How could a table, chart, or diagram help you solve this problem?
- Why does your solution [or answer] make sense?
- How did you reach your answer?
- What have you seen before that looks like this?
- How would an estimate help you decide if your answer makes sense?
- Is there more than one possible correct answer? Explain.
- Is there more than one way to solve this problem? Show it.
- How do you know your answer is reasonable?
- Does your strategy always work? How do you know?
- How can you prove your answer?
- What did you do to check your answer?
- How can you solve this problem in another way?
- Do you see a pattern that can help you solve this problem? Describe it.
- How did you think about this problem?
- Does anyone have a different answer or way to solve the problem?
- What is alike and what is different about your solution and those of others?
- Convince me that your idea makes sense.
- How could you explain your thinking to younger students?

Appendix B:
Reproducible Problems

Number: Problem One

Name ______________________________ Date ________________

If you are counting by tens to make this pattern, what is the next number in the pattern?

71, 81, 91, _______

A. 110

B. 111

C. 101

D. 121

Show how you know.

Number: Problem Two

Name ______________________________ Date ________________

Which of the following is closest to 15 + 18?

A. 40

B. 30

C. 20

D. 50

Show how you know.

Number: Problem Three

Name ______________________________ Date ________________

Last weekend a gas station sold 2,487 gallons of gas on Saturday and 935 gallons of gas on Sunday. What was the total number of gallons of gas sold over the weekend?

A. 2,312

B. 1,552

C. 11,837

D. 3,422

Show how you know.

Number: Problem Four

Name ______________________________ Date _______________

Stacey bought 8 flats of eggs. Each flat held 36 eggs. What was the total number of eggs she bought?

A. 44

B. 2,448

C. 288

D. 248

Show how you know.

Number: Problem Five

Name ______________________________ Date ________________

Which of the following is another way to write 100?

A. 45 + 65 =

B. 63 + 38 =

C. 72 + 28 =

D. 84 + 26 =

Show how you know.

Number: Problem Six

Name ______________________________ Date ________________

Which set of numbers is in order from greatest to least?

A. 148, 164, 235, 276

B. 276, 235, 164, 148

C. 276, 164, 235, 148

D. 164, 276, 235, 148

Show how you know.

Measurement: Problem One

Name ______________________________ Date ________________

One afternoon Ellen set up a lemonade stand. She sold 6 quarts of lemonade. How many cups did she sell? (1 quart = 4 cups)

A. 10 cups

B. 12 cups

C. 24 cups

D. 6 cups

Show how you know.

Measurement: Problem Two

Name ______________________________ Date ________________

The figure below has a perimeter of 15 centimeters. What is the missing measurement?

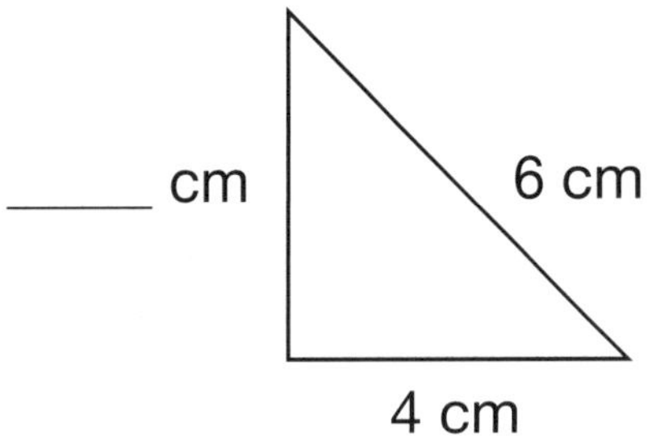

A. 4 centimeters

B. 5 centimeters

C. 6 centimeters

D. 8 centimeters

Show how you know.

Measurement: Problem Three

Name ______________________________ Date ________________

What is the *best* estimate of the area of this figure?

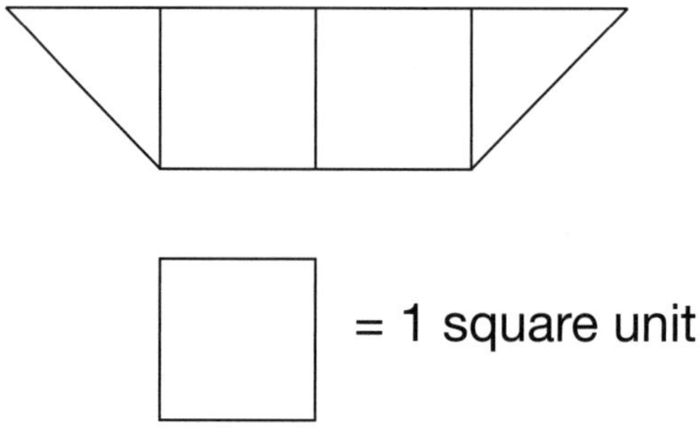

A. 2 square units

B. 3 square units

C. 4 square units

D. 5 square units

Show how you know.

Measurement: Problem Four

Name ______________________________ Date ________________

A skate ramp is 60 meters long. Which of these measurements is the same as 60 meters?

A. 6 millimeters

B. 600 kilometers

C. 6 centimeters

D. 6000 centimeters

Show how you know.

Measurement: Problem Five

Name ________________________________ Date _________________

A desk is 26 inches wide. Which of these best describes the width in feet?

A. less than 1 foot

B. between 1 foot and 2 feet

C. between 2 feet and 3 feet

D. more than 3 feet

Show how you know.

Measurement: Problem Six

Name ______________________________ Date ________________

Sam's bedroom has a perimeter of 64 feet.

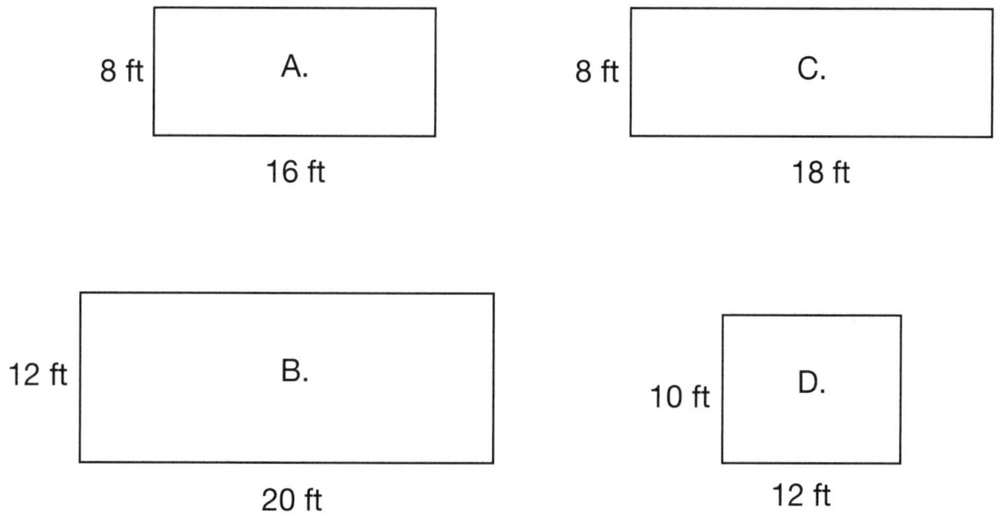

Which rectangle above could represent a room with a perimeter of 64 feet? Circle your answer below.

A. rectangle A

B. rectangle B

C. rectangle C

D. rectangle D

Show how you know.

Algebra: Problem One

Name ______________________________ Date ________________

What number goes in the box to make this number sentence true?

$$13 + 7 = \square + 13$$

A. 13

B. 6

C. 7

D. 20

Show how you know.

Algebra: Problem Two

Name ______________________________ Date ________________

What number goes in the box to make this number sentence true?

$$16 + \square = 30$$

A. 14

B. 4

C. 46

D. 24

Show how you know.

Algebra: Problem Three

Name ______________________________ Date ________________

Angelo had 20 pennies. He found some more. Now he has 43. Which numbe sentence could be used to figure out how many pennies he found?

A. $20 + \square = 43$

B. $20 + 43 = \square$

C. $\square - 43 = 20$

D. $\square - 20 = 43$

Show how you know.

Algebra: Problem Four

Name ______________________________ Date ________________

Which of the following could be used to find out how many inches are in 4 feet?

A. 4×12

B. $12 \div 4$

C. $4 + 12$

D. $12 - 4$

Show how you know.

Algebra: Problem Five

Name ______________________________ Date ________________

What number could go in the blank to make this number sentence true?

$$8 \times 6 < 3 \times \_\_\_$$

A. 17

B. 16

C. 11

D. 14

Show how you know.

Algebra: Problem Six

Name ______________________________ Date ________________

If 8 x 11 x 12 = 1,056, then what is 11 x 8 x 12?

A. 88

B. 100

C. 132

D. 1,056

Show how you know.

Geometry: Problem One

Name ______________________________ Date ________________

Which two shapes can be put together to make a square?

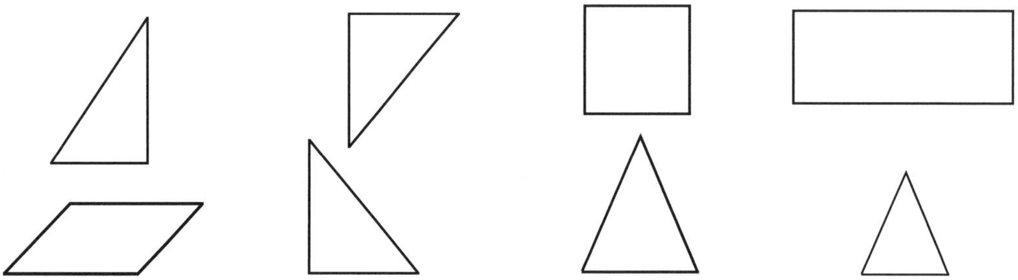

A. B. C. D.

Show how you know.

Geometry: Problem Two

Name ________________________________ Date ________________

Which figure has exactly six faces?

A. 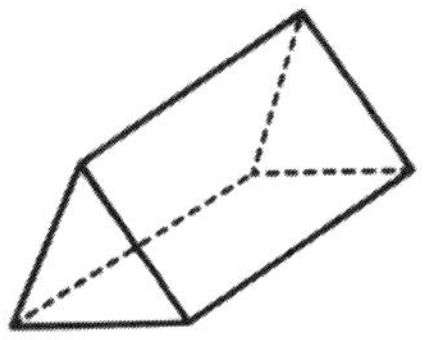

B. 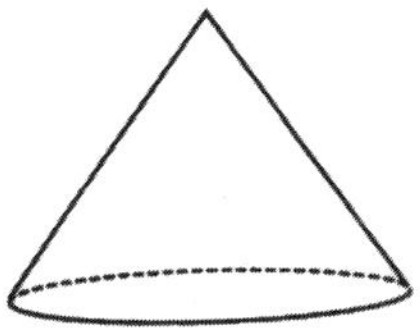

C. 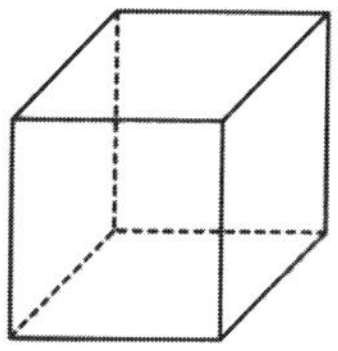

D. 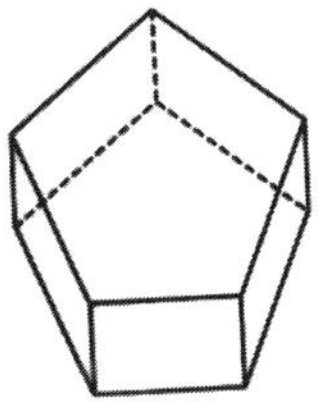

Show how you know.

Geometry: Problem Three

Name ________________________________ Date _________________

Which of these is a true statement about an equilateral triangle?

A. It has no equal sides and no equal angles.

B. It has 2 equal sides and 2 equal angles.

C. It has 4 equal sides and 4 equal angles.

D. It has 3 equal sides and 3 equal angles.

Show how you know.

Geometry: Problem Four

Name ______________________________ Date ________________

Stacy made this wooden shape. What two common figures make up this solid shape?

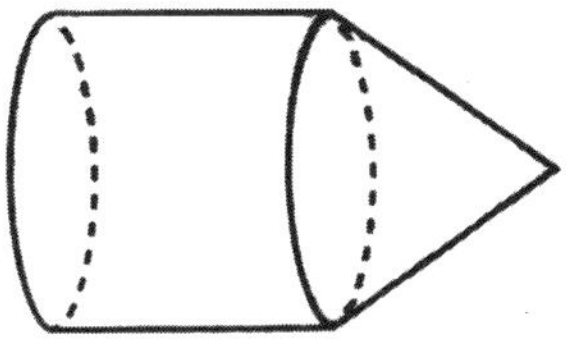

A. sphere and triangular prism

B. cylinder and cube

C. cone and cylinder

D. pyramid and cone

Show how you know.

Geometry: Problem Five

Name ______________________________ Date ________________

Look at the four angles marked on the picture below. Which numbered angle measures *less* than a right angle?

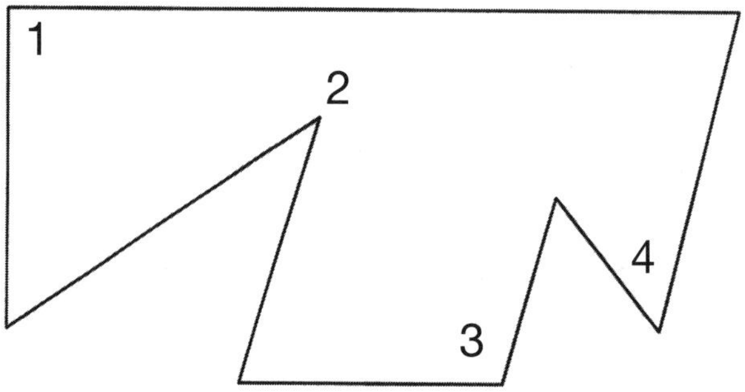

A. angle 1

B. angle 2

C. angle 3

D. angle 4

Show how you know.

Geometry: Problem Six

Name ______________________________ Date ________________

How many faces does a cube have?

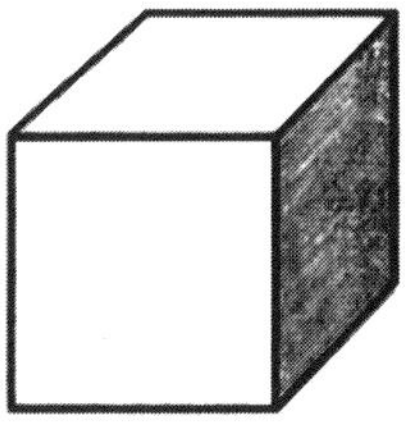

A. 4

B. 6

C. 12

D. 8

Show how you know.

Probability: Problem One

Name ______________________________ Date ________________

A jar had 5 red marbles, 2 blue marbles, 6 yellow marbles, and 8 green marbles. Without looking, Juan reached into the jar and picked 1 marble. What color did he *most* likely pick?

A. blue

B. green

C. yellow

D. red

Show how you know.

Probability: Problem Two

Name ______________________________ Date ________________

Yasmine is tossing a cube with the numbers 2, 4, 6, 8, 10, and 12 on the faces. When the cube lands, is it certain, likely, unlikely, or impossible that the face on the top of the cube will show the number 1?

A. certain

B. likely

C. unlikely

D. impossible

Show how you know.

Probability: Problem Three

Name ______________________________ Date ________________

Sasha tossed a dime 20 times. It landed on heads 9 times and on tails 11 times. Which tally chart shows these results?

A.

heads	tails
𝍸 𝍸	𝍸 𝍸 𝍷

B.

heads	tails
𝍸 𝍷𝍷𝍷𝍷	𝍸 𝍸

C.

heads	tails
𝍸 𝍷𝍷𝍷𝍷	𝍸 𝍸 𝍷

D.

heads	tails
𝍸 𝍷𝍷𝍷	𝍸 𝍸 𝍷

Show how you know.

Probability: Problem Four

Name ______________________________ Date ________________

This line plot shows the results of rolling a number cube with the numbers 1 through 6 on its faces. Which tally chart matches the data in the line plot?

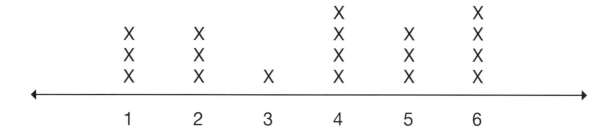

<table>
<tr><td></td><td></td><td></td><td>X</td><td></td><td>X</td></tr>
<tr><td>X</td><td>X</td><td></td><td>X</td><td>X</td><td>X</td></tr>
<tr><td>X</td><td>X</td><td></td><td>X</td><td>X</td><td>X</td></tr>
<tr><td>X</td><td>X</td><td>X</td><td>X</td><td>X</td><td>X</td></tr>
<tr><td>1</td><td>2</td><td>3</td><td>4</td><td>5</td><td>6</td></tr>
</table>

A.

<table>
<tr><td>1</td><td>2</td><td>3</td><td>4</td><td>5</td><td>6</td></tr>
<tr><td>||</td><td>||</td><td></td><td>||||</td><td>||</td><td>|||</td></tr>
</table>

B.

<table>
<tr><td>1</td><td>2</td><td>3</td><td>4</td><td>5</td><td>6</td></tr>
<tr><td>||</td><td>||</td><td></td><td>|||</td><td>||</td><td>|||</td></tr>
</table>

C.

<table>
<tr><td>1</td><td>2</td><td>3</td><td>4</td><td>5</td><td>6</td></tr>
<tr><td>|||</td><td>||</td><td>|</td><td>|||</td><td>||</td><td>||</td></tr>
</table>

D.

<table>
<tr><td>1</td><td>2</td><td>3</td><td>4</td><td>5</td><td>6</td></tr>
<tr><td>|||</td><td>|||</td><td>|</td><td>||||</td><td>|||</td><td>||||</td></tr>
</table>

Show how you know.

Probability: Problem Five

Name ______________________________ Date ________________

There are 14 gumballs in a gumball machine. There are 1 red, 7 yellow, 2 green, and 4 blue gumballs. Is it certain, likely, unlikely, or impossible that the red gumball will come out of the machine next?

A. certain

B. likely

C. unlikely

D. impossible

Show how you know.

Probability: Problem Six

Name ______________________________ Date ________________

Mrs. Parker's class recorded the temperature each day for one week. What was the range in temperature between the highest and lowest temperatures?

Sunday - 60

Monday - 65

Tuesday - 73

Wednesday - 62

Thursday - 75

Friday - 64

Saturday - 70

A. 20

B. 15

C. 62

D. 70

Show how you know.

General Resources

Baratta-Lorton, Mary. 1994. *Mathematics Their Way.* Rev. ed. Menlo Park, CA: Addison-Wesley Longman.

Battista, Michael T., and Douglas H. Clements. 1995. *Exploring Solids and Boxes: 3-D Geometry.* Investigations in Number, Data, and Space. Palo Alto, CA: Dale Seymour.

Burns, Marilyn. 2008. *Do the Math.* New York: Scholastic.

Burns, Marilyn, and Leyani von Rotz. 2002. *Lessons for Algebraic Thinking, Grades K–2.* Sausalito, CA: Math Solutions.

Carpenter, Thomas P., Megan Loef Franke, and Linda Levi. 2003. *Thinking Mathematically: Integrating Arithmetic and Algebra in Elementary School.* Portsmouth, NH: Heinemann.

Chapin, Suzanne H., Catherine O'Connor, and Nancy Canavan Anderson. 2009. *Classroom Discussions: Using Math Talk to Help Students Learn, Grades K–6.* 2nd ed. Sausalito, CA: Math Solutions.

Clements, Doug, Cornelia Tierney, Megan Murray, Joan Akers, and Julie Samara. 2004. *Picturing Polygons: 2-D Geometry.* Investigations in Number, Data, and Space. Glenville, IL: Scott Foresman.

Common Core Standards. 2010. www.corestandards.org.

Confer, Chris. 1994. *Math By All Means: Geometry, Grades 1–2.* Sausalito, CA: Math Solutions.

———. 2007. *Sizing Up Measurement: Activities for Grades 3–5 Classrooms.* Sausalito, CA: Math Solutions.

Cuevas, Gilbert J., and Karol L. Yeatts. 2001. *Navigating Through Algebra in Grades 3–5.* Principles and Standards for School Mathematics Navigations. Reston, VA: National Council of Teachers of Mathematics.

Dacey, Linda, and Anne Collins. 2010a. *Zeroing in on Number and Operations: Key Ideas and Common Misconceptions, Grades 1–2.* Portland, ME: Stenhouse.

———. 2010b. *Zeroing in on Number and Operations: Key Ideas and Common Misconceptions, Grades 3–4.* Portland, ME: Stenhouse.

Economopoulos, Karen, Jan Makros, and Susan Jo Russell. 1998. *From Paces to Feet: Measuring and Data.* Investigations in Number, Data, and Space. Cambridge, MA: TERC; Menlo Park, CA: Dale Seymour.

Fosnot, Catherine Twomey, and Maarten Dolk. 2001. *Young Mathematicians at Work: Constructing Number Sense, Addition, and Subtraction*. Portsmouth, NH: Heinemann.

Goodrow, Anne, Beverly Cory, and Catherine Anderson. 1997. *How Long? How Far? Measurement.* Investigations in Number, Data, and Space. Cambridge, MA: TERC; Menlo Park, CA: Dale Seymour.

Litton, Nancy. 2003. *Second-Grade Math: A Month-to-Month Guide*. Sausalito, CA: Math Solutions.

Litton, Nancy, and Maryann Wickett. 2009. *This Is Only a Test: Teaching for Mathematical Understanding in an Age of Standardized Testing*. Sausalito, CA: Math Solutions.

National Council of Teachers of Mathematics (NCTM). 2006. *Curriculum Focal Points for Prekindergarten Through Grade 8 Mathematics: A Quest for Coherence*. Reston, VA: NCTM.

Richardson, Kathy. 1998a. *Developing Number Concepts: Addition and Subtraction.* White Plains, NY: Dale Seymour.

———. 1998b. *Developing Number Concepts: Place Value, Multiplication, and Division.* White Plains, NY: Dale Seymour.

Ronfeldt, Suzy. 2003. *A Month-to-Month Guide: Third-Grade Math*. Sausalito, CA: Math Solutions.

Russell, Susan J., Karen Economopoulos, and JoAnn Wypijewski. 1997. *Putting Together and Taking Apart: Addition and Subtraction.* Investigations in Number, Data, and Space. Cambridge, MA: TERC; Menlo Park, CA: Dale Seymour.

Scharton, Susan. 2005. *Teaching Number Sense, Grade 2.* Sausalito, CA: Math Solutions.

Tank, Bonnie, and Lynne Zolli. 2001. *Teaching Arithmetic: Lessons for Addition and Subtraction, Grades 2–3.* Sausalito, CA: Math Solutions.

Van de Walle, John. 2006. *Elementary and Middle School Mathematics: Teaching Developmentally.* 6th ed. Boston: Allyn and Bacon.

Wickett, Maryann, and Marilyn Burns. 2002. *Teaching Arithmetic: Lessons for Introducing Place Value, Grade 2.* Sausalito, CA: Math Solutions.

———. 2005. *Teaching Arithmetic: Lessons for Extending Place Value, Grade 3*. Sausalito, CA: Math Solutions.